Leo Strauss, Max Weber,

and the Scientific Study of Politics

Leo Strauss, Max Weber, and the Scientific Study of Politics

Nasser Behnegar

THE UNIVERSITY OF CHICAGO PRESS

Chicago and London

The University of Chicago Press, Chicago 60637
The University of Chicago Press, Ltd., London
© 2003 by The University of Chicago
All rights reserved. Published 2003
Paperback edition 2005
Printed in the United States of America
12 11 10 09 08 07 06 05   5 4 3 2

ISBN (cloth): 0-226-04142-5
ISBN (paperback): 0-226-04143-3

Library of Congress Cataloging-in-Publication Data

Behnegar, Nasser, 1963–
    Leo Strauss, Max Weber, and the scientific study of politics / Nasser
Behnegar.
        p.   cm.
Includes bibliographical references and index.
    ISBN 0-226-04142-5 (cloth : alk. paper)
    1. Strauss, Leo—Contributions in political science.   2. Weber, Max,
1864–1920—Contributions in political science.   3. Cultural relativism.
I. Title.
    JC251.S8 B45 2003
    320′.092′2—dc21
                                                2002006528

⊗ The paper used in this publication meets the minimum requirements of the American National Standard for Information Sciences—Permanence of Paper for Printed
Materials, ANSI Z39.48-1992.

To my mother, Pari Behnegar,

and the memory of my father, Colonel Mansour Behnegar

It is not the victory of science that distinguishes our nineteenth century,
but the victory of scientific method over science.

Nietzsche, The Will to Power

CONTENTS

Acknowledgments *xi*

List of Abbreviations *xiii*

Introduction *1*

Part I

Chapter 1 Political Science in the Age of Relativism *9*

Chapter 2 Political Philosophy in the Age of Relativism *28*

Part II

Chapter 3 The Fact-Value Distinction and Nihilism *65*

Chapter 4 The Fact-Value Distinction and Social Science
as a Theoretical Pursuit *88*

Chapter 5 The Problem of Social Science *112*

Part III

Chapter 6 Strauss's Polemic against the New Political Science *141*

Chapter 7 The New Political Science *148*

Chapter 8 The Revolt against the Old Political Science *169*

Chapter 9 The New Political Science and Liberal Democracy *189*

Concluding Remarks *207*

Works Cited *211*

Index *219*

ACKNOWLEDGMENTS

This study would not have been possible if I had not met the late Allan Bloom. This genius of the heart helped me, then a young student of economics, think about the moral and metaphysical foundations of my science, encouraged me to write my dissertation on Strauss, and introduced me to other teachers from whom I've learned much about Strauss and the love of truth: David Bolotin, Werner Dannhauser, Hillel Fradkin, and Nathan Tarcov.

I am grateful to the anonymous referees for the University of Chicago Press, Robert Bartlett, David Bolotin, Christopher Bruell, Werner Dannhauser, Robert Faulkner, Christopher Nadon, and Devin Stauffer for their helpful criticism of previous drafts of this book. I thank John Tryneski of the University of Chicago Press for his thoughtful assistance throughout the project and Jane Zanichkowsky for her keen copyediting. The generosity of the John M. Olin Foundation and the Earhart Foundation made possible invaluable periods of uninterrupted reflection. My lovely wife, Alice Behnegar, helped her occasionally ghostly husband in every stage of his investigation.

In somewhat difficult circumstances Pari Behnegar lovingly and unhesitatingly supported my decision to become a scholar. Mansour Behnegar introduced me to his love of books and his search for the truth about God. I dedicate this book to both of them.

ABBREVIATIONS

All works are by Leo Strauss.

CM	*The City and Man* (1964)
GS	*Gesammelte Schriften* (1996)
IPP	*Introduction to Political Philosophy* (1989)
JP	*Jewish Philosophy and the Crisis of Modernity* (1997)
LAM	*Liberalism Ancient and Modern* (1968)
LNRH	*Natural Right and History, Walgreen Lectures* (1949)
NRH	*Natural Right and History* (1953)
OT	*On Tyranny* (1963)
PAW	*Persecution and the Art of Writing* (1952)
PL	*Philosophy and Law* (1935)
PPH	*The Political Philosophy of Hobbes* (1935)
RCPR	*The Rebirth of Classical Political Rationalism* (1989)
SCR	*Spinoza's Critique of Religion* (1962)
SPPP	*Studies in Platonic Political Philosophy* (1983)
TM	*Thoughts on Machiavelli* (1958)
WPP	*What Is Political Philosophy?* (1959)

Leo Strauss is a friend, perhaps an indispensable friend, of the scientific study of politics. This is not to say that the impression to the contrary fostered by Strauss's polemic against the scientific study of politics is altogether misleading, for he does deny that political science can be actualized without a radical rejection of the contemporary scientific approach to the study of politics. But unlike the critics of that approach who maintain that "no science of politics is possible; or if possible, desirable" (Charles Beard, quoted in Easton 1953, 68n), Strauss objects to modern social science not because it tries to be scientific but because it is not scientific, not because it insists on precision but because it is not precise regarding the most important issues. In short, Strauss estranges his readers from the social science of his time because on the "fundamental questions our friends of scientific exactness are strangely unexacting" (*WPP*, 24). While leading his readers to what he regards as a more promising path, his polemic obscures a fundamental agreement in intention.

Strauss turned away from the "value-free" social science of his time, which could not understand Hitler's and Stalin's regimes as tyrannies, and turned toward classical political philosophy out of a desire for a genuine social science:

> A social science that cannot speak of tyranny with the same confidence with which medicine speaks, for example, of cancer, cannot understand social phenomena as what they are. It is therefore not scientific. Present-day social science finds itself in this condition. If it is true that present-day social science is the inevitable result of modern social science and of

1

modern philosophy, one is forced to think of the restoration of classical
social science. (*OT*, 189)

Because Strauss returned to classical political philosophy out of a desire for
a genuine social science, his return was "tentative or experimental" (*CM*,
11), a return that could very well lead to the rejection of classical political
philosophy if it turned out that it could not answer the questions that political philosophy or science as such must answer. Yet it is not surprising
that the intention of Strauss's investigations has been generally misunderstood. On the one hand, his preliminary appeal to commonsense judgments
—such as his assertion that tyranny is to the political body as cancer is to the
human body—gives the impression to some that the standards for moral
and political judgment are already available to those who have not been
corrupted by "value-free" social science. But if such standards are already
available it is not clear why a return to classical political philosophy in particular is necessary. On the other, given the contemporary separation of
science from philosophy or the insolubility of questions of ethics and metaphysics by the scientific method, Strauss's tentative restoration of "classical
social science" and even that very expression are apt to appear unintelligible. But the scientific method is not necessarily the standard by which
scientific inquiry ought to be judged. After all, not every achievement of
modern science is the consequence of the scientific method. In particular,
the scientific method was not discovered by the scientific method. Prior to
its discovery there was an idea of science—based on the distinction between opinion *(doxa)* and knowledge *(epistēmē)*—that served as the standard by which that method was judged.

The deepest reason for misunderstanding Strauss's intention and the
most difficult to correct, however, is our lack of awareness of the questions
that he hoped to answer with the help of a more adequate knowledge of
classical political philosophy. That this is Strauss's own judgment is suggested in his request to Alexandre Kojève to review his study of Xenophon's
Hiero: "I know no one besides yourself and Klein who will understand *what
I am after*" (Strauss 1991, 236; emphasis added). It is safe to say that this
judgment was not based on Kojève's status as a Xenophon scholar. After re-
ceiving the review, Strauss wrote: "I am glad to see, once again, that we
agree about what the genuine problems are, problems which are nowadays
on all sides are either denied or trivialized" (ibid., 244).

The only proper access to Strauss's problems is through understanding a problem that has gripped modern man for more than a century: that

of relativism. Strauss did not return to classical political philosophy because he preferred classical politics to modern democratic politics but because he regarded a return to classical political philosophy as a necessary step in achieving clarity about preferences of any kind. Indeed, so far was he from being hostile to modern politics that he tentatively acknowledged that the modern state of the nineteenth century was superior to the ancient city on the basis of the very standards that led classical political philosophers to prefer the city to "the other forms of political association known to classical antiquity, the tribe and the Eastern monarchy" (*WPP*, 65). Since that state "could plausibly claim to be at least as much in accordance" with the standards of freedom (public spirit) and civilization (high development of the arts and sciences) as the Greek city had been, Strauss admitted that in the nineteenth century classical political philosophy did "in a sense become obsolete" (*WPP*, 65). But the difficulty is that in the course of the nineteenth century the very standard of "civilization" became discredited by Nietzsche. This discrediting is at the bottom of the mood that prevailed in the twentieth century, a mood that glorified passions at the expense of reason (see Barrett 1958 for the pervasive influence of this mood). According to Strauss, the deepest reason for the crisis of liberal democracy was Nietzsche's critique of modern rationalism, or of the modern belief in reason (*IPP*, 98). Strauss does not regard the Enlightenment as his enemy, let alone his "archenemy" (Almond 1990, 21). In fact, he begins his perhaps most influential book with a warning about the disappearance of a teaching that was characteristic of the Enlightenment—modern natural right (*NRH*, 1–2). But neither does he regard Nietzsche as an enemy, arguing that Nietzsche's critique of the modern faith in reason cannot be "dismissed or forgotten" by those who understand it because it is sound (*IPP*, 98). Strauss prefers liberal politics to the politics sometimes encouraged by Nietzsche's rhetoric (*WPP*, 54–55; *LAM*, 24; *IPP*, 98), to say nothing of the politics of his great student Martin Heidegger, but he could not be a modern liberal because through the questioning of these thinkers "[a]ll rational liberal philosophic positions have lost their significance and power. One may deplore this but I for one cannot bring myself to clinging [sic] to philosophic positions which have been shown to be inadequate" (Strauss 1995a, 305). Strauss is grateful to Nietzsche, whom he as a young man once described as "the last enlightener" (*GS*, 2:389), not only for showing the inadequacy of the modern belief in reason but also for opening up the possibility of a fresh and untraditional reexamination of the whole tradition of Western thought and for the recovery of the Socratic question of the best life as a real question.

The tradition in its roots has been shaken by Nietzsche. It has completely lost its self-evidence. We stand in the world completely without authority, completely without direction. Now for the first time the question *pōs biōteon* can be raised in its complete sharpness. We can again ask this question. We have the possibility of asking it in its complete seriousness. We can no longer read Plato's dialogues in order to be amazed that the old Plato already knew this and that; we can no longer polemicize against him. And the same is true of the Bible: we can no longer regard it as self-evident that the prophets were right; we ask ourselves seriously whether the kings were not in the right. We must start completely from the beginning. (*GS*, 2:389; translation is my own)

Now, this untraditional reexamination of the roots of the tradition may lead to the possibility of seeing for oneself that the standards first elaborated by classical philosophy were in fact sound, the possibility of seeing for oneself that the life of reason is indeed the best human life.

Strauss, then, introduces his historical studies with discussions of "the crisis of the West" or of "the crisis of liberal democracy" or their equivalents not out of a desire to be relevant but because those studies are responses to that crisis. Today, however, there is so little sense of a crisis of liberal democracy that it seems to be the only game in town, at least in the West. The boundless inhumanity of Islamic terrorists has only strengthened our conviction of the soundness of liberal premises. The distinction between Facts and Values, which according to Strauss is the scientific expression of the doubt about the modern project, has ceased to be the central doctrine of modern social science (*CM*, 6). To be sure, postmodernism is a living sign of the dissatisfaction with modern principles, but postmodernism understands this dissatisfaction in such a way that it is ultimately in the service of modern moral and political principles. We do not live without authority and without direction but in a situation nearly the reverse. We live in a situation similar to that which preceded Nietzsche's questioning: "We have found that in all major moral judgments Europe is now of one mind, including even the countries dominated by the influence of Europe: plainly, one now *knows* in Europe what Socrates thought he did not know and what that famous old serpent once promised to teach—today one 'knows' what is good and evil" (Nietzsche 1967a, #202). The issue is whether the difficulties at the root of the crisis of modern civilization have been resolved or whether the disastrous consequences of communism and national socialism and the victory of liberal democracy over these movements have merely covered over these problems. If the latter, Strauss's work retains its significance. But since according to Strauss the crisis of our time is "the incentive to our *whole* concern with the classics" (*CM*, 11; emphasis added), in losing our sense of this crisis we have lost our access to Strauss's interpretation of classical political philosophy. It is possible and likely that interest in Strauss will continue in this situation, but "Straussianism" is apt to suffer the fate of Platonism, a fate that Strauss describes as merely a "flight from Plato's problem" (Strauss 1988, 185). This study is an attempt to find my way to Strauss's problems by way of Strauss's discussion of the problems of the social science of his time. I have sought to find a path from my questions, those of a young man in search of a science of politics, to Strauss's questions.

Because Strauss's approach is so different from all other contemporary scientific and humanistic approaches to the study of man, one cannot take a serious interest in Strauss's approach without entertaining some doubts about these alternatives. In Part I I do not show the inadequacy of these approaches, but I do show the problems in the light of which the reader can see whether there is any contemporary alternative to Strauss that can fulfill the hope of a science of politics. The rest of the book is an examination of Strauss's critique of social scientific positivism. According to him, the fundamental premise of the social science of his time is the distinction between facts and values (*CM*, 11). Because his essay on Max Weber in *Natural Right and History* is his thematic treatment of that distinction, Part II is devoted to an interpretation of that essay. According to Strauss, the distinction between facts and values is "alien to that understanding of political things which belongs to political life but it becomes necessary, it seems, when the citizen's understanding of political things is replaced by the scientific understanding" (*CM*, 11). Because his thematic examination of the more fundamental assertion of modern social science—that the commonsense understanding of political things prior to scientific corroboration is cognitively worthless—occurs in the epilogue to *Essays on the Scientific Study of Politics* (reprinted in *LAM*), Part III is devoted to an interpretation of that essay. These two essays belong to two different works and have somewhat different intentions. The first is the second chapter of *Natural Right and History*, a chapter that is meant to open up fundamental problems that require extensive historical investigations. The second comes at the end of a book devoted to a criticism of the new political science and seeks to give practical guidance to political scientists who are not necessarily historians of political philosophy. But Strauss makes it clear that he wants them to be read together (Strauss 1963b, 156; compare *NRH*, 76 with *LAM*, 216). At the bottom of both essays is the problem of relativism and hence the question of the possibility of genuine science. There are various responses to relativism—one may reject it, one may welcome it, one may disregard it—but there is only one response that allows one to have access to Strauss's thought, and that is to recognize it as a problem that needs to be solved.

It is not necessary or even proper for the reader of this book to accept in advance what it purports to prove. If my suggestion that Strauss is a friend of the scientific study of politics seems incredible, let the reader begin with the view that Strauss is its enemy. As Georg von Bekesy, a Nobel laureate in physiology, points out, for scientists, human beings who hate error above all else, good enemies are at least as useful as friends:

> [One] way of dealing with errors is to have friends who are willing to spend the time necessary to carry out a critical examination of the experimental design beforehand and the results after the experiments have been completed. An even better way is to have an enemy. An enemy is willing to devote a vast amount of time and brainpower to ferreting out errors both large and small, and this without any compensation. The trouble is that really capable enemies are scarce; most of them are only ordinary. Another trouble with enemies is that they sometimes develop into friends and lose a good deal of their zeal. It was in this way that the writer lost his three best enemies. (Quoted in Backus 1969, xiii)

Much more important for political scientists than methodology is to have a scientific attitude, that is, a state of mind that is open to the discovery of political reality. This is always difficult, but the relativism of our age exacerbates the difficulty. First, one is willing to learn from one's enemies only if one thinks there is something important that can be learned from them. But if human reason cannot solve the conflict between ultimate values, nothing of importance can be learned from those who disagree with us about these values. Second, we are attracted to science through a variety of motives, which may be at odds with each other. This is not the commonly recognized difficulty that "anyone worthy of the name of scientist must be able to struggle with considerable success against jealousy, envy, bigotry, and any other attitude that interferes with clarity of perception and judgment" (Lasswell 1971, 3). There are also other, honorable, motives that may resist clarity, motives that despite being honorable are forced by the relativism of our age to hide themselves in the labyrinths of our souls. The first task of the recovery of the scientific attitude is to call forth these motives and the opinions that accompany them into the daylight so that we can honor them in accordance with their true worth.

PART I

Limits of our hearing.— One hears only those questions for which one is able to find answers.

Nietzsche, *Gay Science*

CHAPTER 1

Political Science in the Age of Relativism

If contemporary social science were fundamentally sound, if it possessed within itself the remedies for the ills from which it suffers, there would be no reason for its adherents to look for help from the outside. The development of social science positivism, however, is largely a history of social science's dissatisfaction with its own achievements. The first step toward understanding Strauss's contribution to social science is to make that dissatisfaction explicit.

To see the predicament of social science positivism, one must first recognize its greatness, and in the first place the great aspirations of its founder, Auguste Comte. Social science positivism emerged in the wake of the partial failure of modern political philosophy. According to Comte, modern political philosophy, which rests on the doctrine of the sovereignty of the people, succeeded in undermining the old social order but failed to produce a political community that combines the demands of progress and order in a coherent form. The political turmoil of Europe in the first half of the nineteenth century was something more than a testimony to the irrational power of the old tradition. The elements of the old order had survived in modern Europe because the new doctrine was no less contradictory than the doctrine it had supplanted. Europe was politically confused because it was morally confused, and it was morally confused because it was intellectually confused. To end the political anarchy, Comte argued, one must first end the intellectual anarchy, and for this a new social science is necessary.

The character of this new science was determined by the realization that the success of one part of modern philosophy, natural philosophy or

natural science, is attributable to its having passed through the theological
and the metaphysical to the positive stage of thought, in which "the mind
has given over the vain search after Absolute notions, the origin and desti-
nation of the universe, and the causes of phenomena, and applies itself to
the study of their laws—that is, their invariable relations of succession and
resemblance" (Comte 1974, 26). A social science modeled after modern
natural science offered the only solid basis for social reorganization, a reorganization in which social scientists would occupy the place formerly
held by priests in the old order and by the people and its representatives in
the new order. Instead of the individualistic teaching characteristic of modern political philosophy, a new altruistic morality, which in addition to being true was also purer than Christian morality, would be the glue that
would keep society together. Such a social science would be the fulfillment
of philosophy, because through it the homogeneity of sciences, that they
are all branches from the same trunk, is revealed. Accordingly, it would
bring modern civilization to perfection by freeing it from "the revolutionary stage in which it has been tossed about for three centuries past" (Comte
1974, 400).

Half a century later, the hopes of Comte were dashed in the thought
of Max Weber—the first social scientist to be profoundly influenced by
Nietzsche. The idea of philosophy as a universal science gave way to the
impossibility of transcending strict specialization. The hope of removing
social anarchy through the discovery of universal principles of action was
replaced by the insistence on the existence of eternal and irreconcilable
conflicts between ultimate values. Whereas Comte had argued that by freeing itself from metaphysical presuppositions modern social science could
solve the moral and political problems of man, Weber insisted that a purely
empirical social science is unable to solve these problems. Yet in admitting
that it is unable to carry out this fundamental task, social science puts its
own value—and indeed the value of science in general—in question. The
doubts about the value of science were accompanied by profound doubts
regarding the goodness of modern civilization, of a secular society based on
the idea of science:

> No one knows who will live in this cage in the future, or whether at the
> end of this tremendous development entirely new prophets will arise, or
> there will be a great rebirth of old ideas and ideals, or, if neither, mecha-
> nized petrifaction, embellished with a sort of convulsive self-importance.
> For of the last stage [lit. "the last men"] of the modern cultural develop-
> ment, it might well be truly said: "Specialists without spirit, sensualists

without heart; this nullity imagines that it has attained a level of civilization never before achieved." (Weber 1958 [original statement made in
1904–5], 182)

The attempt to perfect modern civilization thus gave way to contempt for
that civilization.

In the first half of the twentieth century, "a new science of politics"
emerged that claimed to be more scientific than Comte's in the sense that
it was not only modeled after modern natural science but actually based on
it.[1] This new political science somehow combined Weber's doubts about
the power of reason to solve conflicts of values with Comte's expectation
that an empirical social science would solve the fundamental problems of
society. To understand this mysterious combination, and the ground of the
expectations that animate the new political scientists, one must first understand the problem they faced, as they understood it.

The founders of the new political science, working in the first half of
the twentieth century, were moved by a certain uneasiness about the prospects of modern civilization. As Charles Merriam put it in 1925:

> We complacently assume that all will always be well, but at any time out
> of depths of ignorance and hatred may emerge world-war, anarchy, in-
> dustrial and political revolution, recurring discontent and distress. What
> advantage shall we reap if science conquers the whole world except the
> world's government, and then turns its titanic forces over to a govern-
> ment of ignorance and prejudice, with laboratory science in the hands
> of jungle governors? (1925, 55)

Yet as Churchill pointed out, in the pre-war generation, "statesmen, writers, philosophers, scientists, poets all moved forward in hope and buoy-
ancy, in sure confidence that much was well, and that all would be better"
(Churchill 1942, 71). What was the basis of the new gloomy assessment of
human prudence? First, faith in the necessity of progress was shattered by

---

1. The difference between Comte's sociology and the new political science is manifest in
their different attitudes toward scientific psychology. Comte would have objected to Bentley's attempt to base political science on behavioristic psychology, because in Comte's view social phenomena have a character of their own that cannot be understood by reducing them to nonsocial
phenomena. Durkheim supported Comte by observing that even natural phenomena have a whole-
ness that cannot be understood by reducing them to their elements: the hardness of bronze is not
in the individual ingredients but in their combination (Durkheim 1950, xlviii). Bentley would probably respond that the contention that social phenomena are more than the sum of their parts is
nothing but a mystification of social phenomena.

World War I and the political events that followed it in the first half of the century.[2] Second, faith in democracy was undermined by the transformation of democracy into a mass democracy. The new political scientists paid homage to the claim of classical political philosophers that the extent of the political community should be limited by man's natural powers of understanding and interest by arguing that the modern state had become so extensive—both in territory and responsibility—that man's natural powers were utterly inadequate to meeting its needs:

> At the present stage of civilization and in the present correspondingly complex condition of politics, it is inevitable that the judgment of the plain man should be incompetent in matters well outside the purview of his experience and the compass of his imagination. . . . Questions of foreign policy . . . are regarded with apathy, and the degree of public attention tends to be in inverse proportion to the scale of interests at stake, and to the measure in which they transcend the concern of the moment. India may contain a seventh of the human race, but, as a late Secretary of State used to complain, the British public is not interested in India. (Catlin 1964, 286–87)

Respect for public opinion gave way to contempt, a contempt based on experience. As Learned Hand put it in 1932: "No disclosures, no scandals, can stir the voters from their inertia. Doubtless things might become uncomfortable enough to arouse them, but, given reasonable opportunity for personal favors, and not too irksome control, they are content to abdicate their sovereignty and to be fleeced, if the shepherds will only shear them in their sleep" (Hand 1952, 94). This contempt received support not only from the success of propaganda in World War I but also from the success "of modern advertising, whereby the steady purchase of Listerine has been rendered a social duty taking precedence even over forbearance from homicide" (Corwin 1929, 583).

These observations concerning the new political situation from the beginning were connected with a new understanding of the nature of man. The theory of evolution (Wallas 1921), which suggests that much of hu-

---

2. "The shock of the first World War, the disappointment of renewed hope as the League of Nations proved a broken reed, the lostness of men deprived of the social function by the great depression, the appearance of the irrationalist and racist totalitarianism, the grueling struggle and city-destroying devastation of the second World War, successively undermined the earlier assurance that man's life in society was secure, and would be progressively rewarding" (Cook 1955, 265–66).

man behavior is shaped by instincts that are inherited from our ancestors, behavioristic psychology (Bentley 1967), which denies any efficacy to ideas, and Freudian psychology (Lasswell 1951, 1–282), which in ways that are well known insists on the supremacy of subrational forces, undermine "the 'intellectualist' assumption, 'that every human action is the result of an intellectual process, by which a man first thinks of some end which he desires, and then calculates the means by which that end can be attained'" (Wallas 1921, 5). The consequences of this conclusion for the future of democracy seemed ominous, for it is difficult to defend democracy if human beings are not sufficiently good judges of their own and the public interest (Corwin 1929, 569–92).

The new political scientists, then, came to face the necessary tension between democracy and science, which was somewhat obscured by the Enlightenment. I say necessary because science in all its forms implies a rank ordering of human beings on the basis of knowledge, a rank ordering that the principle of democracy denies.[3] Faced with this conflict, the new political scientists at first chose science rather than democracy. As Harold Lasswell put it:

> Modern reflections on democracy boil down to the proposition, more or less contritely expressed, that the democrats were deceiving themselves. The public has not reigned with benignity and restraint. The good life is not in the mighty rushing wind of public sentiment. It is no organic secretion of the horde, but the tedious achievement of the few. The lover of the good life no longer consults Sir Oracle; he pulls the strings of Punch and Judy. Thus argues the despondent democrat. Let us, therefore, reason together, brethren, he sighs, and find the good, and when we have found it, let us find out how to make up the public mind to accept it. Inform, cajole, bamboozle and seduce in the name of the public good. Preserve the majority convention, but dictate to the Majority! (Lasswell 1927, 4–5)

---

3. That this tension existed even in the Enlightenment doctrine that all men are created equal becomes evident in the debates between Stephen Douglas and Abraham Lincoln. Since this doctrine denied the justice of slavery, Lincoln argued that we must put slavery back on the path of ultimate extinction by preventing its introduction in the federal territories. But Douglas argued that if people are created equal, the people of the territory should decide for themselves whether they want to have slavery: "it is no answer to this argument to say that slavery is an evil, and hence should not be tolerated. You must allow the people to decide for themselves whether it is a good or an evil. . . . Whenever you put a limitation upon the right of the people to decide what laws they want, you have destroyed the fundamental principle of self-government" (Lincoln and Douglas 1965, 28).

The rejection of democracy was primarily a rejection of the justification of the democratic institutions and not of the institutions themselves:

> Political science should borrow by analogy from the new physics [atomic physics] a determination to get rid of intellectual insincerities concerning the nature of sovereignty, the general will, natural rights, the freedom of the individual, the consent of the governed, majority rule, home rule, the rule of public opinion, state rights, laissez-faire, checks and balances, the equality of men and nations, and a government of laws not of men. (Munro 1928, 10)

The new political scientists did not reject the institutions of democracy partly because they seem to have had even more contempt for democracy than did Nietzsche. The masses are so incompetent that regardless of the form of government they will always be ruled by the few: "The dread by which Nietzsche was at one time so greatly disturbed, that every individual might become a functionary of the mass, must be completely dissipated in the face of the truth that while all have the right to become functionaries, few only possess the possibility" (Michels 1966, 167). Since the rule of elites is inevitable, the real issue concerns the character of those elites:

> It is indisputable that the world could be unified if enough people were impressed by this (or by any other) elite. The hope of professors of social science, if not of the world, lies in the competitive strength of an elite based on vocabulary, footnotes, questionnaires, and conditioned responses, against an elite based on vocabulary, poison gas, property, and family prestige. (Lasswell quoted in Storing 1962, 284)

But on what basis could the new political science rescue humanity? First, the belief that social phenomena could be measured, a belief that was buttressed by the appearance of behavioristic psychology, led to the view that the limitation of man's natural powers could be overcome by application of the methods of modern natural science. Whereas earlier political scientists acquired their political knowledge "by listening to wise old men, or, which is the same thing, by reading good historians, as well as by looking around and by devoting themselves to public affairs," the new political scientists living in societies characterized by their "immense complexity and rapid change" acquired their knowledge through such methods as surveys (*WPP*, 15). Second, the very success of propagandists and advertisers, which showed that the masses could be easily manipulated, inspired the hope that social science could save democracy through social engineering. The practical goal of social science became what Merriam called "social and political control" (Merriam 1921, 183–84; Catlin 1964, 349) through the discovery of universally valid laws of political behavior. But here a difficulty arises that was colorfully stated by an early critic of that science: "With modern physics and chemistry brandishing sticks of dynamite with the insouciance of a four-year old, what could be more preposterous than to induct political science into the same nursery of urchins?" (Corwin 1929, 591). Control is always with a view to a purpose, and of the purpose of social control the new political science, according to itself, could not possess any knowledge.

The new political scientists were not troubled by this difficulty, because they did not feel it. They did not find themselves lost in the sea without a compass, because despite their rejection of the traditional justifications for modern democracy and even their doubts about the principle of democracy, they were at bottom democrats. Their sharp comments against democracy were those of despondent democrats, to use Lasswell's own phrase. But they were democrats of a particular kind. They were attracted to the interpretation of democracy that was given by progressive-pragmatic philosophers such as John Dewey: "In the writings of John Dewey, the doctrine of modern democracy is most clearly stated, and in form more truly fraternal perhaps than the socialistic form" (Merriam 1950, 123). Although the progressive philosophy of Dewey overlapped with the new political science, it essentially belongs to an earlier stage of development. Dewey was not a relativist in the sense that Max Weber was a relativist. Although he accepted the historical relativity of values, he still believed in valid normative judgments because he understood history as a progressive movement. This notion of progress allowed him to regard democracy as "the one, the ultimate ethical ideal of humanity" (quoted in Ross 1991, 163). His thought was a modification of the neo-Hegelian political science that prevailed prior to the rise of the new political science, which was rejected by Nietzsche and Weber. If one accepts the historical relativity of values without accepting Hegel's notion of the absolute moment in history, one must abandon the notion of progress because one no longer has a reason for asserting that the values of today are better than the values of yesterday. In short, progressive philosophy and "value-free" social science are mutually exclusive, for the idea of progress implies normative knowledge. The new political science was a blend of these two contradictory views, a contradiction that was overlooked on account of Dewey's rejection of metaphysics and his concern with solving practical problems. A vaguely progressive

understanding of democracy mixed with a sense that only science can solve
the problems of humanity provided the new political science with its ruling values: a firm rejection of religion as superstition, a rejection of old
stern morality, a sense of the priority of addressing the physical needs of
the masses to addressing their spiritual ones, and a belief that science can
eliminate all the important problems of man. In all these ways, the new political scientists were the polar opposite of Max Weber, whose doctrine
concerning values they accepted explicitly.

As the new political science matured, the democratism that originally
coexisted with doubts about democracy came to overpower those doubts.
Whereas the first generation of the new political scientists were social en-
gineers concerned with correcting the shortcomings of democracy, the behavioralists were theoreticians who seemed to see no defects in democracy.
This is a remarkable sea change given that "there is little in behavioralism
that would be completely strange or repugnant to such earlier proponents
of a 'science of politics' as Merriam, Catlin, and Munro" (Somit and Tanenhaus 1967, 179). According to John Gunnell, the behavioral revolution's
"self-understanding, and external image, as basically a revolt against an
obsolescent indigenous idea of political theory and political science is misleading." This revolution was in fact a reaction "against an alien philosophical incursion" by such thinkers as "Friedrich, Hans Morgenthau, Arendt,
Gurian, Franz Neumann, Sigmund Neumann, Strauss, Voegelin, and such
American partisans as John Hallowell" (Gunnell 1993, 142, 144–45). Perhaps it would be more accurate to say that behavioralism was partly a response to an intrinsic difficulty with the new political science, of which the
new political scientists themselves were aware but which was brought out
forcefully by some of the scholars whom Gunnell mentions. The brutality of Hitler's regime at once rehabilitated the discredited democracy and
the very notion that there are objective norms. The question naturally
emerged whether by denying the existence of such norms "value-free" social science hampered the recognition of the dangers of Hitler and weakened the resistance to his movement. Strauss, in particular, raised the question whether "value-free" social science is compatible with the duties that
we have toward liberal democracy (*NRH*, 1–2; *WPP*, 18–20). In response to
this difficulty, some social scientists argued that in fact relativism is the only
foundation for liberal democracy and that the blame for Hilter should be
placed at the door of the "absolutists" (Gunnell 1993, 144; see the discussion of Kelsen in chapter 2). A similar approach was to revise the history of
the new political science by arguing that in its emergence "democratic val-

ues were not in question," that the movement toward science was not a revolt against philosophy but "a *stampede* to complete philosophy," and that the methods of scientific observation "are *certain* to contribute, here and now, to the practice of democratic morals" (Lasswell 1942, 26–27, 48; emphasis added). Another approach was to criticize the early new political scientists for their understanding of science: "among political scientists, as among most other social scientists, no more than a decade ago it was possible to find a considerable number who subscribed to the conviction that complete freedom from value premises is possible" (Easton 1953, 224). All these approaches had the tendency of making political scientists more willing to speak about values. But the issue underlying the notion of "value-free" social science concerns the cognitive status of these value judgments. Do these values have an objective foundation? If the behavioralists had answered yes to this question, they would have rejected the authority of modern logicians and would have returned to the tradition of political philosophy, which they believed was obsolete. If they had answered no, they would have been untrue to the normative claims of democracy. The answer that seemed to have been given was this: the values that direct a political scientist's activity "cannot be scientifically demonstrated to be either true or false," but a political scientist would commit "intellectual treason" if he "place[d] himself at the service of those whose values he disagrees with" (Eulau 1963, 133, 137). More precisely, our values are subjective but we must regard them as if they were objective so that we do not betray the values to which we are committed.[4] Since the values of the new political scientists were a particular interpretation of democratic values, this attitude strengthened the influence of these values even on their theoretical understanding of politics.

In particular, the behavioralists' commitment to their interpretation of democracy influenced the direction of their push toward a more theoretical orientation in political science. David Easton was one of the leaders of this push. He traced the failure of his predecessors to discover "universal generalizations about social relations" to their almost exclusive concern with the collection of information, or their "hyperfactualism," to their premature concern with application, and to their misunderstanding of the

---

4. Eulau's understanding of "intellectual treason" seems to be based on the notion that the highest duty of an intellectual is to a political value. In fact, to avoid political treason he demands that political scientists commit intellectual treason in the precise sense of accepting an inconsistency.

proper role of theory in the development of science (Easton 1953, 66).[5] To advance science, one must not put the emphasis on the accumulation of facts, from which ever broader generalizations would be drawn. Rather, one must search for a theory of the highest level of generality around which political science as a discipline could be organized, just as Newtonian physics is organized by the law of inertia. Because this comprehensive theory would be "a guide to the relevance of political problems and to further research," it would allow political science to address the practical problems of society (Easton 1953, 68). Although Easton's push toward the discovery of a general theoretical framework was a response to "our present social crisis," it in fact led to the denial of the existence of pressing social questions. As Charles Lindblom observed retrospectively:

> The tendency of radicals to turn every apparent strength in democratic politics into a weakness has not gone any further than the mainstream tendency to convert every apparent defect into a strength. Berelson made apathy a strength, Truman made elite privilege a bulwark of democracy, and some of you have read Lindblom on the blessings of fragmentation. (Lindblom 1982, 17n)

Thus, the very observations that troubled the first generation of the new political scientists became signs of the strength of democracy. For instance, instead of being troubled by the existence of apathetic and uninformed citizens, Almond and Verba argued that such citizens contribute to democracy, for their existence allows for a greater governmental power, which would not be possible if all citizens were active, informed, and rational beings. They explained the contradiction between what they called "the rationality-activist" model of democracy and their empirical observation of Western democracies in the following way:

> One possible explanation . . . is that this discrepancy is evidence for the malfunctioning of democracy. Insofar as people do not live up to the ideal of the active citizen, democracy is a failure. If one believes that the reali-

---

5. He thus applied to the early new political scientists the criticism that Lasswell and Kaplan had raised against what they called the descriptive politics of Tocqueville and Bryce: "'brute empiricism'—the gathering of 'facts' without a corresponding elaboration of hypotheses" (Lasswell and Kaplan 1950, x). Although Easton's understanding of the role of theory may have been different than his predecessors', his insistence on theory formation was not a revolutionary change in direction of the new political science but a new resolve to solve the problems of the new political science by being more scientific (Ricci 1984, 133–34).

ties of political life should be molded to fit one's theories of politics, such
an explanation is satisfactory. But if one holds to the view that the theory
of politics should be drawn from the realities of political life—a somewhat easier and probably more useful task—then this explanation of the
gap between the rationality-activist model and democratic realities is less
acceptable. (Almond and Verba 1963, 340)

The difficulty here is that what is taken by Almond and Verba to be
simply an observation of the "way things are" in fact rests on the premises
that the problem of democracy is to maintain a balance "between governmental power and governmental responsiveness," "between consensus and
cleavage, between affectivity and affective neutrality" (Almond and Verba
1963, 340–41), coupled with a view that there is a proper balance between
these needs in existing democracies. But it is not clear on what grounds the
existing balance is found to be acceptable. Moreover, their general notion
of political health appears to be a remnant of a political understanding that
has been transformed by the push toward a theoretical framework, for
underlying the notion of a balance between consensus and cleavage is a belief in the value of pluralism: "Similarly there are required *social* consensus
and cleavage—in effect, pluralism—in politics. Such pluralism makes for
enough consensus to hold the system together and enough cleavage to
make it move. Too much consensus would be deadening and restrictive of
liberty; too much cleavage would be destructive of the society as a whole"
(Berelson et al. 1954, 318; emphasis in original). Underlying this pluralism
is the notion that the aim of the political process is to reconcile "change
with stability" (Herring 1940, viii). And underlying this view is the notion
that change is necessarily a change for the better so long as it is gradual
enough not to threaten the stability of society—in short, progressivism.

To see this marriage between progressivism and "value-free" social
science, we should take a closer look at the theoretical framework of behavioralism. As Easton indicated, the only thing that approximates a general framework in the new political science is what he called the equilibrium theory, a notion borrowed from modern economics and ultimately
from Newtonian physics. According to this theory, "all parts of the political process depend upon all other parts, and collectively they all determine
the state of the political system in the same way that celestial bodies help
to determine one another's position and the general configuration of the
universe" (Easton 1953, 269). Because the parts of the political process are
groups, the equilibrium is the result of pressures that groups exert on each
other. But looking at politics through these lenses makes it difficult to see

or speak of certain political phenomena. The conception of a system consisting of parts interacting with each other obscures the crucial distinction between rulers and ruled and therefore the phenomena of class conflict and injustice in a society parts of which are uninformed and politically inactive while others are not. Moreover, under such a system any meaningful understanding of the distinction between rational and irrational beings disappears and is implicitly replaced by the distinction between active and passive beings. Thus, rational beings become almost indistinguishable from fanatics who resist governmental power regardless of any consideration of the utility and necessity of that power.[6] Finally, the theory implies that the political system gravitates by itself toward stability. As Bentley put it, "order is bound to result, because order is now and order has been, where order is needed" (1967, 267).[7] The assumption is that if one group becomes too powerful other groups will be formed to resist it, and that the power of each group will correspond to the number of individuals. Thus, what seemed to be a value-free theoretical model was informed by a normative outlook that it in turn cultivated. Behavioral political science, then, rests on "the basic premise," made explicit by Seymour Martin Lipset, that democracy, or more precisely, depoliticized liberal pluralistic democracy is "the good society in operation" (1963, 439).

Now, this democratic faith was implicit in the new political science from the very beginning. In my account of the origin of the new political science, I have stressed its implicit acceptance of the aims of democratic society as they were understood by its progressive interpreters, but perhaps no less important is the new political science's departure from progressive philosophy. In the new political science, one sees very little of Dewey's concern with the education of virtuous human beings. Instead, one sees a desire to create a peaceful and free society by turning attention away from the great moral, religious, and political issues that have divided mankind. This is clear in Lasswell's account of his ideal of preventive politics: "The political methods of coercion, exhortation, and discussion assume that the role of politics is to solve conflicts when they have happened. The ideal of

---

6. "True, the highly interested voters vote more, and know more about the campaign, and read and listen more, and participate more; however, they are also less open to persuasion and less likely to change. Extreme interest goes with extreme partisanship and might culminate in rigid fanaticism that could destroy democratic processes if generalized throughout the community" (Berelson et al. 1954, 314).

7. Bentley's work, which was largely ignored by his contemporaries, came to be regarded as a classic in the 1950s because it prefigured the theoretical orientation of behavioral political science.

a politics of prevention is to obviate conflict by the definite reduction of the tension level of society by effective methods, of which discussion will be but one" (Lasswell 1951, 203). The new political science may thus be characterized as an attempt to defend the principles of modern civilization without fully meeting—indeed while giving credence to—the objections of the most serious critics of modern civilization, thinkers such as Nietzsche who objected to its neglect of what is noble and high in man.

In the late sixties, the price that the new political science had to pay for its neglect of man's moral concerns became evident. The behavioralist dream of a pluralistic democracy gravitating toward stability was interrupted by unmistakable signs of disorder: "American society has reached a point where its cities are uninhabitable, its youth disaffected, its races at war with each other, and its hope, its treasure, and the lives of its young men dribbled away in interminable foreign adventures. Our whole world threatens to become anomalous" (S. Wolin 1969, 1081). Wolin's critical discussion of behavioralism, from which the preceding passage is taken, occurs in the same issue of the *American Political Science Review* as David Easton's presidential address. In that address, Easton not only welcomed the new critics of behavioralism but also suggested that they were leading what he called "the post-behavioral revolution." It is revealing that in this very address Easton also implicitly attacked Strauss, who had in effect formulated the difficulties of behavioral political science that the new critics took up and had stated the reasons that would lead a social scientist like Easton to embrace these critics when he argued that "positivism necessarily transforms itself into historicism" (*WPP*, 18–20, 25–27; see Miller 1972 for the historicist presuppositions of the protest against behavioralism).[8] As Easton explained, he welcomed the new critics of behavioralism because they were "future-oriented" whereas the earlier "resistance to the incorporation of scientific method has come in the form of an appeal to the past" (Easton 1969, 1051). Easton was probably quite troubled by the part of Strauss's criticism of behavioralism that showed the contradiction between "value-free" social science and democracy, but his belief in the idea of progress prevented him from taking Strauss's alternative seriously. On the other hand, the contention of the new critics that "behavioral science conceals an ideology of empirical conservatism" (Easton 1969, 1052) troubled

---

8. Because Strauss, on account of *Natural Right and History*, had come to be considered the leading advocate of natural law in political science, it is probable that the following is directed at him: "Those philosophies that seek to revive classical natural law and that *reject the possibility of a science of man* have thereby forfeited their opportunity and put in question their fitness to undertake this creative task of theory" (Easton 1969, 1058; emphasis added).

behavioralists, because it forced them to face the tension between the aims of their left-leaning liberalism and their contention that those aims are self-sustaining. The experience of the sixties made it clear that even the apolitical liberalism of the new political science needs vigilant activism on the part of citizens. Now, with the sudden recognition of the necessity of such virtue, the apparent indifference to morality of the new political science somersaulted into an explicit moralism that combined moral fervor with a desire for freedom from obligation to one's country. Thus, Easton ended his address by exhorting American social scientists to politicize themselves collectively while freeing themselves as much as possible from concerns of national interest: "the social scientist himself needs to be denationalized" while he becomes an intellectual, "the guardian of those civilized, human values known to most men" (Easton 1968, 1059–61).

In the sixties there was a development that, with some exaggeration, one could describe as a scientific revolution. This was a new understanding of science that was popularized by Thomas Kuhn's *Structure of Scientific Revolutions.* According to this understanding, all disciplines rest on certain fundamental assumptions (paradigms) that are not self-evident in principle but appear self-evident to practitioners of that discipline in a particular epoch. When new facts are discovered that are inconsistent with these paradigms, scientists sometimes abandon the old paradigm in favor of a new one, which is not a better representation of reality but somehow makes it easier to solve problems caused by the discovery of the new facts. Kuhn's distinction between "normal" and "revolutionary" science led Easton to interpret the failure of behavioralism to anticipate the social and political problems of the sixties as the kind of anomaly that precedes a scientific revolution. Thus, Kuhn "helped" him interpret his failure to predict the future of politics as a ground for his confidence in predicting the future of political science. Believing that he was presiding over a transitional stage in the history of the discipline, he welcomed postbehavioralism as the verdict of history. Now, Easton seemed to accept Kuhn so easily because, like Kuhn himself, he failed to see that if Kuhn's main argument is correct, one can no longer speak of science without putting the word in quotation marks, for unless the fundamental assumptions of a "science" are evident to man as man nothing that follows from them can be called knowledge.[9] Since Easton, like other social scientists, assumed that modern natural sci-

9. Although Kuhn explicitly abandoned the view that development of science is progress toward a better understanding of reality, he did maintain that this development may constitute progress in problem-solving: "I do not doubt, for example, that Newton's mechanics improves on

ence is a genuine science, he took Kuhn's explanation of the history of that science as an account of science itself. Sheldon Wolin saw the implications of Kuhn's views more clearly when he used it to criticize scientific understanding in general in favor of a humanistic approach. But he too made an error similar to Easton's. He preferred what he called "epic theorists" to normal theorists, but it is not clear on what grounds he could support this preference. Both Easton and Wolin preferred revolutionary forces to conservative forces, a preference that is intelligible if the course of history is necessarily progressive, but the thrust of Kuhn's thesis is to deny the progressive character of "scientific" development. Thus, the idea of progress survived subterraneously even as it was being rejected. Consequently, Easton and Wolin's embrace of Kuhn led to a new kind of empirical conservatism, that is, the idolatry of emerging facts.

The behavioral political science that survived the sixties is quite different from the original behavioralism in two respects. First, the new behavioralism is simultaneously much more appreciative of normative political science and less aware of the obstacles to it. According to Dahl, "the normative orientation has become a rapidly expanding frontier of political science, just as empirical analysis had become earlier" (quoted in Ceaser 1990, 114). Although historicism has led some political "scientists" to reject the distinction between facts and values by asserting that all "facts" are determined by values, behavioral political scientists as a whole have not accepted this rejection of their long-held "commitment to the search for objectivity" (Almond 1990, 29). Sensibly, Almond suggests that the demands of politics and the demands of science could be reconciled by "a logic which will enable us to move from empirical relationships to normative judgments" and that political scientists should search for such a logic. In spite of Almond's suggestion that it is "already to be observed" (Almond 1966, 877), as far as I know the behavioralists have not developed this logic. Instead, they have ceased to discuss the distinction between facts and values. It is remarkable that in a book titled *A Discipline Divided: Schools and Sects in Political Science* (1990), a book that includes short histories of political science, Almond does not even discuss this distinction. Although it remains the basic premise of modern political science, as is evident from the living distinction between its empirical and normative branches,

Aristotle's and that Einstein's improves on Newton's as instruments for puzzle-solving" (1970, 206). But it is difficult, or rather impossible, to understand how a change of a paradigm can result in progress in problem-solving, as Kuhn maintains, if the character and existence of problems is determined by paradigms (166).

political scientists for the most part no longer reflect on it. Second, the new behavioralism is intellectually much less ambitious. Whereas Easton had hoped for an emergence of a political science that would be "in a position to draw generalizations that pass beyond the experience of any one political system or of the systems in any one culture or civilization" (1953, 319), political scientists have come to see that the generalizations that seemed valid in the 1950s are indefensible given the experience of American political life in the 1960s (Almond 1977, 494–97). Accordingly, the new behavioralism seems to be satisfied with finding regularities that are valid at one time or place: "Instead of a need for replication for purposes of verification, our problem has been a need to replicate, because with passage of time social reality inevitably changes" (Pye 1990, 4).

The more modest ambitions of the new behavioralism may explain much of the appeal of rational choice theory—a theory that rests on the premise imported from economics that human beings are rational beings that maximize their utility—to many theoretically minded political scientists, for that theory postulates a broad-gauge theory, which promises to unify the discipline as a whole. Rational choice theory originated in the 1950s and is in a way the natural response to Easton's criticism of the "hyperfactualism" of his predecessors, for its general theory is deduced from axioms. It is the continuation of the tendency of modern social science following modern natural science to understand complex wholes in light of their simple elements. Whereas the behavioralists had shifted the focus of attention away from the state to the groups that composed it, rational choice theory shifts the focus of attention from groups to the individuals that compose them. Like behavioralism, it too has a theory of equilibrium, but because it focuses on self-interested individuals who are parts of groups, it escaped optimistic views about democracy. As Mancur Olson argues, it is possible for rational individuals forming a potentially large group not to act in their collective interest, because they do not have the incentive for such action. Groups do not balance each other, because not all groups are alike:

> They generally take for granted that such groups will act to defend or advance their group interests, and take it for granted that the individuals in these groups must also be concerned about their individual economic interests. But if the individuals in any large group are interested in their own welfare, they will *not* voluntarily make any sacrifices to help their group attain its political (public or collective) objectives. Often the groups that the analytical pluralists expect will organize whenever they

have any reason or incentive to do so are latent groups. Although in relatively small groups ("privileged" or "intermediate" groups) individuals may voluntarily organize to achieve their common objectives, this is not true in large or latent groups. (Olson 1971, 126–27)

By focusing on the conflict between individuals and their own groups, rational choice theorists have not entertained any hopes that groups will automatically balance each other. Accordingly, unlike behavioralists, they were not embarrassed by the experience of the sixties.

This shift of focus toward the individual is connected with a rejection of the basic psychological premise of the new political science. Whereas the new political science began with the denial that man is a rational animal, rational choice theory champions the hypothesis that man is rational in a certain sense. As far as I know, this reversal was not accompanied by a reexamination of the older view. Anthony Downs suggests that a refutation of the evidence presented against human rationality is not necessary, because "theoretical models should be tested primarily by the accuracy of their predictions rather than by the reality of their assumptions" (Downs 1957, 27). To be sure, prediction is possible on the basis of false assumptions, but Downs's indifference to the truth or falsity of the basic assumption of his science betrays an indifference to the idea of science as the attempt to know the truth about the world. Now, this focus on mere prediction would require attention to empirical observation, but Green and Shapiro (1994) have found rational choice theorists wanting precisely on this score. They have identified what they called "pathologies of rational choice," which include crafting experiments to illustrate rather than test their hypotheses and not testing their theories against competing explanations. If these objections are sound (which rational choice theorists dispute), they suggest the following problem. The hypothesis that men are rational beings who maximize their utility is not for rational choice theorists merely any hypothesis but a view around which social science is to be organized. Thus, for them the hope of having a real political science rests on the affirmation of this particular hypothesis; it is not one that can be tested and discarded if found wanting without destroying the possibility of a science of politics. Strangely, then, the commitment to a particular notion of science would have obstructed the performance of the most basic duties of scientists. But even if these objections are not sound, the failure of rational choice theorists to persuade their behavioralist colleagues shows (if one accepts the notion of science to which rational choice theorists ascribe) that this crucial hypothesis has not been scientifically established. What promised to be a universal science of politics has only produced a rather large sect within the profession of political science.

If one compares the achievements of the new political science with its original intentions, one can hardly escape the conclusion that it has been a failure. I, of course, do not deny that political scientists have done useful work that "consists of careful and judicious collections and analyses of politically relevant data" (*WPP*, 14). But this should not obscure the fact that the new political science has failed on its own terms. As Lucien Pye puts it:

> The ambition to discover universal and enduring laws like Boyle's law has been frustrated by the realization that human behavior is too sensitive to the fluctuations of history to yield permanently enduring findings. Instead of a need for replication for purposes of verification, our problem has been a need to replicate, because with passage of time social reality inevitably changes. (1990, 4)

But what is the cause of this failure? According to Pye, political science has failed to discover universally valid laws of human behavior because "social reality inevitably changes." But if there is nothing about social reality that is permanent, there cannot be any political knowledge other than knowledge of history. Therefore, before we attribute the failure of the new political science to the nature of reality and thereby undermine all hopes for a political science, we must consider whether the failure can be traced to the unreasonable intentions of the new political science, for it is not obvious that universal knowledge of politics has to take the form of laws of human behavior. The new political science accepted this understanding of the goal of science because it modeled itself after modern natural science. Since the new political science seeks laws of human behavior for the sake of prediction, and since the effects of morality are uncertain, it deduces these laws by disregarding the moral element in human behavior. But if our moral opinions at least partly determine our actions, disregarding them is apt to impair our ability even to make reasonable guesses about the future.

Moreover, even if the new political science succeeds in discovering general laws of behavior, these laws are apt to be empty and vague and hence useless precisely on account of their generality. Accordingly, as long as such laws remain the goal of political science, the value of political science to political life will remain in doubt. This means that the scientist in the political scientist is apt to be attacked by the citizen in him. Easton's failure to defend "objectivity" is instructive because it brings to light a difficulty that afflicts any political science that is unable to acquire genuine knowledge about the most important issues.

The new political science had urged from the beginning that the scientific study of politics be separated from ethics, partly because "the intrusion of ethical theory into the treatment of political method" is "prejudicial to disinterestedness in thought" (Catlin 1964, 297). The history that I have sketched shows that the ejection of democratic morality from political science only led to an unconscious—hence necessarily unexamined—moralism that elevated democracy to something like a divine machine that automatically solved all of its ills: "Where the rational citizen seems to abdicate, nevertheless angels seem to tread" (Berelson et al. 1954, 311). It was not the detachment of the new political scientist, as their New Left critics maintained, but rather their lack of a genuine detachment that prevented them from seeing the problems of the 1960s.

As Strauss argues, scholarship requires detachment, "but detachment is not easily won and easily preserved—scholarship requires attachment to detachment" (1963b, 155). The only genuinely feasible attachment to detachment is an attachment that is based on detached analysis: scientific scholarship requires a scientific ethics, an ethics that in showing the true good of man shows the goodness of science to man. But we must not forget that in modern times there was an impressive attempt to formulate such an ethics, and the history that I have sketched was set in motion by a sense of the failure of that attempt. Nor can we forget that the founders of the modern natural right teaching would not have engaged in their project if they had thought that such an ethics was already established by the thinkers that Strauss calls classical political philosophers. The primary issue before us is not whether one should be an advocate of the ancient or of the modern social science but to see more clearly the problems of social science. It is only by understanding these problems that one can even begin to consider whether a return to classical political philosophy is possible or necessary.

CHAPTER 2

Political Philosophy in the Age of Relativism

The emergence of relativism has been accompanied by a decline of political philosophy, or political theory understood as normative theory (Cobban 1953). But there has also been a resurgence of political theory in the second half of the twentieth century, a resurgence to which Strauss contributed. But he was not alone. Among his contemporaries and predecessors a few have let posterity know that they "have not loosely through silence permitted things to pass away as in a dream" (Richard Hooker, quoted in Voegelin 1952). Moreover, as I have observed, in the sixties "future oriented" (Easton 1969, 1051), left-leaning, humanistic critics of scientific objectivity led a protest against behavioral political science that paved the way for a more general revival of normative political theory. Although an adequate interpretation of these various political theorists is beyond the scope of this study, their very existence compels me to state as clearly as possible what is distinctive about Strauss's approach to a normative political science: In what sense is Strauss alone?

To answer this question, we must inquire into the original causes of what Cobban called the decline of political theory:

> What I want to do is suggest that modern political theory has largely ceased to be discussed in terms of what ought to be; and the reason, I believe, is that it has fallen under the influence of two modes of thought which have had a fatal effect on its ethical content. These, and they have come to dominate the modern mind, are history and science. (Cobban 1953, 333)

The belief that science cannot establish valid value judgements and the belief that all human thought is essentially historical have undermined the legitimacy of the very goal of political theory, which is to find valid norms. Strauss and other political theorists who have contributed to the revival of political theory agree that there is something wrong with "value-free" social science, but they have radically different views when it comes to the question of the historicity of man. Strauss takes the challenge of historicism very seriously but he insists that political philosophy and historicism are mutually exclusive. Indeed, according to Strauss, historicism, and not positivism, is "the serious antagonist of political philosophy" (*WPP*, 26). But other political theorists, even those who, like Strauss, are inclined to older views, assert "the historicity of human existence" (Voegelin 1952, 1–2; Hallowell 1942, 323–24). The issue before us is not the great question of the truth of historicism, which would require a separate study, but of the possibility of a normative political science on the basis of historicism.

In order to understand why the revival of political theory was accompanied by the acceptance of a view that was responsible for the decline of political theory, one must not forget that one cannot deny something that one believes to be true. Contemporary theorists generally regard the historicity of man as something that has become undeniable after "'the rise of anthropology and allied sciences' or, more precisely stated, after 'the discovery of History'" (Strauss 1961, 148–49). As MacIntyre puts it: "For it was Vico who first stressed the importance of *the undeniable fact*, which is becoming *tedious to repeat*, that the subject matter of moral philosophy at least—the evaluative and normative concepts . . .—are nowhere to be found except as embodied in the historical lives of particular social groups and so possessing the distinctive characteristics of historical existence. . . . Morality that is no particular society's morality is to be found nowhere" (MacIntyre 1987, 413; emphasis added). Moreover, there is a powerful tendency among contemporary political theorists to regard relativism either as unproblematic and even salutary or to believe that its difficulties can be overcome without a radical reappraisal of relativism. As one sympathetic commentary points out: "To oversimplify somewhat: These authors ["proponents of a transformation of philosophy," for example, Habermas, Gadamer, MacIntyre, Taylor, and Putnam] agree with the post-Nietzscheans ["the end-of-philosophy thinkers," for example, Derrida, Rorty, Lyotard, and Foucault] in rejecting ideas of reason, truth, and language as innocent of power and desire, but they argue in differing ways that the normative notion of rational acceptability can also be applied to needs and interests, constraints and prescriptions, thus allowing for post-Platonic conceptions of validity in which it is neither divinized nor naturalized" (Baynes et al. 1987, 12–13). It is characteristic of theorists who seek to establish norms on the basis of relativism to deny or downplay the social crisis that is coeval with relativism, the elaboration of which marks the writings of Nietzsche, Spengler, Weber, Husserl, and Heidegger: no apprehensions of "the last man," of "the decline of the West," of the "meaninglessness" of modern life, of "the crisis of European science" or of "the night of the world" inform the work of the former.

Because contemporary political theorists regard the thesis of the historicity of man as true and largely unproblematic, many of them tend to look at the change in perspective as a "natural" development. Accordingly, they conceive of their own work as somehow a continuation of the tradition of political philosophy begun by Plato and Aristotle. For Strauss this change is a break that, if sound, opens up an abyss. Accordingly, he argues that "a simple continuation of the tradition of classical political philosophy . . . is no longer possible" (*CM*, 2). In this respect, his work is much less traditional than that of even the future-oriented political theorists. But this fact does not prove the soundness of his view, which can only be determined by examining the issue.

For political science to become normative, it must discover a rational ethics, an ethics that establishes the universal validity of at least the value of science. Such an ethics must address arguments that deny its possibility, arguments that have explicitly or implicitly formed the basis of social science at least since Max Weber. Yet John Rawls's *Theory of Justice*, a work celebrated especially for its rigor, passes over this basic difficulty.[1] As a result, it is not clear whether his theory claims to be knowledge about justice or his opinion about justice and hence a liberal ideology. Rawls himself admits that his theory of justice is not a theory for every society but only for constitutional democracies (Rawls 1985, 223). Whereas he presents his postulate of "the original position" as an attempt to take social contract theories to a higher level of abstraction by requiring us to abstract not only from our social life but also from our mental and physical qualities, in reality his theory does not even abstract from the values that are predominant only in a constitutional democracy. According to Richard Rorty, "the frequent re-

---

1. "Simply, historicism, whether that of Marx or that of Nietzsche and the Existentialists, has made it questionable whether an undertaking such as Rawls's is possible at all; yet he does not address himself to these thinkers. He takes it for granted that they are wrong, that they must pass before his tribunal, not he before theirs" (Bloom 1990, 316).

mark that Rawls' rational choosers look remarkably like twentieth-century American liberals is perfectly just, but not a criticism of Rawls. It is merely a frank recognition of the ethnocentrism which is essential to serious, non-fantastical, thought" (1991, 30n). I cannot here examine Rorty's contention regarding the ethnocentric character of all human thought but limit myself to the observation that its acceptance requires a break with the notion of the freedom of mind that underlies liberalism. Our very awareness that other human beings disagree with us compels us as liberals and simply as thinking human beings to explain our rejection of their opinions.

The general difficulty that I have outlined is not unique to Rawls but in one way or another reappears in every historicist normative theory. It stems from the fact, which is denied by the belief in the historical relativity of norms, that every norm requires a final stand. As Strauss shows, this difficulty emerges in Isaiah Berlin's attempt to defend liberalism on relativistic grounds. According to Berlin, there is an irreconcilable conflict between the various ends that men pursue, and a liberal society must prevent at least some collision among these ends. Society must come up with rules that provide a reasonably large area of freedom while placing some limit on individuals' pursuit of their desires. But the question is, what is the cognitive status of the rules that Berlin recommends? According to Berlin, these rules or commandments "are accepted so widely, and are grounded so deeply in the actual nature of men as they have developed through history, as to be, by now, an essential part what we mean by being a normal human being" (quoted in Strauss 1961, 138). Strauss, however, observes: "But Berlin has told us earlier that 'the domination of this ideal has been the exception rather than the rule, even in the recent history of the West,' i.e., that the ideal of negative freedom is not natural to man as man. Let, then, the rules in question be natural to Western man as he is now. But what about the future?" (ibid., 138–39). Berlin obscures the tension between the universal demands of norms and his belief in their merely historical validity by exaggerating the prevalence of the norms that he supports, to the point that they almost seem inescapable. He thus obscures the freedom that we possess. Berlin's procedure has the danger of in effect absolutizing the prevailing view of the present. Strauss's response to Berlin continues as follows: "In entire accord with the spirit of our time, he quotes 'an admirable writer of our time' who says: 'To realize the relative validity of one's convictions and yet stand for them unflinchingly, is what distinguishes a civilized man from a barbarian'" (139). Strauss questions this normative judgment because according to it "every resolute liberal hack or thug would be a civilized man, while Plato and Kant would be barbarians" (140).

This tension between the demands of ethics and those of historical relativism afflicts even thinkers who for moral and political reasons refuse to formulate a normative political theory. According to Derrida, deconstruction is animated by a concern for justice and democracy but it does not examine them thematically because that examination will destroy them: "one cannot speak *directly* about justice, thematize or objectivize justice, say 'this is just' and even less 'I am just,' without immediately betraying justice, if not law" (1990, 935; emphasis in original). But will not this refusal to speak directly about justice lead to the protection of a particular interpretation of justice, which may or may not be the correct interpretation, the just interpretation? Does not justice itself require us to explain our understanding of justice to those who disagree with us?

But one may wonder whether a relativistic ethics could at least allow one to show a decent respect to the opinions that one finds in our society. Can we not base a normative ethics on an immanent criticism of the historically relative values of our society? In this way, instead of merely accepting the prevailing values of our society we could make them coherent and thereby discover adequate but still historically relative values. But we would not have relativism in the first place if we had not inherited traditions that contradict each other. Can an immanent criticism of a tradition composed of traditions that are based on contradictory premises lead to valid normative judgements? For instance, one may seek guidance for the Jewish people through an examination of the Jewish tradition, but if one includes Spinoza as well as Orthodox Jews in this tradition it is difficult to see how that tradition points to a standard for the conduct of Jews.

There is one way in which the tension between normative validity and historical relativity of norms can possibly be overcome. If one lives in the absolute moment in history, then it is at least thinkable that one can have valid normative judgments that are historically relative. But one has to prove that one is living in such a peak moment, and the Hegelian-Marxists have not been able to demonstrate the ultimate validity of the Marxist ideals, especially given Nietzsche's critique of the last man:

> The realm of freedom emerges with the abolition of the division of labor.
> Yet the original form of the division of labor is "the division of labor,"
> not in the generation of offspring, but "in the sexual act." It would seem
> that the realm of freedom, if brought to its perfection, will be the realm
> of homunculi produced in test tubes by homunculi, if it will not be, as is
> more likely, the earth of "the last man," of the one herd without a shep-

herd. For to quote Machiavelli, "as has been written by some moral philosophers, men's hands and tongue, two most noble instruments for en-
nobling him, would not have done their work perfectly nor would they
have carried the works of men to the height to which they are seen to
have been carried, if they had not been driven on by necessity": the jump
from the realm of necessity into the realm of freedom will be the inglori-
ous death of the very possibility of human excellence. (Strauss 1961 148;
WPP, 128–31)

Given these difficulties one may wonder why the revival of normative
theory has not been accompanied by a critical reappraisal of relativism.
This reappraisal is possible because the historicity of man is not an undeniable fact. From the fact that every view about morality emerges in a
particular society it does not follow that every view about morality is "a
particular society's morality." For instance, it is by no means clear that
Socrates' view of justice was the same as the view of the city of Athens, of
those who put him to death. As Strauss argues, "it has always been known
that different notions of justice obtain at different times and in different
nations. It is absurd to claim that the discovery of a still greater number
of such notions by modern students has in any way affected the fundamental issue" (*NRH*, 9–10). According to Strauss, the historicity of man can
only be established through a philosophic critique of philosophy, and the
thinker who was most aware of this necessity was Martin Heidegger. But
given the controversial character of Heidegger's attempt, it is certainly permissible to doubt that all human thought is essentially limited by changing
historical circumstances.

The difficulties of a relativistic ethics did not lead to a critical reappraisal of relativism, because there were countervailing ethical and political reasons that inclined political theorists to relativism. To see these reasons, we must return to normative political theory's and existentialist
historicism's common antagonist: positivism. The failure of positivistic social science to reflect on politically and morally important issues is the unintended consequence of the appropriation by modern man of what one of
the fathers of modern mathematics and therefore of the scientific method
called the "problem of all problems, which is: to leave no problem un-
solved" (Vieta 1968, 353). The method by which all problems are to be
solved, however, requires a seeming reversal of man's natural priorities.
Whereas according to our natural judgement "the slenderest knowledge
that may be obtained of the highest things is more desirable than the most

certain knowledge obtained of the lowest things," the scientific method demands that "we should attend only to those objects of which our minds
seem capable of having certain and indubitable cognition" (Descartes 1988,
"Rules for the Direction of Our Native Intelligence," Rule 2; see also
Aquinas 1945, *Summa Theologica*, q1.a5.r1). But the original intention of
this reorientation is not to ignore but to solve the great problems of metaphysics and ethics. As Husserl argues, it is in light of this intention that

> we can understand the energy which animated all scientific undertakings,
> even the merely factual sciences of the lower level; in the eighteenth
> century (which called itself the philosophical century) it filled ever
> widening circles with enthusiasm for philosophy and for all the special
> sciences as its branches. Hence the ardent desire for learning, the zeal
> for a philosophical reform of education and of all of humanity's social
> and political forms of existence, which makes that much abused Age of
> Enlightenment so admirable. We possess an undying testimony to this
> spirit in the glorious "Hymn to Joy" of Schiller and Beethoven. It is only
> with painful feelings that we can understand this hymn today. (1970, 10)

As the last sentence of Husserl's statement indicates, modern man has
come to believe that the hope of solving moral and metaphysical problems
is a delusion. Positivism, the positivism that has abandoned Comte's hope,
is a child of this belief. For in light of the failure to establish a rational ethics
and metaphysics, the modern mind could sustain its problem-solving orientation only by limiting its attention to problems that are susceptible of a
solution by its methods. Thus, the seeming reversal of man's natural priority became an actual reversal. Yet this disregard of metaphysical and ethical problems is possible only if they cease to be recognized as problems. It
therefore became necessary to annihilate the problems that we cannot
solve, to argue, for example, that questions such as those that concern the
existence and nature of god, the soul, and justice are not only insoluble but
meaningless.

But the very intention that animates modern man, to say nothing
about the concern for one's humanity, finds this new situation revolting.
Positivism turns its gaze away from genuine human problems toward the
discovery of the regularities of behavior, because these regularities—unlike questions of value—can be objectively verified. Since the concern for
objectivity is the cause of the abandonment of interest in serious human issues, those who rebel against such an abandonment are inclined to ques-

tion the value and the possibility of objectivity, especially once they realize that the shortcoming of positivism is symptomatic of a general shortcoming of what passes for objective knowledge. Strauss brings this point out in a brief statement about Heidegger's rejection of ethics: "Heidegger on the other hand explicitly denies the possibility of ethics because he feels that there is a *revolting* disproportion between the idea of ethics and those phenomena which ethics pretended to articulate" (*WPP*, 246; emphasis added). Heidegger does not reject ethics because he thinks that immorality is better than morality. He rejects ethics because as "objective" knowledge it obscures what it tries to see, and it obscures it in such a way that it makes one indignant with its pretensions. Even Kantian ethics, through its claim to be universal knowledge, does an injustice to ethical phenomena. The authority of modern natural science no longer stands in the way of this questioning of objectivity, because Heidegger along with others has seen that modern natural science rests on premises that it has not demonstrated. Accordingly, modern science came to be seen as a historical project supported by a free and hence irrational decision. From the notion that our most fundamental views rest on our free decisions follows a kind of formal ethics that distinguishes authentic beings who take responsibility for their commitments from shallow beings who refuse to take such a responsibility.

An ethics of this sort informed the New Right in Germany between the wars and the New Left in the United States in the sixties. In fact, the relativism that one finds among those who supported the Caucus for a New Political Science Association is a mixed one. Some of them were influenced by an earlier liberal relativism that, fearing all absolutes, feared the search for objective knowledge, at least regarding norms. Christian Bay, for example, found "the Straussian position" more objectionable than that of the behavioralists, because it "is more authoritarian [than the position of the behavioralists] and far less respectful of the right to radical dissent, as is to be *expected when a corner on objective truth is being claimed*" (Bay 1967, 22; emphasis added). But the more powerful relativism was the relativism that demands free and irrational commitment to a cause. As a disappointed supporter of the Caucus reported:

> The main implication through all of this was that there was nothing at all wrong with the fact that the APSA might have been guilty for many years of collectively encouraging individual research along lines that had important social and intellectual biases. The only thing wrong was that the biases were not the ones with which the typical Caucus member had

complete sympathy. The intention of the Caucus, as spelled out in the letter and spirit of the platforms, was simply to take over the Association in order to have it serve a different set of masters. The improvements would be that, under Caucus rule, *the Association would serve the new masters explicitly and unashamedly rather than the old masters covertly and unconsciously* (Lowi 1972, 17–18; emphasis added).

We may add that this committed relativism was typically combined in a necessarily incoherent manner with a view that the American involvement in Vietnam was objectively unjust. But the development of both committed relativism and tolerant relativism makes clear not only that moral convictions have survived relativism but also why many people who felt these convictions have sought to advance relativism, and therefore, why the turn to urgent moral and political issues has not been accompanied by a critical reappraisal of relativism.

Political scientists embraced the critique of objectivity because they believed it allowed them to replace an apolitical politics with a genuine politics. But the critique of objectivity cannot truly rehabilitate the perspective of political actors, because that perspective does not presuppose a rejection of objectivity. One cannot restore contact with our original problems by merely reversing the process that led to our alienation from them, because citizens and statesmen who are devoted to the principles of their community also want those principles to be known to be true. In this respect, an important aspect of the ideal of objectivity is implicit in the political perspective as such. Although a political man may recognize the futility of debating with some human beings, he is in principle, if not always in practice, open to debates. A political man would not, for instance, say: "By entering into the arena of argument and counterargument, of technical feasibility and tactics, of footnotes and citations, *by accepting the presumption of legitimacy of debate on certain issues, one has already lost one's humanity.* This is the feeling I find impossible to repress when going through the motions of building a case against the American war in Vietnam" (Chomsky 1967, 9; emphasis added). Moreover, the relativistic opposition to the ideal of objectivity still retains in disguised form that aspect of that ideal—the notion of neutrality—which is alien to nonscientific political life. Only someone who is indifferent to all principles can honestly praise those who are committed to any principle. The ideal of commitment—not to one's principles but to principles that are consciously unsupported by objective evidence—is not a political perspective but a new perspective that somehow combines detachment with something akin to zealotry.

▲ ▲

In contrast to both positivistic political science and its humanistic critics, Strauss sought to reexamine the problem of relativism from scratch. His examination is fully open to the possibility that relativism reveals the truth about our situation. This difference points to a more general difference between Strauss and his and our contemporaries: whereas the new political science and its humanistic critics focus their attention on solving problems,[2] Strauss's political science is concerned above all with understanding problems. He went so far as to say that philosophy "is nothing but genuine awareness of the problems, i.e., of the fundamental and comprehensive problems" (*WPP*, 116; *TM*, 14). He too wanted to solve these problems, for it is impossible to confront a genuine problem without wanting to solve it, but he argued that "a philosopher ceases to be a philosopher at the moment at which the 'subjective certainty' of a solution becomes stronger than his awareness of the problematic character of that solution" (*WPP*, 116). Only by understanding this attitude, which determined Strauss's entire being, can we understand why a friend of philosophy would state the objections to it with such clarity (*NRH*, 29–31, 74–75). Regardless of what Strauss's ultimate view may be, the general path that he indicated is clearly the right path, for just as problems precede their solutions the understanding of a problem must necessarily precede the understanding of its adequate resolution or mitigation.

But what is the character of the problems that face us? All political action is informed by some understanding of the good: "All political action aims at either preservation or change. When desiring to preserve we wish to prevent a change to the worse; when desiring to change, we wish to bring about something better. All political action is then guided by some thought of better and worse. But thought of better or worse implies thought of the

---

2. As Easton made clear, the critics of behavioral political science argued that "the immediate issues of the day" require timely answers that could not be given by "slow moving basic research" (Easton 1969, 1055). Similarly, Strauss asserted that, from the point of view of Husserl, the demand for immediate answers to urgent questions—a demand which by itself is legitimate—led Heidegger to abandon philosophy as a rigorous science in favor of *Weltanschauungsphilosophie*. Strauss's Husserl implied that a thinker who at one time understood that the task of philosophy was to surrender man radically to anxiety found it impossible to resist the urgent need for immediate "consolation and exaltation" (*SPPP*, 36).

good" (*WPP*, 10). Now, one's understanding of the good is informed by one's understanding of justice, for every decent man denies himself many things that he thinks are good for him out of his concern for justice. Similarly, our understanding of justice is informed by our understanding of the good, for law-abiding men would not accept the sacrifices that justice demands if they did not think that somehow justice itself is good. The most profound political disagreements—those that tend to tear a community apart—are based on disagreements about the good and the just: "Agreement can always be reached in principle about the means to an established end, whereas the ends are always controversial: we disagree with one another and with ourselves always only about the just and the good" (*SCR*, 347). The task of political philosophy, a task that according to relativism is a delusion, is to resolve these controversies. Accordingly, relativism has a tendency of dismissing the questions that naturally emerge in political life. This is true of liberal relativism even more than of existentialist relativism. For instance, relativism allowed a member of the Supreme Court of the United States in the midst of a world war to write:

> What we most love and revere generally is determined by early associations. I love granite rocks and barberry bushes, no doubt because with them were my earliest joys that reach back through the past eternity of my life. But while one's experience thus makes certain preferences dogmatic for oneself, recognition of how they came to be so leaves one able to see that others, poor souls, may be equally dogmatic about something else. And this again means skepticism. Not that one's belief and one's love does not remain. Not that we would not fight and die for it if important—we all, whether we know it or not—are fighting to make the kind of world that we should like—but that we have learned to recognize that others will fight and die to make a different world, with equal sincerity or belief. Deep-seated preferences can not be argued about—you can not argue a man into liking a glass of beer—and therefore, when differences are sufficiently far reaching we try to kill the other man rather than let him have his way. But that is perfectly consistent with admitting that, so far as appears, his grounds are just as good as ours. (Holmes 1952, 311–12)

According to Holmes, it is perfectly consistent to kill one's enemy while insisting that his "grounds are just as good as ours." But would not such killing be unjust? Is this not the reason that led the young Holmes as a soldier in the Civil War to inform a friend that "if one did not believe this war was a crusade in the cause of the whole Christian world it would be hard to keep the hand to the sword" (quoted in Burton 1992, 30)? It seems, then, that relativism led the older Holmes to regard the question of justice, the question of which side in a dispute is in the right, as a moot question.

Although liberal relativism is a less advanced form of relativism, it is proper to begin with it because it is the first obstacle to a critical reappraisal of relativism. For unlike existentialist relativism, it seems to regard relativism not so much as a problem but as a blessing. Many today regard relativism as the only solid basis for liberal democratic values and therefore a cause for celebration. To be sure, this view is not often explicitly stated, for relativism faces certain obvious difficulties that have been exploited by, among others, defenders of illiberal institutions in Asia, of genital mutilation in Africa, and even of cock fighting in rural America, who have pointed out that their critics want to impose Western or urban values on them while constantly preaching the equality of all cultures and values. But many of those who do not consider themselves relativists, and many relativists who are too sophisticated to argue that it is the only basis of democratic values, implicitly embrace relativism insofar as they regard absolutism as the source of closed-mindedness and intolerance and insofar as they cannot find a solid middle ground between relativism and absolutism (Geertz 1989, 12–34).

Hans Kelsen was one of the earliest and most influential advocates of this view, which gained currency shortly after World War II. According to him, philosophical absolutism (any doctrine that claims to be "true not only in relation to the knowing subject but to everybody, always and everywhere" [Kelsen 1948, 907]) inherently supports political absolutism (autocracy), and philosophical relativism (any doctrine that only claims to be true relative to the knowing subject but not to others) inherently supports political relativism (democracy): "If one believes in the existence of the absolute . . . good—to use Plato's terminology—is it not meaningless to let a majority vote decide what is politically good?" Similarly, he argued that only philosophical relativism allows for respect for the rights of minorities: "It may be that the opinion of the minority, and not the opinion of the majority, is correct. Solely because of this possibility, which only philosophical relativism can admit—that what is right today may be wrong tomorrow—the minority must have a chance to express freely their opinion and must have full opportunity of becoming the majority" (ibid., 913). Kelsen, however, put the greatest emphasis on the claim that his contention is amply supported by empirical evidence: "Almost all outstanding representatives of a relativistic philosophy were politically in favor of democracy, whereas followers of philosophical absolutism, the great metaphysicians, were in favor of political absolutism and against democracy" (ibid., 911).

Now Kelsen's arguments, which have some weight in a nonrelativistic context, are manifestly inadequate as a defense of relativism. There is indeed a tension between the claims of political knowledge and the claims of democracy, but if no opinion as far as we can know is intrinsically superior to another, it follows that the opinion of an autocrat cannot be inferior to that of the majority of the citizens, and this observation can easily be the basis for preferring autocracy to democracy, since even the friends of popular government admit that autocrats in general can make decisions more quickly and carry them out more energetically than assemblies. There is indeed a tension between dogmatic certainty that the truth is already available and the view that freedom of discussion is good, but if no opinion as far as we can know is intrinsically superior to another, no reason is left to justify freedom of discussion, for that freedom is given with the hope of discovering the truth, a hope that according to relativism is a delusion. Moreover, Kelsen's appeal to empirical evidence is even weaker than his theoretical arguments, for the original advocates of liberal democracy based their advocacy on certain "self-evident truths" (*NRH*, 1). And they did not deny that some individuals are better judges of what is politically good and that "that form of government is best, which provides the most effectually for a pure selection of [the] natural *aristoi* into offices of good government" (Jefferson, "Letter to John Adams," October 28, 1813, quoted in *WPP*, 86; see also Spinoza 1951, 385–87 consider also Paine's criticism of the nobility, which he called the "no-ability," 1969, 128). Relativism, in contrast, emerged in Germany, the Western country in which liberal democracy faced the greatest resistance. Strauss reminds us of this historical fact by referring to an observation made between the wars by Ernst Troeltsch that "the West still attached decisive importance to natural right, while in Germany the very terms 'natural right' and 'humanity' 'have now become almost incomprehensible'" (*NRH*, 1). To illustrate this point, Troeltsch mentioned the following story:

> It was only the other day that a judge of the Supreme Court of the
> United States, C. E. Hughes, delivered a course of lectures to students,
> describing democracy as the form of government which . . . was yet the
> form dictated by God, by nature, and by Humanity. In his introduction
> to the German translation of these lectures, D. J. Hill, the former
> American ambassador in Berlin, makes the characteristic remark, that
> the lecturer never mentions the essential premise on which his lectures

are based—the natural and divine foundation of the rights of men—
simply because it is self-evident to all Americans. (1934, 209)

What is self-evident to Americans needed to be explained to Germans.
Writing after the war, Strauss noted that American social science, to the extent that it was not Roman Catholic social science, had adopted the same attitude toward natural right that was characteristic of German thought prior
to the war: "It would not be the first time that a nation, defeated on the
battlefield and, as it were, annihilated as a political being, has deprived its
conquerors of the most sublime fruit of victory by imposing on them the
yoke of its own thought" (*NRH*, 2; compare Heidegger 1968, 66).[3] By comparing America and Germany to Rome and ancient Israel, Strauss warned
of a possible decline and fall of America. There are two ways humans and
their institutions can be destroyed: they can die or they can cease to be themselves. They cease to be themselves when they give up their aspirations. It is
this danger that was of concern to Strauss in this context. Now, America's
noblest aspiration is the actualization of a political society based on principles of nature and not on myths: "It was the general opinion of ancient nations that the Divinity alone was adequate to the important office of giving
laws to men. . . . The United States of America have exhibited, perhaps, the
first example of governments erected on the simple principles of nature"
(John Adams, quoted in Pangle 1988, 78; see also *Federalist Papers*, #1).

By suggesting that relativism is inimical to liberal democracy, Strauss
almost turned Kelsen's thesis on its head. He did not suggest that all relativists are illiberal (he spoke of "liberal relativism") nor did he suggest that
relativism or any other intellectual or social condition made the rise of
Hitler necessary, but he did suggest that by obscuring the meaning of the
notion of humanity relativism undermined resistance to Hitler's movement. At the very least, relativism weakened the resistance to illiberal politics by encouraging contempt for morality and the fundamental political

---

3. Indeed, American political scientists, "many of whom were trained in German schools"
(Merriam 1968, 306), had already begun to reject natural rights in the nineteenth century: "The
present tendency in American political theory is to disregard the once dominant ideas of natural
right and social contract, although it must be admitted that the political scientists are more agreed
upon this point than is the general public" (ibid., 311, 307). Earlier he said that the ideas in question were "discredited and repudiated," rather than disregarded. As Merriam explains, after the
civil war American political theorists sided with Calhoun's contention that liberty is not the natural and inherent right of all men while rejecting his use of this idea to support slavery: "The mistaken application of the idea had the effect of delaying recognition of the truth in what had been
said until the controversy over slavery was at an end" (312). Although they argued that the state
was the source of liberty, they still supported liberty because they judged it necessary for progress.

principles of liberalism. In 1925, the year in which Field-Marshal Von Hindenburg was elected to presidency of the Weimar Republic (*SCR*, 1), Kelsen himself said:

> The assertion that in despotism there is no rightful order but only the rule of the arbitrary will of the despot is completely meaningless. . . . In a despotically ruled state there is also some sort of an order of human affairs. . . . This order is precisely the rightful order. To deny its rightful character is only a natural right naiveté or presumption. . . . What is referred to as an arbitrary will is only the rightful possibility of the autocrat to appropriate every decision to himself in order to determine unconditionally the activity of subordinate agents and to change or invalidate the legal norms at any time with general or special authority. Such a position is a rightful position, even if it is perceived as disadvantageous. But it also has its good side. This is shown most clearly by the not infrequent calls for dictatorship in the modern legitimate state. (*NRH*, 4n; the translation is my own)

In light of this passage, which Kelsen eliminated from the English translation of his work, his thesis about the necessary connection between relativism and democracy appears to be the result not of naiveté but of an attempt to conceal—perhaps from himself no less than from others—the implications of his relativism. Since Kelsen could neither abandon his abhorrence of Hitler nor renounce his relativism, he ignored the contradiction he had so ably articulated.[4]

A more thoughtful response to the experience of Hitler would have been to reevaluate the whole question of natural right and relativism.[5] But a reevaluation of the question of natural right is difficult for most liberals, because

---

4. His subsequent argument has the added bonus of putting part of the blame for the rise of Hitler on his intellectual opponents. In this respect, he has not been altogether unsuccessful (Gunnell 1993, 212).

5. Carl Becker, who had rejected the notion of natural right in his study of the Declaration of Independence, felt compelled to state in a new postwar preface to his study that "the incredible cynicism and brutality of Adolph Hitler's ambitions . . . have forced men everywhere to re-appraise the validity of half-forgotten ideas, and enabled them once more to entertain convictions as to the substance of things not evident to senses. One of these convictions is that 'liberty, equality, fraternity' and 'the inalienable rights of men' are phrases, glittering or not, that denote realities—the fundamental realities that men will always fight for rather than surrender" (1948, xvi). This is not, however, a reappraisal of the issue in the precise sense of the term: Whereas Jefferson posited the inalienable rights of men as self-evident truths, Becker returned to them even though they are "not evident to senses." As Becker's allusion to Hebrews 11 indicates, he accepted the teachings of political philosophy concerning faith.

they associate liberalism with relativism and National Socialism with absolutism. It is easy to interpret liberalism as a kind of relativism, because intolerance often has its roots in the belief that one has certain knowledge of right and wrong.[6] Yet the belief that those who are governed by firm principles cannot be tolerant of others ignores the fact that only a firm adherence to toleration allows one to resist the intolerance that is directed against unpopular opinions. It is easy to interpret National Socialists as absolutists, because they surely claimed that they were right and others wrong. But right about which doctrines? Strauss pointed to the peculiar lack of clear principles of the Nazi regime by observing that it was the only regime anywhere "which had no other clear principle than murderous hatred of Jews, for 'Aryan' had no clear meaning other than 'non-Jewish'" (*SCR*, 3). The absolutist philosopher is Hegel, who claimed to have transformed love of wisdom to wisdom. Strauss observed: "It has been said, not without reason, that Hegel's rule over Germany came to an end only on the day Hitler came to power" (*SCR*, 2). Hitler's rule was not a rule based on absolute knowledge of ideas. As Heidegger said in 1933: "Let not doctrines and 'Ideas' be the rules of your Being. The Fuehrer alone *is* the present and future German reality and its law" (quoted in R. Wolin 1995, 8). Moreover, Strauss suggested that the professors and writers who knowingly or unknowingly paved the way for Hitler—Oswald Spengler, Moeller van den Bruck, Carl Schmitt, Alfred Baeumler, Ernst Juenger, Martin Heidegger—were all relativists, if relativists who were dissatisfied with relativism or with some versions of it (Strauss 1999, 362).

But it is not necessary for us to determine whether National Socialism was a relativistic or an absolutistic movement. It may even be the case that the inculcation of relativism may foster toleration in certain societies for some time. What is important is to know the logical consequence of relativism, for only this knowledge can help us take our bearing toward it. To acquire this understanding, we turn to Strauss's brief discussion in his introduction to *Natural Right and History* of the consequences of the contemporary rejection of natural right.

▲   ▲

To see the consequences of the contemporary rejection of natural right, Strauss suggests, we must first understand man's perennial "need for natural right," for "political life in all its forms necessarily points to natural

6. "It is hard to see how a political scientist can be either a Nazi or a Communist. The spirit of compromise and relativism inherent in political science, the appreciation of the relativity of means to ends and of ends to means can, I think, be a protection against absolutistic beliefs whether of the right or the left, of the church or of the state" (Wright 1950, 8).

right as an inevitable problem" (*NRH*, 2–3, 81). To deny that there is a standard of right and wrong independent of societal conventions is to imply that "what is right is determined exclusively by the legislators and the courts of various countries" (*NRH*, 2). But certain experiences—for example, that of slavery—make it "meaningful and sometimes even necessary to speak of unjust laws or unjust decisions," and by implication of "a standard of right and wrong independent of positive right and higher than positive right" (*NRH*, 2). Now opponents of natural right may deny the need for a transcendent standard to give an account of such experiences, for one can criticize bad laws on the basis of a standard that is immanent in society: one may regard slavery as an evil not because it contradicts the inalienable right to liberty but because it contradicts the ideal of our society. But this implies that no standard higher than the ideal adopted by our society exists and that the worth of that ideal rests on nothing but its adoption by our society. As soon as we make this implication clear, we realize that the denial of a standard higher than the ideal adopted by our society contradicts itself, for by stating that our ideal rests only on its adoption by our society, we undermine that very ideal:

> All societies have their ideals, cannibal societies no less than civilized ones. If principles are sufficiently justified by the fact that they are accepted by a society, the principles of cannibalism are as defensible or sound as those of civilized life. From this point of view, the former principles can certainly not be rejected as simply bad. And since the ideal of our society is admittedly changing, nothing except dull and stale habit could prevent us from placidly accepting a change in the direction of cannibalism. (*NRH*, 3)

Ignorance of this difficulty constitutes much of the charm of cultural relativism for those who regard relativism, and the related thesis that "we have no other criterion of reason than the example and ideas of the opinions and customs of the country we live in," as a remedy for "provincialism," that is, as a means of freeing us from the grip of the opinions and customs of the country we live in (Geertz 1989, 14–15). Yet the very openness of anthropologists to such practices as cannibalism and human sacrifice, that is, their very questioning of the principles of their own society, speaks against cultural relativism: "If there is no standard higher than the ideal of our society, we are utterly unable to take a critical distance from that ideal. But the mere fact that we can raise the question of the worth of the ideal of our society shows that there is something in man that is not altogether in slavery to his society, and therefore that we are able, and hence obliged, to look for a standard with reference to which we can judge of the ideals of our own as well as of any other society" (*NRH*, 3). But how does Strauss deduce our obligation to search for such a standard from our ability to do so? Our primary obligation is not to this search but to our community, the community in which we are born and which has nourished and raised us. As soon as we become aware, however, that the ideal of our community is questionable, our obligation to our community obliges us to answer those questions, and we cannot answer them without finding a "standard with reference to which we can judge the ideals of our own as well as of any other societies." This transcendence of our society's ideal on behalf of that ideal presupposes a genuine openness to other societies, a willingness to learn from them instead of just refusing to criticize them, a possibility that cultural relativism denies. Even a practice as bizarre as cannibalism leads one, as Strauss demonstrates, to raise questions about Western civilization that require serious answers:

> Can one say that the bodily needs of the individual have first claim over against the spiritual props of society, over against beliefs, however erroneous? Are firmly held beliefs not much more important for getting an integrated culture in which man can find mental security than what modern medicine declares to be adequate satisfaction of bodily wants? Is there no support for the view that the interests which arise out of the bodily needs are divisive, whereas beliefs—agreements regarding fundamentals—have a unifying effect? (*LNRH*, lecture 1.3)

One cannot judge the ideals of societies without knowing what the good society in principle is, but we cannot deduce the structure of that society from "the needs of the various societies, for the societies and their parts have many needs that conflict with one another: the problem of priority arises." The problem posed by the conflicting needs of a society cannot be solved in a rational manner if we do not have a standard "with reference to which we can distinguish between genuine needs and fancied needs and discern the hierarchy of the various genuine needs," that is, if we do not have knowledge of natural right (*NRH*, 3). Knowledge of natural right is something that is of interest not merely to historians but to every intelligent and honest citizen living today. This understanding of natural right is brought out clearly in Edward Banfield's recollections of his conversations with Strauss:

When in my capacity as a student of planning I put to [Strauss] the problem of budgeting—given limited funds, which should get more, schools
or hospitals?—he answered unhesitatingly, "schools, because education
is more important than health." Later, teasing me for my failure to appreciate the contribution that natural law made to the theory of planning, he remarked that being an honest man I must act on principles.
"And natural law," he went on, "is nothing but an attempt to spell out
the principles on which honest men act and have acted and will act as
long as there are men." (1991, 496)[7]

By articulating man's need for natural right, Strauss is preparing us for
the consequences of rejecting natural right. Although he maintains that
any rejection of natural right "would seem" to lead to disastrous consequences, he argues that it is "obvious" that disastrous consequences would
follow from the *contemporary* rejection of natural right (*NRH*, 3; emphasis
added). Whereas nihilism is the consequence of or rather identical with the
contemporary rejection of natural right, it is not obvious that the same is
true of, say, Machiavelli's rejection of natural right. This is because the
contemporary rejection of natural right is more radical insofar as it denies
man knowledge of the good as well as of the right:

> Such a science is instrumental and nothing but instrumental: it is born
> to be the handmaid of any powers or any interests that be. What Machi-
> avelli did apparently, our social science would actually do if it did not
> prefer—only God knows why—generous liberalism to consistency:
> namely, to give advice with equal competence and alacrity to tyrants as
> well as to free peoples. (*NRH*, 4)

There are two consequences: one potential and the other actual. According to the first, this social science would serve its own interests by giving
advice to any powers that be because it does not recognize the claims of re-
publican principles to be more just than the maxims of tyrants. But Strauss
suggests that it does not follow this mercenary policy. It does not make use
of liberalism but is attached to liberalism. Having rejected modern natural
right and the individualism characteristic of it, this social science cannot

---

7. Strauss's preference for schools to hospitals must be qualified in certain circumstances,
"for one has to consider not only which of the various competing objectives is higher in rank but
also which is most urgent in the circumstances. What is most urgent is legitimately preferred
to what is less urgent, and the most urgent is in many cases lower in rank than the less urgent"
(*NRH*, 162).

decide whether one's own good or that of one's community is more important. According to modern social science, "no goals that are pursued with tolerable consistency can be called 'irrational': if a person seeks above all else a life of poverty and abnegation, and if he pursues that goal consistently and efficiently, his behavior is rational" (Rogowski 1978, 299). But if the choice of our ends is arbitrary, what reason do we have for insisting on consistency? Instrumental rationality is a kind of irrationality that places us "in the position of beings who are sane and sober when engaged in trivial business and who gamble like madmen when confronted with serious issues—retail sanity and wholesale madness" (*NRH*, 4). Accordingly, Strauss concludes, "if our principles have no other support than our blind preferences, everything a man is willing to dare will be permissible" (*NRH*, 4–5).

Now, Strauss observes that in spite of the fact that the contemporary rejection of natural right is identical with nihilism "generous liberals view the abandonment of natural right not only with placidity but with relief" (*NRH*, 5). It would seem that liberals should be troubled by nihilism because by permitting everything it permits harming others. But if the most intractable motive for harming others is intolerance of their opinions and preferences, and if the basis of this intolerance is the belief that one has knowledge of good or right, this very nihilism appears to undermine the most intractable reason for harming others: "They [generous liberals] appear to believe that our inability to acquire any genuine knowledge of what is intrinsically good or right compels us to be tolerant of every opinion about good or right or to recognize all preferences or all 'civilizations' as equally respectable. Only unlimited tolerance is in accordance with reason" (*NRH*, 5). The very esteem for tolerance that has been fostered by modern natural right leads some of those who have been shaped by it to welcome the rejection of that natural right because it leads to the replacement of a limited tolerance with an unlimited one.

But Strauss observes that the acceptance of unlimited tolerance necessarily leads one to put a limit on tolerance. In particular, he shows that the rejection of natural right leads to an affirmation of a rational or natural right: "[T]his leads to the admission of a rational or natural right of every preference that is tolerant of other preferences or, negatively expressed, of a rational or natural right to reject or condemn all intolerant or all 'absolutist' positions. The latter must be condemned, because they are based on a demonstrably false premise, namely, that man can know what is good" (*NRH*, 5). If only unlimited tolerance is in accordance with reason, preferences that do not tolerate other preferences cannot be rational: not all preferences but only those that are tolerant of other preferences ought to be tolerated. More precisely, according to this view one must reject only preferences that do not tolerate other preferences on the basis of a claim to knowledge. This permits some intolerance. Whereas it rejects all "civilizations" that have hitherto existed, this view seems to allow respect for "the simple preliterate people who cherish their values without raising exorbitant claims on their behalf" (*RCPR*, 12). But what is the basis of this view? At first it seems to be a rational right teaching, since it condemns all "absolutist" positions because they violate the limits of human knowledge as they are allegedly known by our reason. But Strauss suggests that it in fact is a natural right teaching: "At the bottom of the passionate rejection of all 'absolutes,' we discern the recognition of a *natural* right or, more precisely, of that particular interpretation of *natural* right according to which the one thing needful is respect for diversity or individuality" (*NRH*, 5; emphasis added). The affirmation of diversity or individuality is the reverse side of the rejection of all absolutes, but why is this rejection a passionate rejection? The rejection would not be passionate if absolutist positions did not deny human beings something that they need, something that is good for them. Accordingly, the passionate rejection of all absolutes implies some claim to knowledge about human nature. According to Strauss, the liberal respect for diversity is a consequence of the more fundamental respect for individuality, for if human beings are by nature individuals, they should be allowed to develop themselves, either individually or collectively, as they see fit. The deduction of unlimited tolerance from our inability to acquire genuine knowledge about good or right leads to a view that claims just such knowledge.

But Strauss observes that the notion of natural right that maintains that the one thing needful is respect for diversity or individuality suffers from an internal tension, for "there is a tension between the respect for diversity or individuality and the recognition of natural right" (*NRH*, 5). Strauss alluded to this tension when he referred alternatively to the condemnation and the passionate rejection of all absolutes. Those who regard individuality or diversity as the one thing needful can reject all absolutes only with passion. Every notion of natural right imposes a certain uniformity and social constraint on individuals. But one cannot accept these impositions if one regards respect for diversity or individuality as the one thing needful. Faced with this tension, one could either affirm natural right and accept some limitations on diversity or individuality, as earlier liberals had done, or else make a complete break with natural right. According to Strauss, the liberals chose the latter: "When liberals became impatient of the absolute limits to diversity or individuality that are imposed even by the most liberal version of natural right, they had to make a choice between natural right and the uninhibited cultivation of individuality. They chose the latter" (*NRH*, 5).

To understand the choice between natural right and the view that individuality or diversity is the one thing needful, we briefly turn to Strauss's account of the history of modern thought, for "the quarrel between the ancients and the moderns concerns eventually, and perhaps even from the beginning, the status of 'individuality'" (*NRH*, 323). Modern liberalism—the liberalism of Hobbes and Locke—began with an attempt to deduce natural rights from the assumption that human beings are by nature free and individual. According to Strauss, the inconsistency of this teaching was brought to light by Rousseau: "Hobbes is grossly inconsistent because, on the one hand, he denies that man is by nature social and, on the other hand, he tries to establish the character of the natural man by referring to his experience of men, which is the experience of social man" (*NRH*, 268). By following Hobbes's premise in a consistent manner, Rousseau deduces a state of nature that is at once superior to political society and incompatible with it. Accordingly, in Rousseau's thought the tension between individualism and the demands of society resurfaces: "At one moment he ardently defends the rights of the individual or the rights of the heart against all restraint and authority; at the next moment he demands with equal ardor the complete submission of the individual to society or the state and favors the most rigorous moral or social discipline" (*NRH*, 254). Although according to Strauss Rousseau did not believe that this conflict was soluble, the most powerful interpretation of Rousseau—that of Kant and Hegel—maintained that Rousseau saw, if somewhat vaguely, the solution of this problem in a certain type of society (*NRH*, 254–55, 255n. 4). According to Kant, the full actualization of this society requires a world order, a reshaping of the existing states and of their relation to each other (Kant 1949, 123–27). This interpretation of Rousseau underlay the French Revolution, understood as a revolution that must be spread to the rest of the world, and it was against this idea that the German historical school arose. The imposition of the Napoleonic code on German states revealed once again the tension between natural right, which as such is universal, and respect for diversity or individuality. According to Strauss, the conservatives who founded the historical school rejected the principles of the revolution by further clarifying them, that is, by making them more consistent:

> The revolutionists assumed, we may say, that the natural is always individual and that therefore the uniform is unnatural or conventional. The

human individual was to be liberated or to liberate himself so that he could pursue not just his happiness but his own version of happiness. This meant, however, that one universal and uniform goal was set up for all men: the natural right of each individual was a right uniformly belonging to every man as man. But uniformity was said to be unnatural and hence bad. (*NRH*, 14).

By rejecting the value of universal principles, the conservative members of the historical school came to maintain a position that was more consistent with the notion of nature underlying modern liberalism: "The only kinds of rights that were neither incompatible with social life nor uniform were 'historical' rights: rights of Englishmen, for example, in contradistinction to the rights of man. Local and temporal variety seemed to supply a safe and solid middle ground between anti-social individualism and unnatural universality" (*NRH*, 14). But as Strauss observes, the expectation that historical studies can yield standards that are both objective and relative to particular situations rests on "assumptions that stemmed directly or indirectly from the natural right doctrine of the eighteenth century": "that nations or ethnic groups are natural units or that there exist general laws of historical evolution" (*NRH*, 16). According to Strauss, Max Weber saw this difficulty and rejected historical rights because they rest on assumptions that are metaphysical inasmuch as they contradict the premise that "the real is always individual" (*NRH*, 37). The liberal rejection of natural right is a clarification of the modern liberal understanding of reality and perhaps of modern understanding as such.

But by remaining true to the premise of liberalism, liberal relativists moved away from its intention, for the rejection of natural right undermined any reason for preferring tolerance to intolerance: "Once this step was taken, tolerance appeared as one value or ideal among many, and not intrinsically superior to its opposite. In other words, intolerance appeared as a value equal in dignity to tolerance" (*NRH*, 5). Both tolerance and intolerance can be rejected insofar as they claim to rest on universal principles that are known, but insofar as they claim to be based on a human choice they are of equal worth.

But as Strauss observes, "it is practically impossible to leave it at the equality of all preferences or choices" (*NRH*, 5), for human beings cannot live without some sort of guidance. As a result, the need for guidance that led to the emergence of natural right re-emerges in a magnified form, but now it must be addressed without recourse to a natural right teaching. This need can be fulfilled only by reflection on the human situation as it is disclosed by relativism: "If the unequal rank of choices cannot be traced to the unequal rank of their objectives, it must be traced to the unequal rank of acts of choosing; and this means eventually that genuine choice, as distinguished from spurious or despicable choice, is nothing but resolute or deadly serious decision" (*NRH*, 5–6). This new understanding of the primacy of choice paves the way for the distinction between two types of choice. It thus becomes possible to distinguish between those who see or face up to the truth about man's situation, who choose to posit their ultimate ends, and who thereby become authentic in the sense of owning themselves, and those who do not see or face up to the truth about man's situation, who avoid this fundamental choice by letting their values be determined for them by others, and who thereby become inauthentic in the sense of letting others own them.[8] The alleged truth about man's situation is the realization that man's fundamental choice is a "groundless choice," one not based on adequate reasons (Strauss 1995a, 309). A genuine choice is a "resolute decision" because only such a choice is made in full awareness of the alleged fact that our highest principles, including the principles of modern natural science, are based on a free choice. The difference between choice in general and decision is that one can make a choice while being open to the alternatives not chosen, whereas a decision closes one to these alternatives. A resolute decision is one made in full awareness that one is making a decision. To illustrate the difference between choice and resolute decision, let us consider Strauss's claim that one must choose between philosophy and theology:

> No one can be both a philosopher and a theologian, or, for that matter, some possibility which transcends the conflict between philosophy and theology, or pretends to be a synthesis of both. But every one of us can be and ought to be either one or the other, the philosopher open to the challenge of theology, or the theologian open to the challenge of philosophy. (*JP*, 116)

We ought to make a choice, Strauss argues, but whatever choice we make we ought to be open to the challenge of its alternative, because we may have made the wrong choice and because we may discover that error through examination. But if one knows that one's fundamental choice is a

---

8. Authenticity as a standard presupposes relativism and is therefore a phenomenon peculiar to twentieth-century thought: "Nietzsche *prepares* decisively the replacement of the natural by the authentic" (*SPPP*, 186; emphasis added).

"groundless choice," one realizes that a theologian who is open to the challenge of philosophy and a philosopher who is open to the challenge of theology are living on the basis of a delusion that their examinations will reveal the correctness or the error of their choice.

By focusing on the view that man's principles have no support other
than irrational decisions, one derives a standard that on the basis of liberal
premises rehabilitates intolerance, or more precisely, is "akin to intolerance" (*NRH*, 6). This becomes clear by the way Strauss identifies genuine
and spurious choices. A spurious choice is a choice to travel on tracks laid
by others without realizing that one is making such a choice, that is, without realizing that one is free to choose otherwise. Those who unknowingly
let others determine their principles may be foolish but they are not blame-
worthy. But if their failure to see the truth stems from a lack of courage,
then their choice can plausibily be described as despicable. If the fundamental truth of the human situation is so ugly that it requires courage to
see it, this relativism not only rehabilitates courage as a virtue but also raises
it to a new height. We are here at the opposite pole of the modern natural
right, which maintained that self-preservation is man's most important
end. Similarly, since a resolute decision is one that determines one's ultimate principles, principles for which men are willing to die, resolute decision can plausibly be identified as a "deadly serious decision." But can one
be intolerant toward the enemy in good conscience if one does not think
there is something wrong with the substance of his principles? Strauss
raises this difficulty in his criticism of Carl Schmitt's criticism of liberalism:

> Whoever affirms the political as such, respects all who are willing to
> fight; he is quite as tolerant as liberals, but with the opposite intention.
> Whereas the liberal respects and tolerates all 'honestly held' convic-
> tions, so long as these respect the legal order or acknowledge the sanc-
> tity of *peace*, whoever affirms the political as such respects and tolerates
> all 'serious' convictions, in other words, all decisions leading up to the
> possibility of *war*. Thus the affirmation of the political as such proves to
> be liberalism preceded by a minus sign. (*SCR*, 350)

Accordingly, Strauss characterizes a resolute decision as one that is only
akin to intolerance.

Although the position that I have just sketched is characteristic of critics of liberalism, Strauss describes it as liberal relativism because it is based
on liberal premises and because it has not succeeded in freeing itself from
liberalism. Whereas liberal relativism is "a seminary of intolerance," its

own principle is only "akin to intolerance." It itself cannot do what it preaches. The thinkers in question wish for intolerance not because they were ruled by some perverse human impulse but because they were concerned with humanity:

> The First World War shook Europe to its foundation. Men lost their sense of direction. The faith in progress decayed. The only people who kept that faith in its original vigor were the communists. But precisely communism showed to the non-communists the delusion of progress. Spengler's *Decline of the West* seemed to be much more credible. But one had to be inhuman to leave it at Spengler's prognosis. Is there no hope for Europe and therewith for mankind? It was in the spirit of such hope that Heidegger perversely welcomed 1933. (Strauss 1995a, 315–16)

In one sense of the term, it is possible to leave it at the equality of all preferences or choices; it is possible to live an utterly aimless and irrational life. But as members of a society we can not live an aimless life, for a society that tolerates everything will soon disintegrate. Equality of all preferences or choices fosters an extreme liberalism that is tolerant of views that do not tolerate it and the society that it was meant to protect (*WPP*, 224). Whereas the need for natural right stemmed especially from the need to judge the ideals of one's own society, the rejection of natural right leads especially to a need to find ways to support one's primary concern with one's society. Since they could not return to the past, the more advanced relativists sought to find their standards within the nihilistic liberalism to which they belonged. They sought to overcome nihilism by thinking it through to its ultimate consequence.

But Strauss suggests that they failed to overcome nihilism because they could not truly establish the view that genuine choice is a resolute decision. The distinction between resolute decision and spurious choice cannot overcome the difficulties that afflicted value relativism, because what one must resolutely decide is not some action but the principles of our actions. Principles of action are higher than the individual's choice of a particular action inasmuch as they govern the latter. Realizing that the principles of our action have no support other than our blind choice is like realizing that one's god is one's own fabrication. Accordingly, Strauss writes: "Once we realize that the principles of our actions have no other support than our blind choice, we no longer believe in them any more" (*NRH*, 6). By realizing that our principles of action cannot be derived from different acts of choosing, we realize that we cannot replace the old transcendent ideals with our free and conscious creations. Indeed, we realize that the individual can never be simply the basis of the values that obligate him, and "precisely through characterization of something as 'a value' what is so valued is robbed of its worth. That is to say, by the assessment of something as a value what is valued is admitted only as an object for man's estimation" (Heidegger 1977, 228). Once we no longer believe in our principles, "we cannot wholeheartedly act upon them any more. We cannot live any more as responsible beings. In order to live, we have to silence the easily silenced voice of reason, which tells us that our principles are in themselves as good or as bad as any other principles" (*NRH*, 6). We cannot live without living as responsible beings, because we are social beings who feel the obligation to give an account of ourselves to our community, and therefore we want to act wholeheartedly on the principles of our community.[9] Thus, a profound conflict emerges between our moral and political needs and the rational conclusion of the modern rejection of natural right: "The more we cultivate reason, the more we cultivate nihilism: the less are we able to be loyal members of society." According to Strauss, "the inescapable practical consequence" of this conflict is "fanatical obscurantism" (*NRH*, 6).

To understand this necessity and the meaning of "fanatical obscurantism," it is helpful to consider Heidegger's thought, for according to Strauss Heidegger saw the difficulty of overcoming nihilism by establishing historicism more clearly than anyone else. If our ends rest on blind choice, we can transcend our historical circumstances, for there would be no reason to prevent, for example, a contemporary American from worshiping Zeus. But we notice that not even those who claim to be pagans fear Zeus' thunderbolts. We today cannot worship Zeus as his genuine devotees did. Since, according to relativism, the existence of Zeus was never refuted and could never be refuted, our limitation must be traced to our historical circumstance. But here we run into a difficulty: on one hand, we assert that all human thought and action depends on history, but on the other, history is the product of human thought and action. We can remove this difficulty and thus clarify the insight that human reason rests on presuppositions that it cannot validate or even recognize by maintaining that the real ground of history is not the thoughts and actions of men but mysterious fate:

---

9. Although Heidegger criticizes the public for depriving the individual of his responsibility, his concern with responsibility is no less a concern for the public. The inauthentic individual is despicable, because he is not responsible. But responsible to whom? To himself, but that self is thoroughly social: "Man is essentially a social being: to be a human being means to be with other human beings. To be in an authentic way means to be in an authentic way with others: to be true to oneself is incompatible with being false to others" (Strauss 1995a, 311).

> A single comprehensive view is imposed on us by fate. . . . Strictly speaking, we cannot choose among different views. All human thought depends on fate, on something that thought cannot master and whose workings it cannot anticipate. Yet the support of the horizon produced by fate is ultimately the choice of the individual, since that fate has to be accepted by the individual. We are free in the sense that we are free either to choose in anguish the world view and the standards imposed on us by fate or else to lose ourselves in illusory security or in despair. (*NRH*, 27)

"Fanatical obscurantism" is in the first place, then, a thesis about Being: the ground of the world is unintelligible (obscure). It rejects the opposite thesis, characteristic of science and philosophy, which is that the world is ruled by an intelligible necessity. It is fanatical because one can only see it on the basis of evidence that is not in principle available to man as man but only to those who freely commit themselves to it: "Only to thought that is itself committed or 'historical' does the true meaning of the 'historicity' of all genuine thought disclose itself" (*NRH*, 27). If we understand mysterious fate as the ground of history and understand that understanding as "an unforeseeable gift of unfathomable fate" (*NRH*, 28), historical relativism becomes an apparently consistent view of the world that makes possible again deadly serious decision. It seems to overcome modern subjectivism because it recognizes the source of our principles in nonhuman fate.

But does it overcome modern subjectivism? Does it not in fact obscure something of importance? At the time that Heidegger was moving toward this position, Strauss was questioning the meaning of accepting the verdict of fate:

> From the fact that mankind has a present it does not follow that one needs to heed it: our *fate* is not our *task*. This is the principle error to which the modern man succumbs: the attempt to determine one's task out of fate. This attempt is nonsense, for if there is no God then fate is chance and if God exists then fate is providence and we are not permitted to want to play with providence. This error reveals itself in the will to synthesis: factually every standpoint may be a synthesis but it was *never willed as* synthesis; it was willed as the *truth*. (*GS*, 2 : 384; emphasis in original; translation is my own)

Heidegger's position obscures the choice between atheism and theism that every human being must make. Nor does Heidegger overcome modern subjectivism, according to Strauss, for his attempt to establish historicism led him to insist that Being does not exist independent of man. But what happens if mankind ceases to exist? Heidegger believed that "if and when there are no human beings, there may be *entia*, but there cannot be *esse*, that is, there can be *entia* while there is no *esse*" (*NRH*, 32). Heidegger made this statement in the "Nachwort" of the fourth edition of *Was ist Metaphysik?*, but in the fifth edition he silently reversed his position by asserting that a being can never be without Being (Lukàcs 1981, 833–34). According to Strauss, this and similar difficulties "led Heidegger to a very thorough revision of his doctrine" but he never succeeded in overcoming this difficulty (*SPPP*, 30; *NRH*, 32; Strauss 1961, 155–56).

I have interpreted Strauss's contention that fanatical obscurantism is the inescapable consequence of the contemporary rejection of natural right not as a sociological prediction but as a logical thesis. If it were not a logical thesis, it would not give us any compelling reason to reconsider the issue of natural right. If it were a sociological thesis, it would be a manifestly false assertion. Although such mass movements as National Socialism were encouraged by the reasoning that I have just suggested, Strauss did not mean that such movements are the inescapable destiny of the modern West. He was perfectly aware of the transformation of "Heil Hitler" into "Heil Unheil" (*SPPP*, 30). Fanatical obscurantism is simply the inescapable consequence of establishing the thesis that genuine choice is a resolute decision, which was the only view that had the potential of establishing a standard derived from relativism. It is a phenomenon that was fully actualized only by Martin Heidegger, because he is the only thinker who has attempted to establish historicism in a thoroughgoing manner.[10] Others may escape fanaticism for a time at least, but they cannot escape mere obscurantism, for the problem that led to fanatical obscurantism—the tension between the nihilistic consequences of modern individualism and the demands of social life, understood not as the need to get along with others but as the need to be dedicated to one's community, whether it be one's family or one's political community—is a conflict that cannot be resolved and therefore is apt to be obscured in one way or another by those who are unwilling to abandon modern individualism. And the persistence of this

---

10. That by "fanatical obscurantism" Strauss does not mean mass movements such as National Socialism is confirmed by his preface to the American edition of *The Political Philosophy of Hobbes*, a work that was originally published in 1935: "I had seen that the modern mind had lost its self-confidence or its certainty of having made decisive progress beyond pre-modern thought; and I saw that it was *turning* into nihilism, or what is in practice the same thing, fanatical obscurantism" (*PPH*, xv; emphasis added).

problem is apt to have social consequences in the sense that society will continue to be torn between an easygoing moral indifference and moral fanaticism. I know of no better antidote to liberal antipathy toward Strauss than an unflinching attempt to solve this problem, for such an attempt is apt to arouse interest in the investigations of someone who sought for guidance outside of liberalism.

Alexis de Tocqueville, the greatest liberal analyst of liberal society, did not think that the problem posed by the conflict between individualism and devotion is susceptible of a solution. For this reason he was not wholeheartedly attached to liberalism, but, wishing to help liberal societies, he opted for a practical substitute. Whereas the individualism of modern democracy is incompatible with the kind of dedication that is fostered by premodern democracy, he argued that self-interest properly understood is a doctrine that could allow democratic masses to make "sacrifices" that are necessary for the welfare of society. He praised American women in particular for willingness to give up some of their ambitions for the sake of their families, which are so essential to their happiness. I do not need to refer to empirical evidence from modern life to show the limits of what can be expected from self-interest as a guide. It suffices to point out that self-interest properly understood requires understanding one's self, but we cannot understand ourselves properly without understanding our love for duty, for excellence, for devotion and hence the pleasures associated with self-restraint, and this understanding is undermined if we begin with the assumption that self-interest should be our guide.

Unlike the liberalism that understood self-preservation as the most important end of man, the utilitarian liberalism of Mill and the progressive liberalism of Dewey regarded the cultivation of individuality understood as a kind of human excellence as the most important end of man. They remained liberals because they believed that the maximum freedom from restraint is the best condition for the cultivation of individuality in our current historical situation, but this belief has been questioned not only by Nietzsche but by liberals themselves. As Isaiah Berlin put it, "Integrity, love of truth and fiery individualism grow at least as often in severely disciplined communities or under military discipline, as in more tolerant or indifferent societies" (quoted in Strauss 1961, 136). Once liberals begin to wonder whether intolerant societies may foster these virtues more than liberal societies, they become entangled with relativism and therefore with the development that I have just sketched.

Paradoxically, what Strauss called "fanatical obscurantism" was for him actually the clarification of the meaning of the contemporary rejection of natural right and even of modern thought as a whole. Although Strauss recognized that Lukàcs had a point in accusing Heidegger of "mystification," he argued that "Lukács only harmed himself by not learning from Heidegger," for "in all important respects Heidegger does not make things obscurer than they are [prior to him]" (Strauss 1995c, 330). He did not, however, regard the history of modern thought as simply a development.[11] While maintaining that Heidegger's thought is the culmination of modern thought, he did not deny the possibility that some earlier modern thinkers may have had "insights" that Heidegger failed to appreciate. The early modern philosophers may have had greater clarity about the fundamental problems than did Heidegger, but the latter's position may be the result of the working-through of the premises of the former, and for this reason his position is superior to theirs. Accordingly, the alternative that Strauss took seriously was that between Heidegger and Plato: "the question Plato or existentialism is today the ontological question" (Strauss 1993, 63).

The notion that modern thought culminates in Heidegger is an aspect of Strauss's thought that has troubled some contemporary political theorists who have wondered why Strauss apparently rejected Kant or Hegel without stating his reasons for this rejection in a detailed way. But as we have seen, he gave the decisive reason for his rejection of modern natural or rational right, namely, that the modern premise of individualism is in principle incompatible with morality and that the rejection of modern natural right leads to fanatical obscurantism. Despite their attempt to restore the high morality of classical political philosophy, Kant and Hegel, Strauss argued, entertained the delusion that the moral order can be achieved by "the blind selfish passion" (*WPP*, 53–54). This point is made even more clearly in Strauss's exchange with Kojève:

> Kojève knows as well as anyone living that Hegel's fundamental teaching regarding Master and Slave is based on Hobbes's doctrine of the state of nature. If Hobbes's doctrine of the state of nature is abandoned *en plain connaissance de cause* (as indeed it should be abandoned), Hegel's fundamental teaching will lose the evidence which it apparently still possesses for Kojève. Hegel's teaching is much more sophisticated than Hobbes's, but it is as much a construction as the latter. Both doctrines

11. Consider, for instance, the following comments: "[Rousseau's] disciples clarified his views indeed, but one may wonder whether they preserved the breadth of his vision" (*NRH*, 252). "[Karl Loewith's] understanding of Goethe enables him to see that the way leading from Hegel through Marx, Kierkegaard and historicism to Nietzsche and beyond is necessary, not absolutely, but only on the basis of Hegel" (*WPP*, 269).

construct human society by starting from the untrue assumption that man as man is thinkable as a being that lacks awareness of sacred restraints or as a being that is guided by nothing but a desire for recognition. (*WPP*, 111)

But there is a more profound dissatisfaction with Strauss among students of his who are inclined to the principles of the Declaration of Independence. Strauss begins *Natural Right and History* by pointing to the threat that German thought poses to these principles. Yet, within few pages he suggests that these principles are the roots of our trouble: "Liberal relativism has its roots in the natural right tradition of tolerance or in the notion that everyone has a natural right to the pursuit of happiness as he understands happiness; but in itself it is a seminary of intolerance" (*NRH*, 6). Strauss's original appeal to the principles of the Declaration of Independence, however, is not a self-destructive tease that attracts lovers of those principles only to disappoint them, for Strauss's distinction between tolerance and individuality is that between the intention of a doctrine and its substance. Because this substance is inadequate to the intention that it serves, Strauss rejects it in order to be loyal to that intention. Now, the modern natural right teaching is concerned with toleration above all because it is concerned with independence of thought. By suggesting that modern natural right has culminated in fanatical obscurantism, Strauss gives us reason to consider whether the only way to remain loyal to the intention of the principles of the Declaration of Independence is the restoration of classical political philosophy. If one cannot establish natural right on that understanding of nature according to which the natural is always individual, then the only natural right teaching that is potentially open to us is the classical one. It is for this reason that Strauss ends his introduction by drawing our attention to an objection to natural right that is in fact only an objection to classic natural right (*NRH*, 7–8).

▲　▲

Strauss begins the final section of his introduction with a warning to those who want to return to natural right: "Our aversion to fanatical obscurantism must not lead us to embrace natural right in a spirit of fanatical obscurantism" (*NRH*, 6). He warns us that we who are concerned with truth should never confuse truth with utility: "Even by proving that a certain view is indispensable for living well, one proves merely that the view in question is a salutary myth: one does not prove it to be true." The bad consequences of the rejection of natural right do not guarantee that there is any remedy to them or that this rejection is unwarranted: "The fact that reason compels us to go beyond the ideal of our society does not yet guarantee that in taking this step we shall not be confronted with a void or with a multiplicity of incompatible and equally justifiable principles of 'natural right'" (*NRH*, 6). The bad consequences of relativism do not prove the existence of natural right, but they do give us good reasons for examining the problem of natural right, which examination requires "a detached, theoretical, and impartial discussion" (*NRH*, 7).

It is to support that attitude, that is, to lift the issue of natural right from the realm of partisanship—the partisan struggle between "the liberals of various descriptions" and "the Catholic and non-Catholic disciples of Thomas Aquinas"—that he points out that classic natural right "is connected with a teleological view of the universe" and that this view of the universe "seems" to have been discredited by modern natural science:[12]

> Two opposite conclusions could be drawn from this momentous decision. According to one, the nonteleological conception of the universe must be followed up by a nonteleological conception of human life. But this "naturalistic" solution is exposed to grave difficulties: it seems to be impossible to give an adequate account of human ends by conceiving of them merely as posited by desires or impulses. Therefore, the alternative solution has prevailed. This means that people were forced to accept a fundamental, typically modern, dualism of a nonteleological natural science and a teleological science of man. This is the position which the modern followers of Thomas Aquinas, among others, are forced to take, a position which presupposes a break with the comprehensive view of Aristotle as well as that of Thomas Aquinas. (*NRH*, 8)

In this way, Strauss shows that the contemporary followers of Aquinas are in the same boat as the liberals whom they combat. More comprehensively, "we all are in the grip of the same difficulty." We are all in the same boat, but it seems that our boat is sinking. If modern natural right ultimately leads to nihilism and fanatical obscurantism, and if we cannot return to classic natural right because it is connected with an antiquated notion of the universe, then we are left with nothing.

But if this were the judgment of Strauss he never would have attempted a return to classical political philosophy. We must here limit our-

---

12. For the difference between Aristotle's own understanding of his natural science and Aristotelianism see Bolotin 1998.

selves to the answer that Strauss suggests in his very formulation of that problem. Our problem seems to be that the nonteleological account of the whole seems to provide a more adequate explanation of natural things, while the teleological account seems to provide a more adequate explanation of human beings, but only one of these accounts can be true. But can an account of the whole that does not seem to explain adequately a part of the whole be known to be the true account? This is a sufficient reason for us to conclude that the issue has not yet been settled. Because that is so, and because we as social scientists are not competent to examine whether modern natural science did in fact deserve to win, it is reasonable for us to limit our attention to "that aspect of the problem of natural right which can be clarified within the confines of the social sciences" (*NRH*, 8).

I have discussed this objection to classical political philosophy not because I intend to return to classical political philosophy in this book but because it was necessary to address the despair caused by relativism's claim that knowledge of norms is impossible. For this despair makes it even more difficult to solve the problem of relativism. The abandonment of the hope for valid knowledge of morality has led social scientists to focus their attention on the study of empirical data at the expense of moral arguments, and historians on interpretations of texts that are concerned not so much with the soundness of arguments as with their historical context. The only way to free ourselves from despair is to find reasons for hope, and we today can find these reasons only by working through relativism to its end, for only the full awareness of our own perplexity can lead to the realization of the possibilities that remain open to us.

PART II

The genuine, the only, and the deepest theme of world and human history, to which all else is subordinate, remains the conflict between unbelief and belief.

Goethe

CHAPTER 3

The Fact-Value Distinction and Nihilism

If knowledge of natural right is necessary for the actualization of social science, our first duty as would-be social scientists is to understand more fully the difficulty that led to the rejection of natural right in modern times. According to Strauss, natural right is rejected today "in the name of History and in the name of the distinction between Facts and Values" (*NRH*, 8). Although in Strauss's own judgment historicism is the "serious antagonist of political philosophy" (*NRH*, 8, 36, 38–39; *WPP*, 25, 26), he allocated almost twice as many pages to an explicit examination of the distinction between facts and values as to an examination of the historical approach, and this in a book that bears the title *Natural Right and History* (*NRH*, 9–34, 35–80). No doubt this choice was partly due to the prevalence of positivism in academic circles at his time. But there is also a deeper reason. According to Strauss, the superiority of historicism consists in its greater consistency. If "positivism necessarily transforms itself into historicism" (*WPP*, 25; *NRH*, 36–37), historicism and the distinction between facts and values are likely to be two different responses to the same fundamental difficulty. Radical historicism, the attempt to establish historicism by Heidegger, has the advantage of clarifying the modern response to this difficulty. But Strauss suggested that this clarification was bought at the price of a certain estrangement from the primary issues:

> Modern thought reaches its culmination, its highest self-consciousness, in the most radical historicism, i.e., in explicitly condemning to oblivion the notion of eternity. For oblivion of eternity, or, in other words, estrangement from man's deepest desire and therewith from the primary

issues, is the price which modern man had to pay, from the very beginning, for attempting to be absolutely sovereign, to become the master and owner of nature, to conquer chance. (*WPP*, 55)

Although Strauss regarded Weber's notion of "timeless values" as a form of decayed Platonism, he seems to have thought Weber's social science to be a more fertile ground for bringing out this difficulty (*WPP*, 26). At any rate, it is in his treatment of Weber that he placed his explicit discussion of the most fundamental alternative that faces man (*NRH*, 74–76). If Strauss is correct that "no one since Weber has devoted a comparable amount of intelligence, assiduity, and almost fanatical devotion to the basic problem of the social sciences," it is doubtful that one can find a better way to understand that problem than through an examination of Weber's attempt to solve it (*NRH*, 36).

▲   ▲

Strauss introduces his analysis of Weber with a discussion of the relation between historicism and the distinction between facts and values (*NRH*, 35–39).[1] This discussion has two parts: a general discussion in which no mention is made of the distinction between facts and values and a more specific discussion of Weber's relation to historicism.

He begins the first discussion by pointing to the more limited scope of Weber's position. Whereas historicism rejects the possibility of natural right by rejecting the possibility of philosophy in the full sense of the term, the position that underlies the distinction between facts and values rejects natural right without rejecting the possibility of philosophy. According to Strauss, in order to establish philosophy, one only needs to know that the fundamental problems are coeval with man:

> In grasping these problems as problems, the human mind liberates itself from its historical limitations. No more is needed to legitimize philosophy in its original, Socratic sense: philosophy is knowledge that one does not know; that is to say, it is knowledge of what one does not know, or awareness of the fundamental problems and, therewith, of the fundamental alternatives regarding their solution that are coeval with human thought. (32)

---

1. All unspecified references in chapters 3, 4, and 5 are to Strauss's "Natural Right and the Distinction between Facts and Values," in *Natural Right and History*. In interpreting Strauss's argument I have occasionally made use of the original Walgreen lectures (*LNRH* [1949]).

Now, the adherents of the view underlying the distinction between facts and values do not deny but insist on the permanence of the fundamental problems, for they reject natural right because they maintain that there is an eternal conflict between ultimate values. Accordingly, we would not expect that Strauss's discussion of the distinction between facts and values would lead to the questioning of the idea of philosophy. Yet that discussion does culminate in an examination of Weber's view that "the idea of philosophy or science suffers from a fatal weakness" (75–76).

Strauss prepares us for this development by pointing to a difficulty that faces political philosophy in particular. Unlike theoretical philosophy, political philosophy is meant to be an activity that is of practical value, but "if political philosophy is limited to understanding *the* fundamental political alternative, it is of no practical value" (35; emphasis added). Strauss suggests that there are a number of fundamental problems but only one fundamental political problem. He does not immediately identify this problem. Instead, he maintains that "the whole galaxy of political philosophers from Plato to Hegel, and certainly all adherents of natural right, assumed that" it "is susceptible of a final solution" (36). Indeed, Strauss goes on to suggest that they were inclined to the same answer, for "[t]his assumption ultimately rested on the Socratic answer to the question of how man ought to live." The very awareness of fundamental problems such as those of justice provides the basis for a solution to the fundamental political problem: "By realizing that we are ignorant of the most important things, we realize at the same time that the most important thing for us, or the one thing needful, is quest for knowledge of the most important things or quest for wisdom" (36). The difficulty that Socratic argument seeks to resolve is that it is not obvious that wisdom (knowledge of the whole) is the most important thing. What is of paramount importance in the first place are the affairs of one's community (*NRH*, 83). By realizing that one lacks knowledge of justice, one realizes that the most important thing is the search for knowledge of justice. Since originally the way of one's community was understood as a gift from gods (*NRH*, 83–84), the search for knowledge of justice becomes part of a more general search for knowledge about the whole. Philosophy, the quest for wisdom understood as knowledge about the whole, is "the one thing needful."[2] But as it is

---

2. Strauss's use of the expression "one thing needful" draws our attention to the similarity and the opposition between the philosophic position and the biblical position. When Martha complains to Jesus that her sister Mary, who has been sitting at Jesus' feet, had left her to serve her guest alone, Jesus responds that one thing is needful and Mary has chosen that good part (Luke 10:38–42). Philosophy and the Bible agree that service to one's community is not the most important thing. But they disagree as to what is the one thing needful.

"known to every reader of Plato's *Republic* or Aristotle's *Politics*," this conclusion is "not barren of political consequences" (36), for if the philosophic
life is the best way of life the right political order is the one that directs man
toward that life, an order in which philosophers have the decisive say. The
kinds of democracy supported by modern philosophers and the kinds of aristocracy supported by ancient philosophers are merely different practical
versions of this fundamentally aristocratic answer to the fundamental political problem, the problem of who should rule the society. Accordingly, the
issue of whether the fundamental political problem is susceptible of a final
solution depends on the soundness of the Socratic answer. The difficulty
with the Socratic answer seems to be that it maintains that the quest for wisdom is the best way of life while leaving open the possibility that the acquisition of wisdom might lead to the rejection of the philosophic life as the best
way of life. But so long as we have not acquired this wisdom this difficulty
need not lead to the rejection of the Socratic answer: "It is true that the successful quest for wisdom might lead to the result that wisdom is not the one
thing needful. But this result would owe its relevance to the fact that it is the
result of the quest for wisdom: the very disavowal of reason must be reasonable disavowal" (36). Yet it does leave the door open for what Strauss calls
"the anti-Socratic answer," because not having knowledge about the whole,
we cannot rule out the possibility that the wisdom that we need is provided by a source other than our own reason. Now, the very fact that the
Socratic answer could not vanquish "the anti-Socratic answer" creates the
impression that the perennial conflict between these two alternatives is insoluble. Accordingly, Strauss concludes, many present-day social scientists
reject natural right "because it is thought that there is a variety of un-
changeable principles of right or of goodness which conflict with one another, none of which can be proved to be superior to others" (36).[3]

Strauss limits his discussion of this position to a critical examination of
Weber. His critique brings to mind Weber's argument that what Wilhelm
Roscher says about economic policy is not an expression of a clear ideal that
has been thought through to its logical end but the consequence of his
mild, moderate, and conciliatory personality (Weber 1975, 89), for Strauss

---

3. Whereas knowledge of other fundamental problems does not lead to "any assignable limits to the progress of understanding," the conflict between the Socratic and the anti-Socratic answer is apparently of such a nature that it creates the impression that one can know that the conflict
cannot be resolved: "modern man is a dogmatic skeptic, whereas Socrates was a Zetetic skeptic, a
seeking skeptic" (*LNRH*, 2:5). This transformation of skepticism leads to doubts about the value of
philosophy or science, doubts that at first glance are compatible with affirmation of the validity of
scientific propositions.

argues that Weber's articulation of his own doctrine is incoherent partly because it was influenced by "a tradition in which he was brought up" and by "his character" even though that doctrine undermines that tradition and the value of his character (43, 48). Strauss arrives at this view not by imposing his own framework on Weber but rather by allowing himself to be guided by the contradictions of Weber's own thought.[4] Once one becomes aware of the contradictions in Weber's thought that Strauss brings out, it becomes impossible to accept Weber's own self-understanding. By revealing Weber's confusions, however, Strauss also reveals Weber's remarkable grasp of "*the* basic problem of the social sciences" (36; emphasis added). Accordingly, his criticism of Weber demonstrates, in a way that no other interpretation of Weber that I am aware of does, why Weber "is the greatest social scientist" of the twentieth century (36).

Strauss begins his discussion of Weber by examining the relation between his thought and historicism. According to Strauss, "a strong case can be made for the view that [Weber's] reservations against historicism were half-hearted and inconsistent with the broad tendency of his thinking" (36–37). Weber abandoned the historical school on two grounds that were accepted by the historical school: that reality is not rational and that the real is always the individual. Although the historical school had rejected Hegel's notion of the universal as the real, Weber showed that this notion surreptitiously survived in its attempts to derive rights from unique folk minds and to explain historical phenomena by general laws. The latter attempt rests on a confusion of the notion of the general (which, being an abstraction from historical phenomena, cannot be their cause) and the notion of the universal (which, being a metaphysical reality, can be the cause of historical phenomena as a whole can be the cause of its parts). Because Weber rejected the rationality of reality as a dogmatic opinion, he concluded that the only meaning in history is that of the intentions of actors, which often lead to an unintended outcome, which "molds not only our way of life but our very thoughts, and especially does it determine our ideals" (38).

This reasoning would have led Weber to unqualified historicism if it were not for his attachment to the idea of science:

---

4. Although Strauss is known for his insistence that one should understand a thinker as he understood himself, his work on Weber shows clearly that he did not believe that social science should confine itself to this approach, for otherwise the social scientist "would have to bow without murmur to the self-interpretation of his subjects" (55–56). This approach is merely preparatory: before judging or explaining a doctrine in sociological or other terms, one must understand it exactly as its originator understood it (57). But if self-interpretations can be erroneous, understanding a thinker better than he understood himself may be the true understanding.

Weber was, however, still too much impressed by the idea of science to
accept historicism without qualification. In fact, one is *tempted* to suggest that the primary motive of his opposition to the historical school
and to historicism in general was devotion to the idea of empirical science as it prevailed in his generation. (38; emphasis added)

Strauss observes two possible motives in Weber's opposition to historicism: the idea of science in general and the idea of empirical science as it
prevailed in his generation. Both of these motives are present in his account
of Weber's initial resistance to historicism:

The idea of science forced him to insist on the fact that all science as
such is independent of Weltanschauung: both natural and social science
claim to be equally valid for Westerners and for Chinese, i.e., for people
whose "world views" are radically different. The historical genesis of
modern science—the fact that it is of Western origin—is wholly irrele-
vant as regards its validity. Nor did Weber have any doubt that modern
science is absolutely superior to any earlier form of thinking orientation
in the world of nature and society. That superiority can be established
objectively, by reference to the rules of logic. (38)

But Weber came to sense that these rules of logic are not sufficient to
establish the superiority of modern science, and hence could not resist
historicism:

There arose, however, in Weber's mind this difficulty in regard to the
social sciences in particular. He insisted on the objective and universal
validity of social science in so far as it is a body of true propositions. Yet
these propositions are only a part of social science. They are the results
of scientific investigation or the answers to questions. The questions
which we address to social phenomena depend on the direction of our
interest or on our point of view, and these on our value ideas. But the
value ideas are historically relative. Hence the substance of social science is radically historical; for it is the value ideas and the direction of
interest which determine the whole conceptual framework of the social
sciences. (38)

The distinction between facts and values is an attempt to separate the objective or transhistorical element of science (findings regarding facts and
their causes) from its subjective or historically relative element (the impor-

tance and the significance of any findings). But the problem is that the latter element is absolutely decisive, for one would be interested in science if science is worthless knowledge. The same difficulty applies to natural sciences: "All science presupposes that science is valuable, but this presupposition is the product of certain cultures, and hence historically relative" (39). Now, we understand Strauss's suggestion that Weber's reservations against historicism were halfhearted. Weber could not have been wholeheartedly devoted to the idea of science or that idea as it prevailed in his generation, because he was aware that all science presupposes that science is valuable and that this presupposition is historically relative. But devotion to the idea of science may be possible if the value of science is something that is transhistorical. Indeed, Weber insisted that the concrete and historical value ideas have elements of transhistorical character: "the ultimate values are as timeless as the principles of logic" (39). Weber's notion of timeless values requires a break with the view that the real is always individual, for the acceptance of that view would have led him to conceive of historical values as emanations from timeless values and this consequence would have been unacceptable to him on account of its dogmatic assumption that reality is rational.[5] But because Weber did not consistently reject the view that the real is always individual, one may conclude that his reservation against historicism was inconsistent with the broad tendency of his thought. Since the notion that the real is always individual underlies the idea of empirical science as it prevailed in Weber's generation, the acceptance of timeless values amounts to a rejection of that notion of science. Accordingly, Strauss argues that underlying the notion of timeless values is "a relapse into a decayed Platonism" (*WPP*, 26). Accordingly, I conclude that it was a peculiar notion of timeless values—and not his acceptance of timeless principles of logic—that distinguished Weber's position most significantly from historicism, and that the primary motive behind this notion was Weber's devotion to the idea of science in general (39).

I have suggested that Weber's opposition to historicism was based on his devotion to the idea of science and that motive has two elements: concern for valid knowledge of facts and concern for valid knowledge of values. It is this combination that makes intelligible much of the structure of

---

5. Weber's understanding of the dogmatic character of this assumption becomes visible in his approval of Roscher's rejection of the evolutionists who wanted to reconcile the principle of evolution with religion: "Whoever simply gazes upon the ascent out of matter will look upon sin, especially the highly cultivated sin, with great composure. He will see it as a state of completeness not yet attained. But in truth, it is absolute evil, that which is antagonistic, even fatal, to the innermost core of our nature" (Roscher, quoted in Weber 1975, 235–36).

Strauss's chapter. By arguing that Weber's thesis led to nihilism, Strauss shows that Weber's thesis cannot adequately address his moral concerns (42–49); by arguing that social science as a theoretical pursuit is not possible on the basis of the distinction between facts and values, Strauss shows that Weber's thesis could not adequately address his theoretical concerns (49–62). Finally, by showing that Weber's position was postulated under the impulse of a specific moral preference, which he himself did not submit to adequate examination on account of the power of the modern criticism of commonsense understanding, Strauss shows that a clarification of moral-political phenomena as understood by moral actors themselves will lead to a more adequate position (62–80). He begins this whole argument by showing that Weber's thesis is not a logical but an axiological thesis.

▲ ▲

Strauss begins his explanation of Weber's position with a remarkable observation: "Weber never explained what he understood by 'values'" (39). His view of the relation of values to facts is governed not by a clear understanding of values but by a particular understanding of facts, an understanding borrowed from modern natural science: "We have already learned from the natural sciences, and hopefully will learn ever more, of the manner in which one treats facts purely as facts" (Weber 1924, 478; translation is my own). "Value-free" social science seems to follow from modern natural science's notion of nature. As Nietzsche pointed out, there is a tension between modern natural right teaching, according to which self-preservation is the most important end of man, and modern natural science's claim that there are no natural ends (Nietzsche 1967a, #9). If one accepts modern natural science's understanding of nature as authoritative, one must admit that we cannot have any knowledge of natural ends. Accordingly, Strauss asserts that Hobbes "prepares the 'value free' political science of our time" by his attempt to base his political philosophy—and hence the ideal of civilization—on modern natural science (*WPP,* 181):

> There was only one reason why it was temporarily possible to attempt
> to ground the modern ideal, the ideal of civilization, by means of natural
> science: It was believed that the new concept of nature was the adequate
> foundation of the new ideal precisely because the old concept of nature
> had been the adequate foundation of the old ideal. But this was a delu-
> sion. It had yet to be ascertained that the "end-free" and "value-free"
> nature of modern natural science can say nothing to man about "ends

and values," that the "Is," understood in the sense of modern natural science, involves no reference at all to the "Ought," and that the traditional view that the right life is a life according to nature becomes meaningless under the modern premise. (*PL*, 34)

The acceptance of the modern notion of nature led Weber to insist on the absolute heterogeneity of questions of fact and questions of value. If one cannot derive values from facts, every attempt to derive values from the historical process becomes untenable. Both the liberal-Marxist notions of progress and the conservative attempts to bolster the value of religion and morality on account of their influence in history must be rejected:

> No conclusion can be drawn from any fact as to its valuable character, nor can we infer the factual character of something from its being valuable or desirable. Neither time-serving nor wishful thinking is supported by reason. By proving that a given social order is the goal of the historical process, one does not say anything as to the value or desirable character of that order. By showing that certain religious and ethical ideas had a very great effect or no effect, one does not say anything about the value of those ideas. To understand a factual or possible evaluation is something entirely different from approving or forgiving that evaluation. (39–40)

Since evaluations are also facts to be observed, one may understand them but one cannot approve or forgive them. According to Weber, "the absolute heterogeneity of facts and values necessitates the ethically neutral character of social science: social science can answer questions of facts and their causes; it is not competent to answer questions of value" (40).

The very understanding of facts that led Weber to limit the scope of empirical social science to the study of facts and their causes led him "to insist very strongly on the role played by values in social science" (40). If there are no natural wholes, there are potentially infinite objects of social science. Social scientists must choose from this infinity a number of relevant social facts, and what is relevant is determined by the values of the social scientists. Although Weber insisted that the "objects of social science are constituted by 'reference to values,'" he insisted "no less strongly on the fundamental difference between 'reference to values' and 'value judgments': by saying that something is relevant with regard to political freedom, for example, one does not take a stand for or against political freedom" (40). The value of a scientific investigation of a particular subject may be legitimately questioned, but its thesis, if correct, must be so acknowledged even by those who do not share the investigator's values (Weber 1949, 58–59).

Having stated Weber's view, Strauss begins to expose its basis: "Weber contended that his notion of a 'value-free' or ethically neutral social science is fully justified by what he regarded as the most fundamental of all oppositions, namely, the opposition of the Is and the Ought, or the opposition of reality and norm or value" (40–41). According to Weber, his notion of social science requires something that is so uncontroversial that it is "utterly trivial in itself," namely, that a researcher should keep separate his factual statements and his own practical evaluations because they involve different kinds of problems:

> The issue is not really the question of the extent to which practical evaluations, in particular ethical ones, may claim for themselves normative dignity—in other words, whether they are different in character from, for instance, the often cited question whether blondes are preferable to brunettes or any other similarly subjective judgment of taste. These are problems of axiology [*Wertphilosophie*], not of the methodologies of empirical disciplines. (Weber 1949, 12)

But Strauss argues that the radical heterogeneity of the Is and the Ought cannot be the basis of a "value-free" social science. He invites the reader for the sake of the argument to assume that "we had genuine knowledge of right and wrong, or of the Ought, or of the true value system" (41). Because social science seeks to find means for given ends, that knowledge would guide social science, regardless of whether it was obtained in a different manner from the knowledge of the means. Modern natural science's understanding of facts is not a sufficient basis for the separation of social science from social philosophy. Strauss points out the insufficiency of Weber's account of his position not in order to reject that position but rather to show the true reason underlying it and thus its true character: "The true reason why Weber insisted on the ethically neutral character of social science as well as of social philosophy was, then, his belief that there cannot be any genuine knowledge of the Ought" and his denial "to man [of] any science, empirical or rational, and knowledge, scientific or philosophic, of the true value system" (41). Indeed, Weber spoke not only of the logical distinction between questions of fact and questions of values but also, and at times on the same page, of the irreconcilability of the conflicts between various value spheres. In "Science as a Vocation," he even concedes that the "deeper reason" for the impossibility of scientific pleading for practical stands is not the heterogeneity of the questions of facts and values but this irreconcilability (Weber 1946, 147). Weber's social science is intelligible only if it is understood to rest on an axiological as opposed to a logical thesis.

But what difficulty led to Weber's confusion about the basis of his own position? Weber failed to see in a clear manner that his understanding of social science rests on the denial of the possibility of genuine knowledge of the Ought, because he was inclined to believe that there were objective norms in the sphere of ethics. Strauss brings this to our attention through the contrast between what he asked us to assume in order to see the true basis of Weber's position and his formulation of that basis:

> Let us assume that we had *genuine knowledge of right and wrong*, or *of the Ought*, or *of the true value system*. . . . The true reason why Weber insisted on the ethically neutral character of social science as well as of social philosophy was, then, not his belief in the fundamental opposition of the Is and the Ought but his belief that there cannot be any *genuine knowledge of the Ought*. He denied to man any science, empirical or rational, any knowledge, scientific or philosophic, of *the true value system:* the true value system does not exist; there is a variety of values which are of the same rank, whose demands conflict with one another, and whose conflict cannot be solved by human reason. (41–42; emphasis added)

Strauss does not say that Weber denied the possibility of genuine knowledge of right and wrong. Weber insisted on the ethically neutral social science precisely because he was inclined to believe in the existence of objective (neo-Kantian) ethics. Yet this formal ethics cannot guide social science because of the tension between it and the demands of social life. Given this tension, it is possible, at least it seemed to Weber, to insist on the objectivity of this ethics and to deny at the same time the existence of a genuine knowledge of the Ought and of the true value system. Moreover, given this tension, any social science that seeks ethical imperatives is apt to obscure the dignity of ethics. Accordingly, as we shall see, the first thing that Strauss does to show the nihilistic consequence of Weber's thesis is to show that Weber was unable to sustain the dignity of ethics.

To summarize: The opposition of the Is and the Ought is a consequence of the modern understanding of nature. By showing that this opposition is not a sufficient basis for Weber's notion of an ethically neutral social science, Strauss suggests that Weber's notion of science is based not only on the recognition that the modern ideal of civilization cannot be based on modern science but also on a sense that this ideal cannot be defended on any grounds. Accordingly, Strauss virtually begins each of the three remaining sections of his essay by referring to Weber's well-known comments on the prospects of Western civilization (42, 49, 62).

▲   ▲

Strauss follows his discussion of Weber's contention regarding the basis of his thesis with a contention of his own regarding its consequence: "I contend that Weber's thesis necessarily leads to nihilism or to the view that every preference, however evil, base, or insane, has to be judged before the tribunal of reason to be as legitimate as any other preference" (42). He presents Weber's statement about the prospects of Western civilization as a sign of the truth of this contention:

> He saw this alternative: either a spiritual renewal ("wholly new prophets or a powerful renaissance of old thoughts and ideals") or else "mechanized petrifaction, varnished by a kind of convulsive sense of self-importance," i.e., the extinction of every human possibility but that of "specialists without spirit or vision and voluptuaries without heart." Confronted with this alternative, Weber felt that the decision in favor of either possibility would be a judgment of value or faith, and hence beyond the competence of reason. This amounts to an admission that the way of life of "specialists without spirit or vision and voluptuaries without heart" is as defensible as the ways of life recommended by Amos or by Socrates. (42)

Strauss, however, asks us to compare this statement with two other passages that suggest that Weber may have had moral and theoretical reasons for resisting nihilism (42n). According to the first, the very realization that we live in a world of irreconcilably antagonistic values could be the basis for condemning the shallowness of those of our contemporaries who are unwilling to face this fact:

> The shallowness of our routinized daily existence in the most significant sense of the word consists indeed in the fact that the persons who are caught up in it do not become aware, and above all *do not wish to become aware*, of this . . . motley of irreconcilably antagonistic values. They avoid the choice between "God" and the "Devil" and their own ultimate decision as to which of the conflicting values will be dominated by the one, and which by the other. (Weber 1949, 18; emphasis added)

According to the second passage, social science and social philosophy can give us some guidance by informing us of the consequences of our actions, by clarifying our ultimate values, and even by rejecting some of these values if they proved to be contradictory (Weber 1949, 53–54). To show that Weber's thesis leads to nihilism, that is, to explain why Weber could not objectively prefer the ways of life recommended by Amos or by Socrates to the way of life of "specialists without spirit or vision and voluptuaries without heart," Strauss has to show the groundless character of Weber's relativistic ethics and his notion of rationality.

To make his case, Strauss follows Weber's thought step by step. He begins with Weber's apparent affirmation of a rational norm, shows that this affirmation cannot be consistently maintained by Weber and that Weber himself abandons it and arrives at a more permissive standard, and then repeats these steps with this new standard until he arrives at nihilism. In this way, he first shows that on the basis of Weber's thesis one cannot distinguish between human excellence and depravity, between human excellence and baseness, and finally between sanity and insanity. But before proceeding, he addresses a reluctance that some of his contemporaries may have in following the argument to the end: "In following this movement toward its end we shall inevitably reach a point beyond which the scene is darkened by the shadow of Hitler. Unfortunately, it does not go without saying that in our examination we must avoid the fallacy that in the last decades has frequently been used as a substitute for the *reductio ad absurdum;* the *reductio ad Hitlerum.* A view is not refuted by the fact that it happens to have been shared by Hitler" (42–43).[6]

FROM MORAL DUTIES TO RELATIVISTIC IDEALISM

Strauss begins his demonstration of the nihilistic consequence of Weber's thesis by considering Weber's attempt to reconcile two opposing schools of thought: "Weber started out from a combination of the views of Kant as they were understood by certain neo-Kantians and of the views of the historical school" (43). He accepted the historical school's rejection of the universal politics of Kant and more generally its view that there is "no

6. Guenther Roth's interpretation of this passage testifies to the strength of these temptations. He writes: "But Strauss is fair enough to denounce *Reductio ad Hitlerum,* the assertion that Weber's thinking led to fascism" (Bendix and Roth 1971, 64). Strauss, however, argues that even if Weber's thoughts led to fascism, one cannot dismiss them, because they can still be true.

possible social or cultural order which can be said to be *the* right or the rational order" while maintaining the neo-Kantian notion of science as well as of *individual* ethics, "which rejected utilitarianism and every form of eudemonism" (43). This combination is possible to the extent that the ethics in question is merely an individual ethics. Weber combined his Neo-Kantian notion of ethics with cultural relativism by insisting on the fundamental difference between ethical imperatives and cultural values: "Moral commands appeal to our conscience, whereas cultural values appeal to our feelings: the individual ought to fulfill his moral duties, whereas it depends on his arbitrary will whether he wishes to realize cultural ideals or values" (43). On account of this difference, ethics would only compromise itself if it claimed to legislate in matters that are beyond its province: "Whereas gentlemen, or honest men, necessarily agree as to things moral, they legitimately disagree in regard to such things as Gothic architecture, private property, monogamy, democracy, and so on" (43).

Weber's distinction between moral imperatives and cultural values gives the impression that he recognizes "the existence of absolutely binding rational norms, namely, the moral imperatives" (43). But this impression, Strauss argues, is misleading, for "what [Weber] said about moral commands is not much more than the residue of a tradition in which he was brought up and which, indeed, never ceased to determine him as a human being" (43). If moral commands have a validity that cultural values lack, in the case of a conflict between the two one would be obligated to prefer the former to the latter. Accordingly, in case of conflict between politics and morality, Kant insists that politics must bend its knee before morality (Kant 1949, 469). But, according to Weber, it is just as legitimate to bear the burden of ethical guilt for the sake of politics as it is to bear the burden of political irresponsibility for the sake of ethics (1949, 15). Accordingly, Strauss maintains: "What he really thought was that ethical imperatives are as subjective as cultural values. According to him, it is as legitimate to reject ethics in the name of cultural values as it is to reject cultural values in the name of ethics, or to adopt any combination of both types of norm which is not self-contradictory" (43–44). Now, although Strauss does show a contradiction in Weber's statements about the status of ethical imperatives, one may ask how he knows which of these statements express what Weber "really thought"? Answer: "This decision [that ethical imperatives are as subjective as cultural values] is the *inevitable* consequence of his notion of ethics. He could not reconcile his view that ethics is silent about the right social order with the undeniable ethical relevance of social questions, except by 'relativizing' ethics" (44, emphasis added). Weber's combination of

Kantian ethics and cultural and social relativism is untenable, because moral and social spheres are not separate. Similarly, Weber's distinction between moral commands and cultural values obscures the fact that economic, social, and political questions cannot be conflated with cultural questions. Ethics may be silent about Gothic architecture, but it cannot be silent about private property, monogamy, and democracy.

Weber's admission that ethical imperatives are as subjective as cultural values did not lead him immediately to nihilism. Rather, it became the basis for a new kind of standard, his notion of personality, which he presented in opposition to the romantic-naturalistic notion of personality. What distinguishes human beings from animals is freedom. Accordingly, "the true meaning of 'personality' depends on the true meaning of 'freedom'" (44). Weber began with a notion of freedom according to which "human action is free to the extent to which it is not affected by external compulsion or irresistible emotions but is guided by rational consideration of means and ends" (44). This view is compatible with the traditional notion that human freedom consists in the discovery of our natural ends by reason and the rational pursuit of these ends. But the true meaning of freedom must be based on the true situation of man. Since according to Weber human beings cannot discover their ultimate ends, true freedom must be based on the recognition that man is free to choose his ends:

> Yet true freedom requires ends of a certain kind, and these ends have to be adopted in a certain manner. The ends must be anchored in ultimate values. Man's dignity, his being exalted far above everything merely natural or above all brutes, consists in his setting up autonomously his ultimate values, in making these values his constant ends, and in rationally choosing the means to these ends. The dignity of man consists in his autonomy, i.e., in the individual's freely choosing his own values or his own ideals or in obeying the injunction: "Become what thou art." (44)

From Idealism to Fanatical Resoluteness

Now, Weber's notion of "personality" seems to provide "something resembling an objective norm, a categoric imperative: 'Thou shalt have ideals.'" Although it tells us nothing about the content of the ideals to which one ought to be devoted, it seems "to establish an intelligible or nonarbitrary standard that would allow us to distinguish in a responsible manner between human excellence and depravity," that is, between good and evil preferences. It seems to allow one to oppose depraved men who turn their backs on all ideals with "a universal brotherhood of all noble souls; of all men who are not slaves to their appetites, passions, and self-interest; of all 'idealists'—of all men who can justly esteem or respect one another" (45).

But according to Strauss this is a delusion: "What seems at first to be an invisible church [universal brotherhood of all noble souls] proves to be a war of everybody against everybody or rather, pandemonium" (45). Weber's idealism does not lead to a war of everybody against everybody, because not everybody has different ideals. But it does lead to pandemonium, for "Weber's own formulation of his categoric imperative was 'Follow thy demon' or 'Follow thy god or demon.'" The second formulation implies the existence of good and evil ends. Although these ends may exist, according to Weber there is no objective criterion for distinguishing them, "for there is an insoluble, deadly conflict between the various values among which man has to choose" (45). Accordingly, Strauss argues, Weber's "categoric imperative actually means 'Follow thy demon, regardless of whether he is a good or evil demon'" (45). But given the character of the values that are in conflict, this pagan formulation is inadequate: "it is really a question of not only of alternatives between values but of an irreconcilable death-struggle, like that between 'God' and the 'Devil'" (Weber 1949, 17). Accordingly, Strauss reformulates Weber's categoric imperative: "'Follow God or the Devil as you will, but whichever choice you make, make it with all your heart, with all your soul, and with all your power.' What is absolutely base is to follow one's appetites, passions, or self-interest and to be indifferent or lukewarm toward ideals or values, toward gods or devils" (45). Since one must arbitrarily choose an end that as far as we know may be evil, Weber's notion of personality cannot provide an intelligible standard that would allow us to distinguish between good and evil preferences. But it does seem to provide a nonarbitrary standard for distinguishing between noble and base preferences. Nobility is fanatical devotion to any cause, and baseness is following one's appetites, passions, or self-interest. The universal brotherhood of all idealists is transformed into a war among fanatical votaries of various demons.

FROM RESOLUTENESS TO PHILISTINISM

At this stage, Strauss argues, we still have some kind of criterion inasmuch as one may judge that any kind of resolute life is good (*LNRH*, 2, 9). But a further contradiction inherent in Weber's idealism makes even the praise of resolute life untenable. On one hand, Weber's recognition of all causes "seems to permit of a nonarbitrary distinction between excellence and baseness." On the other, it "culminates in the imperative 'Follow God or the Devil,' which means, in nontheological language, 'Strive resolutely for excellence or baseness.'"[7] Thus, resolute striving for baseness becomes a form of human excellence. This contradiction is testimony to the fact that "for Weber, in his capacity as a social philosopher, excellence and baseness completely lost their primary meaning," that is, the meaning they have in "the dimension of action," in "the world in which we have to make decisions." His notions of excellence and baseness "are the correlates of a purely theoretical attitude toward the world of action," of an attitude that implies "equal respect for all causes." According to Weber, "excellence is devotion to a cause, be it good or evil, and baseness is indifference to all causes." But only someone who respects all causes equally can identify excellence with devotion to any cause, and only a man who is not devoted to a cause can respect all causes equally. Weber's notion of excellence is a correlate of an attitude that it condemns as base. Thus, Weber's own theoretical attitude led him to the devaluation "of theory, of science, of reason, of the realm of the mind, and therewith of both the moral imperatives and the cultural values" (46).[8]

This devaluation forced Weber "to dignify what he called purely 'vitalistic' values to the same height as the moral commands and the cultural values." By "vitalistic values" Weber meant "the principle, *Sich Ausleben*, which means to follow one's instincts without restraint, or to live freely accordingly to one's appetites, or live the life of the senses" (*LNRH*, 2, 9). On one hand, Weber suggested that these values are merely another kind of

---

7. "For if Weber meant to say that choosing value system A in preference to value system B is compatible with genuine respect for value system B or does not mean rejecting value system B as base, he could not have known what he was talking about in speaking of a choice between God and Devil; he must have meant a mere difference of tastes while talking of a deadly conflict" (45–46). Weber confirmed this judgment by his suggestion that from a mundane perspective the Christian exhortation that one should not resist evil is an ethic of "undignified conduct" (Weber 1946, 148).

8. "From a purely empirical point of view, however, it follows that the 'value' of science is thoroughly problematical. From an empirical-psychological standpoint, the value of science 'pursued for its own sake' is not only practically opposed to certain religious positions and conceptions of 'reason of state.' It is also logically inconsistent both [*sic*] with a radical commitment to purely 'vitalistic' values. And it is inconsistent with the contrary of this commitment—a radical negation of the value of life. Anyone who accepts one of these positions has not thereby committed himself to a logically self-contradictory view, at least as long as he realizes that his position is only a way of making the following claim: It is not the value of scientific truth, but rather other values, which have a preeminent status" (Weber 1975, 116–17).

values to which a personality may be devoted (1949, 55). On the other, he indicated that the acceptance of these values constitutes a break with his notion of personality and that they are not even values.[9] It is the latter view that is consistent with Weber's own articulation of his notion of personality. Accordingly, Strauss maintains:

> The "purely 'vitalistic' values" may be said to belong entirely to "the sphere of one's own individuality," being purely personal and in no way principles of a cause. Hence, they are not, strictly speaking, values. Weber contended explicitly that it is perfectly legitimate to take a hostile attitude toward all impersonal and superpersonal values and ideals, and therewith toward every concern with "personality" or the dignity of man as previously defined; for, according to him, there is only one way to become a "personality," namely, through absolute devotion to a cause. (46–47)

But while breaking with Weber's notion of personality, the recognition of vitalistic values seems to lead to a new basis for distinguishing between excellence and baseness:

> At the moment when the "vitalistic" values are recognized as of equal rank with cultural values, the categoric imperative "Thou shalt have ideals" is being transformed into the command "Thou shalt live passionately." Baseness no longer means indifference to any of the incompatible great objects of humanity, but being engrossed with one's own comfort and prestige. (47)

Whereas earlier following one's appetites, passions, or self-interest was considered base, now only following one's appetites or interest is considered base. For instance, the recognition of vitalistic values seems to allow one to

---

9. "If a man says of his erotic relationships with a woman, 'at first our relationship was only a passion, but now it is a value—the cool matter-of-factness of the Kantian *Critique* would express the first half of the sentence as follows: 'At first each of us was a means for the other.' . . . The negative predicate itself, which was expressed in the words 'only a passion,' can be regarded as degradation of what is most genuine and most appropriate in life, of the only, or at any rate, the royal road away from the impersonal or super-personal 'value'-mechanisms which are hostile to life, away from enslavement to the lifeless routine of everyday existence and from the pretentiousness of unrealities handed down from on high. At any rate, it is possible to imagine a conception of this standpoint which—although scorning the use of the term 'value' for the concrete facts of experience to which it refers—would constitute a sphere claiming its own 'immanent' dignity in the most extreme sense of the word. Its claim to this dignity would not be invalidated by its hostility or indifference to everything sacred or good, to every ethical or aesthetic law, and to every evaluation of cultural phenomena or personality" (Weber 1949, 17).

prefer "one who openly flaunts all conventions and is prepared to shoulder full responsibility for his choice" to "one who surreptitiously and hypocritically gratifies his instincts" (*LNRH*, 2, 10).

But Strauss asks: "[W]ith what right except that of arbitrary whim can one reject the way of life of philistines in the name of 'vitalistic' values, if one can reject the moral commands in the name of 'vitalistic' values?" (47). He implies that the objection to the way of life of a philistine is at bottom a moral objection, for the rejection of "one who surreptitiously and hypocritically gratifies his instincts" in favor of "one who openly flaunts all conventions and is prepared to shoulder full responsibility for his choice of the life of the senses" is based on a rejection of hypocrisy:

> It is hard to defend hypocrisy, but I cannot help noting that while I may be duly impressed by the moral courage of number one [who flaunts all conventions], I am equally impressed by his impudence, and I consider it perfectly legitimate to waver when confronted with the choice between the impudent and brutal he-man, and the sober and easy-going moral coward. (*LNRH*, lecture 2.10)[10]

Indeed, Strauss points out that "it was in tacit recognition of the impossibility of stopping on the downward path that Weber frankly admitted that it is merely a subjective judgment of faith or value if one despises 'specialists without spirit or vision and voluptuaries without heart' as degraded human beings" (47). This recognition leads to the final revision of Weber's ethical principle: "'Thou shalt have preferences'—an Ought whose fulfillment is fully guaranteed by the Is," that is, an Ought that offers no guidance whatsoever.

From Philistinism to Insanity

Although at this stage one can no longer make a nonarbitrary distinction between excellence and baseness, it seems that one may still have reason to oppose insanity, inconsistency, and irrationality: "Whatever preferences I

---

10. Strauss admits that one may establish the superiority of the so-called vitalistic values to selfish desires without reliance on moral commands, and this is the only way they may be established: "It is obvious that the superiority of the so-called vitalistic values to selfish desires can be defended only by reference to the natural superiority of the former, e.g., health, strength, beauty to the latter, say money. But Weber rejects in principle all attempts to derive ideals from reality, from the natural order" (*LNRH*, lecture 2.10).

may have or choose, I must act rationally: I must be honest with myself, I must be consistent in my adherence to my final objectives, and I must rationally choose the means required by my ends." Strauss responds: "we cannot take seriously this belated insistence on responsibility and sanity, this inconsistent concern with consistency, this irrational praise of rationality" (47). The demand that one ought to adhere to one's fundamental objectives is a residue of moral imperatives. If it is permissible to reject the obligatory character of moral imperatives, one may reject those who consistently adhere to their fundamental objectives in favor of those who undergo in their lives "a number of radical changes—of conversions from one value system to another, from one demon to another" (*LNRH*, lecture 2.11). If it is permissible to make vitalistic values one's supreme values, one may reject even instrumental rationality, for if it is permissible to follow one's instincts without restraint, one may let the moment decide one's actions, instead of rationally choosing the means required by one's ends (ibid.). Finally, Strauss gives voice to Weber's potential objection that "whatever preference one adopts, one has to be honest, at least with one's self, and especially that one must not make the dishonest attempt to give one's preference an objective foundation which would necessarily be a sham foundation" (48). But Weber could not consistently insist on the value of being honest with oneself, "for, according to him, it is equally legitimate to will or not to will the truth, or to reject truth in favor of the beautiful and the sacred" (48; Weber 1946, 148). If it is permissible to reject truth in favor of the beautiful and the sacred, one may be dishonest with oneself by embracing pleasing delusions or edifying myths. Despite his own devotion to science and his own rejection of myths, Weber's position prevented him from denying the legitimacy of the acceptance of myths. It prevented him from insisting that sanity is preferable to insanity. Accordingly, Strauss concludes: "Weber's regard for 'rational self-determination' and 'intellectual honesty' is a trait of his character which has no basis but his nonrational preference for 'rational self-determination' and 'intellectual honesty'" (48). Whereas Strauss had traced Weber's views concerning ethics to a tradition in which he was brought up, he traces Weber's love of science to his character. In this way, he indicates his own delight in Weber's character while revealing Weber's inability to justify that character and hence to sustain it. In order not to allow his own assessment of Weber's character to obscure the consequence of Weber's position, he adds:

> One may call the nihilism to which Weber's thesis leads "noble nihilism." For that nihilism stems not from a primary indifference to

everything noble but from the alleged or real insight into the baseless character of everything thought to be noble. Yet one cannot make a distinction between noble and base nihilism except if one has some knowledge of what is noble and what is base. But such knowledge transcends nihilism. In order to be entitled to describe Weber's nihilism as noble, one must have broken with his position. (48)

Strauss ends his discussion of the nihilistic consequence of Weber's thesis by considering an objection to his own argument:

> What Weber really meant cannot be expressed in terms of "values" or "ideals" at all; it is much more adequately expressed by his quotation "Become what thou art," i.e., "Choose thy fate." According to this interpretation, Weber rejected objective norms because objective norms are incompatible with human freedom or with the possibility of acting. (48)

Whereas the argument that we have been following begins with Weber's attempt to protect objective ethical norms from relativism, this possible interpretation suggests that Weber actually wanted to get rid of objective norms. These are two interpretations of Weber's suggestion that those who demand objective norms from social scientists should be told, "become what thou art" (Weber 1975, 87). Strauss apparently interpreted this injunction to mean that we should choose our own values or ideals because objective norms are not available, and hence only someone who does not understand his true situation would ask a scientist to give him objective norms. But according to the alternative interpretation, objective norms are bad in themselves because they limit the possibility of acting. Strauss rejects this alternative interpretation on the following ground:

> We must leave it open whether this reason for rejecting norms is a good reason and whether the nihilistic consequence would be avoided by this interpretation of Weber's view. It is sufficient to remark that its acceptance would require a break with the notions of "value" and "ideal" on which Weber's actual doctrine is built and that it is that actual doctrine, and not the possible interpretation mentioned, which dominates present-day social science. (48–49)

Whereas according to the interpretation in question there are no norms outside of the individual, according to Weber's doctrine there are timeless values and ideals that the individual has not made but that the individual is free to choose. Whereas Weber's notion of timeless values is at least partly a consequence of his devotion to the idea of science, the existentialist rejection of objective norms for the sake of protecting the possibility of practice seeks to destroy theory (*NRH*, 320–21). This latter interpretation cannot express the deepest intention of Weber, a thinker who impressed the young Strauss "by his passionate devotion to the idea of science, a devotion that was combined with a profound uneasiness regarding the meaning of science" (Strauss 1995a, 304).

I conclude with two reflections on what Strauss has proved. He does not prove that any understanding of the existence of irreconcilable conflict between values leads to nihilism. In fact, elsewhere he denies that the existence of such conflicts necessarily leads either to value-free social science or to nihilism:

> It is prudent to grant that there are value conflicts which cannot in fact be settled by human reason. But if we cannot decide which of two mountains whose peaks are hidden by clouds is higher than the other, cannot we decide that a mountain is higher than a molehill? If we cannot decide, regarding a war between two neighboring nations which have been fighting each other for centuries, which nation's cause is more just, cannot we decide that Jezebel's actions against Naboth [were] inexcusable? (*WPP*, 23)

What he proved was that Weber's understanding of these conflicts, the understanding that led Weber to insist on value-free social science, leads to nihilism. The key moment, the moment that makes nihilism inevitable, is that in which the shadow of Hitler emerges, for once fanatical devotion to values is recognized as a sign of nobility the theoretical attitude that gave rise to it is undermined as base, and nihilism is the inevitable consequence of the self-destruction of reason.

Second, although Strauss argues that Weber's thesis leads to nihilism, he argues elsewhere that this thesis "fosters not so much nihilism as conformism and philistinism" (*WPP*, 25). This is not a contradiction because a logical consequence of a view is not necessarily the same as what it fosters. Nihilism is an unpleasant position, and facing it requires a certain toughness and honesty. By undermining all standards, Weber's thesis on one hand leads us to nihilism and on the other makes it difficult for us to face it. Contemporary conformism and philistinism are partly the consequences of the failure to face nihilism. Accordingly, it is important to remember that by showing that Weber's thesis leads to nihilism, Strauss does not solve the problem underlying that thesis. Strauss's argument is chiefly a step in his attempt to clarify Weber's thesis. Such a clarification is necessary not least to counteract the easygoing philistinism and conformism that Weber's thesis in practice fosters, and it is therefore an indispensable preparation for a serious examination of that very thesis.

CHAPTER 4

The Fact-Value Distinction and Social Science as a Theoretical Pursuit

Strauss follows his explicit discussion of the nihilistic consequences of Weber's thesis (42–49) with a demonstration of the impossibility of social science as a theoretical pursuit on the basis of that thesis (49–62) because "[m]any social scientists of our time seem to regard nihilism as a minor inconvenience which wise men would bear with equanimity, since it is the price one has to pay for obtaining that highest good, a truly scientific social science" (49). Like the position of the liberals who welcome nihilism on account of their concern for toleration (*NRH*, 5–6), this position is incoherent, for nihilism is not consistent with the view that a truly scientific social science is the highest good. But this view requires a response because nihilism may well be compatible with the possession of knowledge, and if Weber's distinction between facts and values is the only way we can have a truly scientific social science, then Strauss himself, I suggest, would feel the inclination to accept it. In other words, as long as truth is possible, it has a hold on the souls of at least some human beings who cannot help but want to live in truth: "They [many social scientists] seem to be satisfied with any scientific finding, although they cannot be more than 'barren truths which generate no conclusion,' the conclusions being generated by purely subjective value judgments or arbitrary preferences" (49). Strauss suggests that the heirs of Bacon have forgotten Bacon's criticism of pre-modern science. To revitalize that criticism, Strauss shows that one cannot understand social phenomena without knowing important truths, and in particular without knowing truths that allow one to make value judgments.

Strauss begins his critique by referring us back to Weber's statement about the prospects of Western civilization:

> As we observed, Weber saw the following alternative: either a spiritual
> renewal or else "mechanized petrifaction," i.e., the extinction of every
> human possibility except that of "specialists without spirit or vision and
> voluptuaries without heart." He concluded: "But by making this state-
> ment we enter the province of judgments of value and faith with which
> this purely historical presentation shall not be burdened." It is not
> proper, then, for the historian or social scientist, it is not permissible,
> that he truthfully describe a certain type of life as spiritually empty or
> describe specialists without vision and voluptuaries without heart as
> what they are. (49)

It would indeed be improper for the historian or the social scientist to make a value judgment that is not true, but the problem is that Weber himself regarded the characterization in question as true.[1] This raises the question of the ground of Weber's objection to value judgments in social science. By claiming that according to Weber value judgments are not only "improper" but also "impermissible" in scientific discussion, Strauss implies that Weber's objection was both theoretical and moral. Weber both rejected and prohibited value judgments. Strauss responds with an argument that has five parts:

> But is this not absurd? Is it not the plain duty of the social scientist
> truthfully and faithfully to present social phenomena? How can we give
> a causal explanation of a social phenomenon if we do not first see it as
> what it is? Do we not know petrifaction or spiritual emptiness when we
> see it? And if someone is incapable of seeing phenomena of this kind, is
> he not disqualified by this very fact from being a social scientist, just as
> much as a blind man is disqualified from being an analyst of painting?
> (49–50)

These questions appear to be rhetorical, but Strauss judged that they require elaboration in order to make his argument demonstrative. In fact,

---

1. Weber explicitly maintained that his characterization of the last men of the Western civilization was truthful: "Dann allerdings könnte für die 'letzten Menschen' dieser Kulturentwicklung das Wort zur *Wahrheit* werden: 'Fachmenschen ohne Geist, Genussmenschen ohne Herz' . . ." (Weber 1920, 1:204, emphasis added).

they determine the structure of Strauss's discussion of this whole issue, a discussion that cannot be fully intelligible if we do not realize that it seeks to give answers to these questions, starting with the last one.[2] One cannot understand the argument of this section if one does not realize that it is an elaboration of the above argument but in reverse.

The Qualifications of a Social Scientist

The following is an interpretation of paragraph 18 of Strauss's discussion, which I argue is a response to the question "And if someone is incapable of seeing phenomena of this kind, is he not disqualified by this very fact from being a social scientist, just as much as a blind man is disqualified from being an analyst of painting?" By reflecting on Weber's own practice as a social scientist, Strauss argues that a man who cannot see moral and religious phenomena such as petrifaction for what they are is by this very fact disqualified from being a social scientist.[3] He argues that Weber's sociology of ethics and sociology of religion are not possible without moral and religious value judgments. To study ethics one must distinguish ethical phenomena from nonethical phenomena, for to study a subject one must distinguish it from other subjects. Weber, for example, argued that a sociologist should not confuse what he called "'techniques of living' (or 'prudential rules')" with "ethos" (50). The maxim "honesty is the best policy" was for Weber not a maxim of ethics, because it does not recommend honesty for its own sake but as an activity that serves one's self-interest. Now, Weber admitted that to recognize an ethos a sociologist must have a feel for and an appreciation of ethos, but Strauss argues that this appreciation necessarily implies

2. For instance, the meaning of paragraph 19 (52–53), which otherwise seems to serve no other purpose than to be repetitive and insulting, remains unclear unless we realize that it is a response to the all-important question: "Do we not know petrifaction or spiritual emptiness when we see it?" Similarly, his ending of paragraph 20 with a sentence that begins with "[a]s for the question whether the inevitable and unobjectionable value judgments should be expressed or suppressed" is not fully intelligible if one does not realize that he is beginning to respond to the question: "Is it not the plain duty of the social scientist truthfully and faithfully to present social phenomena?" Moreover, some aspects of the formulation of these questions themselves remain dark if one does not regard them as setting the framework for the discussion that follows. For instance, the original mentioning of the historian along with the social scientist and the dropping of the former (49) becomes intelligible only if one realizes that it refers in reverse order to the movement from social science (50–57) to history (57–62).

3. A sign that paragraph 18 is a response to the final question in the passage quoted in the text is Strauss's insertion of the following question in a discussion that deals with the sociologies of ethics and of religion: "Would one not laugh out of a court a man who claimed to have written a sociology of art but who actually had written a sociology of trash?" (50)

a value judgment insofar as it implies "the realization that a given phenomenon is a *genuine* 'ethos' and not a *mere* 'technique of living'" (50; emphasis in original). Thus, for instance, Weber's notion of ethos presupposes a rejection of utilitarianism as a pseudo-ethics. The correct value judgment is essential, for the sociologist of ethics who confuses a pseudo-ethics with a genuine ethics is like the sociologist "who claimed to have written a sociology of art but who actually had written a sociology of trash" (50). Similarly, Strauss argues that one cannot study religion without some understanding of what religion is, for how else can one distinguish religious from nonreligious phenomena? Weber, for example, distinguished magic from religion on the ground that they have entirely different attitudes toward gods. Now, Strauss argues in opposition to Weber that this understanding forces one to distinguish not only "between genuine and spurious religion" but also "between higher and lower religions: those religions are higher in which the specifically religious motivations are effective to a higher degree" (50). Accordingly, the sociologist of religion not only can but must rank religions on the basis of the motivations that animate them:

> The sociologist of religion cannot help noting the difference between those who try to gain the favor of their gods by flattering and bribing them and those who try to gain it by a change of heart. Can he see this difference without seeing at the same time the difference between a mercenary and a nonmercenary attitude? Is he not forced to realize that the attempt to bribe the gods is tantamount to trying to be the lord or employer of the gods and that there is a fundamental incongruity between such attempts and what men divine when speaking of gods? (50–51)

The notion of god that men divine is a regulative standard by which one can judge various religions. Those who try to gain the favor of their gods by flattering them are confused, because they are in effect trying to be lords over beings whom they believe are their lords. Flattery of gods is self-contradictory, for flattery presupposes that those who are flattered need the approval of the one who flatters them, but divine beings cannot need the approval of human beings.[4] Similarly, those who try to gain the favor of their gods by bribing them are confused because they in effect are

---

4. This argument seems to be part of Nietzsche's preference for Buddhism rather than Christianity: "Buddha says: 'Do not flatter your benefactor!' Repeat this saying in a Christian Church: right away it clears the air of everything Christian" (1974, #142). To make his case, however, Nietzsche would have had to show that the Christian praise of God is a kind of flattery.

trying to be employers of beings whom they believe they ought to serve. Accordingly, one can objectively state that a religion that suggests that one can buy one's salvation is a confused religion and therefore a religion of lower order than one that has purified itself from such relics of a nonreligious attitude. Despite Weber's contention that one cannot judge among religions, Strauss points out through a series of quotations that Weber's whole sociology of religion rests on value judgments:

> In fact, Weber's whole sociology of religion stands or falls by such distinctions as those between "ethics of intention" and "priestly formalism" (or "petrified maxims"); "sublime" religious thought and "pure sorcery"; "the fresh source of a really, and not merely apparently, profound insight" and "a maze of wholly unintuitive, symbolistic images"; "plastic imagination" and "bookish thinking." His work would be not merely dull but absolutely meaningless if he did not speak almost constantly of practically all intellectual and moral virtues and vices in the appropriate language, i.e., in the language of praise and blame. I have in mind expressions like these: "grand figures," "incomparable grandeur," "perfection that is nowhere surpassed," "pseudo-systematics," "this laxity was undoubtedly a product of decline," "absolutely unartistic," "ingenious explanations," "highly educated," "unrivaled majestic accounts," "power, plasticity, and precision of formulation," "sublime character of ethical demands," "perfect inner consistency," "crude and abstruse notions," "manly beauty," "pure and deep conviction," "impressive achievements," "works of art of the first rank." (51)[5]

5. Strauss gives nine quotations from Weber to show that his sociology of religion rests on value judgments and seventeen quotations to show that he refers to intellectual and moral virtues and vices in the language of praise and blame. According to Strauss, "[t]wenty-six is the numerical value of the letters of the sacred name of God in Hebrew, of the Tetragrammaton" (*SPPP*, 223). The only proper use of numerology that I am aware of is to alert the reader that the author is following two different arguments at the same time. The superficial argument shows that social scientists can distinguish between "genuine and spurious religion, between higher and lower religions" in the loose sense of the term. The deeper argument indicates how a social scientist may be able to distinguish between genuine and spurious religion in the strict sense of the term. Strictly speaking, the genuine religion is the true religion. Strauss suggests that one can test the claims of a religion to be true by discovering the truly religious motivation. The motivation characteristic of the true religion is that whose perception is coeval with a genuine grasp of the true ethics, for a religion that commands us to be immoral cannot be the true religion. If "moral principles have greater evidence than the teachings even of natural theology," then knowledge of morality is the arena where theological disputes must be settled (*NRH*, 164). This suggestion is supported by the reference to "ethos" in an argument that was only meant to rank religions (50) and by the number of quotations that Strauss gives in his discussion of virtues and vices, for seventeen is the number of nature (Strauss 1991, 275).

Both by argument and by example, Strauss shows that the social scientist cannot study ethics and religion without making value judgments.

Strauss concludes this paragraph by considering a matter that leads him to address the question whether Weber was qualified to be a social scientist. After showing that Weber referred to virtues and vices in the language of praise and blame, he suggests that Weber's assessment of those virtues and vices[6] led him to remark on the negative effect that Puritanism had on art:

> Weber paid some attention to the influence of Puritanism on poetry, music, and so on. He noted a certain negative effect of Puritanism on these arts. This fact (if it is a fact) owes its relevance exclusively to the circumstance that a genuinely religious impulse of a very high order was the cause of the decline of art, i.e., of the 'drying-up' of previously existing genuine and high art. For clearly, no one in his senses would voluntarily pay the slightest attention to a case in which a languishing superstition caused the production of trash. In the case studied by Weber, the cause was a genuine and high religion, and the effect was the decline of art. (51–52)

Now, many secular readers of Weber would probably read Weber's account as if it were a case in which a languishing superstition caused the production of trash. In fact, it was the case of a genuine and high religion that sought to suppress everything that smacked of superstition, and in doing so it was willing to tolerate the decline of some arts. As Strauss observes, Weber could not have seen this phenomenon without having made sound value judgments. In other words, he was qualified to be a social scientist because he was willing and able to make largely sound value judgments: "Weber had to choose between blindness to the phenomena and value judgments. In his capacity as a practicing social scientist, he chose wisely" (52).

The Posssibility of Valid Value Judgments

The following is an interpretation of paragraph 19 of Strauss's discussion, which is in fact a response to the question "Do we not know petrifaction or spiritual emptiness when we see it?"

But if Weber was willing and able to make value judgments, why did

---

6. The connection between the two subjects is indicated by the last quotation in the list of moral virtues and vices: "works of art of the first rank" (51).

he think that he could not portray a way of life as spiritually empty? I discuss Strauss's full answer to this question in chapter 5, but here it is sufficient to mention that Strauss suggests that Weber avoided value judgments at least partly for moral reasons. By showing the moral consequences of his *prohibition* against value judgments, he shows that that prohibition in fact undermined those moral concerns: "The prohibition against value judgments in social science would lead to the consequence that we are permitted to give a strictly factual description of the overt acts that can be observed in concentration camps and perhaps an equally factual analysis of the motivation of the actors concerned: we would not be permitted to speak of cruelty" (52). Now, Strauss's point is not that this prohibition will prevent the readers from seeing the cruelty of these actions, for "every reader of such a description who is not completely stupid would, of course, see that the actions described are cruel" (52). Rather, he argues that the prohibition will force the writer of this description to become dishonest or just plain silly:

> The writer would deliberately suppress his better knowledge, or, to use Weber's favorite term, he would commit an act of intellectual dishonesty. Or not to waste any moral ammunition on things that are not *worthy* of it, the whole procedure reminds one of a childish game in which you lose if you pronounce certain words, to the use of which you are constantly incited by your playmates. (52; emphasis added)[7]

Whereas Weber denied the possibility of a rational ethics partly out of concern for intellectual honesty, Strauss shows that his prohibition against value judgments leads to just such lack of honesty. Moreover, Strauss's contention that the prohibition against value judgments leads to childish games being played by adults is not just heated rhetoric but a response to the other element of Weber's moral objection to rational ethics:

> After Nietzsche's devastating criticism of those 'last men' who 'invented happiness,' I may leave aside altogether the naïve optimism in which science—that is the technique of mastering life which rests upon science—

---

7. For an example of this game, consider the following episode from a lecture that Weber gave: "Was bedeutet den für die künstlerische Entwicklung beispielsweise, die Klassenevolution des modernen Proletariats, sein Versuch, sich als eine Kultergemeinschaft in sich—denn das war ja das Grossartige an dieser Bewegung—hinzustellen (Der Vortsitzende [Sombart] will den Redner unterbrechen). Das 'Grossartige' soeben ein Werturteile, wie ich offen zugestehe, und ich nehme es wieder Zurück (Gross Heiterkeit)" (quoted in Bruun 1972, 66n).

has been celebrated as the way to happiness. Who believes in this?—aside from a few *big children* in university chairs or editorial offices. (Weber 1946, 143; emphasis added)

According to both Weber and Nietzsche, modern man's belief that he has solved the moral problem, his belief that he has invented happiness, has turned human life into a game, a life that lacks any seriousness. Accordingly, Weber suggested that those who still believe in the possibility of rational ethics are not only wrong but lack seriousness. They are big children. But Strauss shows that Weber's prohibition against value judgment leads to the same lack of seriousness that he wanted to avoid. In making this objection, Strauss points to a better approach. His objection preserves the spirit of Weber's, for while he speaks of the attitude in question as not being worthy of moral condemnation he actually suggests that it is beneath contempt. Weber's and Nietzsche's objection to the "last men" was really a moral objection, but because they believed that this immorality is the result of the belief in morality, they could not present their objection as a moral objection. According to Strauss, the problem with the "last men" is not that they "invented happiness" but they invented a false understanding of happiness, an understanding that makes them morally contemptible.

Having argued that the prohibition against value judgments undermines the very moral concerns that Weber sought to protect, Strauss articulates Weber's sober moral insights: "Weber, like every other man who ever discussed social matters in a relevant manner, could not avoid speaking of avarice, greed, unscrupulousness, vanity, devotion, sense of proportion, and similar things, i.e., making value judgments" (52–53). Social scientists cannot avoid value judgments, not because they must necessarily provide normative guidelines but because they must necessarily formulate questions about social matters. Now, one cannot formulate questions about social matters unless one is interested in social problems, but one cannot see a problem without making a value judgment. Something that seems to be a problem for one person is not a problem for another, because the other person has different value judgments. There are those who are troubled with pseudo-problems and there are those who fail to see genuine problems: a mental patient who washes himself all day does have a problem, but it is not the problem that he thinks he has. Accordingly, social science must concern itself with genuine problems. Weber, for instance, objected to the defenders of prostitution who maintained that it is good for public health, because they do not see the problem of prostitution:

He expressed indignation against people who did not see the difference
between Gretchen and a prostitute, i.e., who failed to see the nobility
of sentiment present in the one but absent from the other. What Weber
implied can be formulated as follows: prostitution is a recognized subject of sociology; this subject cannot be seen if the degrading character
of prostitution is not seen at the same time; if one sees the fact "prostitution" as distinguished from an arbitrary abstraction, one has already
made a value judgment. (53)

According to Weber, the proponents of hygienic prostitution do not see
the fact of prostitution because their utilitarianism prevents them from
seeing the repulsive character of mercenary sexual intercourse. By imply-
ing that one can see the degrading character of prostitution, Weber himself admitted that one can see petrifaction and spiritual emptiness, for the
way of life of prostitutes is one instance of the way of life of "specialists
without spirit and voluptuaries without heart."

After showing that Weber could see phenomena such as spiritual emptiness or petrifaction, Strauss implicitly asks us to compare Weber's own political science with one that more consistently attempts to avoid value judgments: "What would become of political science if it were not permitted to
deal with phenomena like narrow party spirit, boss rule, pressure groups,
statesmanship, corruption, even moral corruption, i.e., with phenomena
which are, as it were, constituted by value judgments?" With this list, Strauss
completes his repetition of the previous paragraph. Whereas in the preceding paragraph he had quoted seventeen expressions that showed that Weber
referred to human virtues and vice in the language of praise and blame and
nine expressions that referred to religious phenomena that are constituted
by value judgments, he now refers to seven value judgments and six political
phenomena constituted by value judgments without placing them in quotation marks.[8] By repeating himself and by avoiding quotation marks, Strauss
indicates that he is presenting Weber's moral judgments in an adequate
manner. In the list of political phenomena constituted by value judgments
there is only one phenomenon that is a sign of excellence (statesmanship)
and in the list of value judgments there are two virtues (devotion and sense
of proportion). By referring to "similar things" in his list of value judgments,

8. Strauss explains "the method of repeating the same thing with apparently insignificant,
but actually highly important variations" in the following way: "[t]he purpose of repeating conventional statements is to hide the disclosure, in the repetition, of unconventional views. What
matters is . . . the slight additions to, or omissions from the conventional view which occur in the
repetition" (*PAW,* 63–64).

Strauss draws our attention to Weber's well-known statement that a statesman must have three qualities: passion, sense of proportion, and responsibility, a passage that he cites in a footnote to the paragraph in question.
Strauss has omitted responsibility and passion because they are not precisely
value judgments. We praise those who have a passion for their work and are
responsible to their cause, yet every human being has passions and every
human being with a tongue or a hand can give an answer to others. The notion of responsibility is silent about the quality of the answer. This notion is
a substitute for public virtue that has become necessary on account of modern individualism. As Strauss observes, "[w]e frequently say of a man that he
is a responsible man, where people of former generations would have said
that he is a just man or a conscientious man or a virtuous man" (*LAM*, 10).
Similarly, when Weber said that nothing has value for man as man that he
cannot do with passion, what he meant is that nothing has value for man as
man to which he cannot be devoted; but he could not make his real meaning
explicit because moral judgments had become questionable to him (Weber
1951b, 531).[9] By purifying Weber's language of pseudo-value judgments,
Strauss clarifies Weber's understanding of what makes a good statesman. According to Strauss's correction, a good statesman must have devotion and a
sense of proportion. Strauss illustrates this understanding by referring to
Weber's discussion of the manner in which German and English political
leaders treated the working class during World War I (53n). The Germans
tried to manipulate the workers through deception and demagoguery. The
English, on the other hand, explained to the workers in a frank manner the
aims of the war, and they did this precisely when the workers were disgrun-
tled and were threatening strikes. The English were successful in retaining
the support of the workers but the German deceptions ultimately backfired.
According to Weber, German leaders believed that they were being
"clever," but their cleverness was really a form of vanity, which is the quality that is most harmful to a statesman. Just as in the case of prostitution, the
sophisticated saw things less clearly than the morally serious.[10]

Now, to turn to a political science that is not permitted to speak of

9. Gerth and Mills divine Weber's meaning, the meaning that Weber hides from himself,
when they mistranslate the above passage in the following way: "For nothing is worthy of man as
man unless he can pursue it with passionate devotion" (Weber 1946, 135).

10. Consider also the following comment of Strauss's: "I believe that Nietzsche is substantially correct in asserting that *the* German tradition is very critical of the ideals of modern civilization, and those ideals are of *English* origin. He forgets however to add that the English almost
always had the very un-German prudence and moderation not to throw out the baby with the
bath, i.e., the prudence to conceive of modern ideals as a reasonable adaptation of the old and
eternal ideal of decency, rule of law, and of that liberty which is not license, to changed circum-

phenomena that are constituted by value judgments, Strauss suggests that two possibilities remain open. Political science may treat these phenomena by placing them in quotation marks, a procedure that Strauss likens to "a childish trick which enables one to talk of important subjects while denying the principles without which there cannot be important subjects—a trick which is meant to allow one to combine the advantage of common sense with the denial of common sense" (53). By placing these phenomena in quotation marks, political science acknowledges its dependence on value judgments while undermining the examination of the soundness of those judgments because of its claims to know in advance that they are not sound. The other possibility is for political science to turn its attention toward phenomena that are not constituted by value judgments. Strauss argues that value judgments are necessary even in dealing with these phenomena:

> Or can one say anything relevant on public opinion polls, for example, without realizing the fact that many answers to the questionnaires are given by unintelligent, uninformed, deceitful, and irrational people, and that not a few questions are formulated by people of the same caliber— can one say anything relevant about public opinion polls without committing one value judgment after another? (52)

Strauss, of course, does not object to the use of polls here. Rather, he argues that if one uses them in the spirit of value-free social science, one will place oneself at the mercy of unintelligent, uninformed, deceitful, and irrational people. This is not an antidemocratic sentiment, for no one on reflection can deny the existence of such people or deny that some of them could be found in departments of political science. There is a world of difference between a democratic statesman who speaks frankly to the people so that they may see their duties and a social scientist who tries to deceive his subjects, some of whom may also try to deceive him.

THE NECESSITY OF VALUE JUDGMENTS FOR CAUSAL EXPLANATIONS OF SOCIAL PHENOMENA

The following is an interpretation of paragraph 20 of Strauss's discussion, which is in fact a response to the question "How can we give a causal ex-

---

stances. . . . Whatever may be wrong with the peculiarly modern ideal: the very Englishmen who originated it, were at the same time versed in the classical tradition, and the English always kept in store a substantial amount of the necessary counterpoison" (Strauss 1999, 372).

planation of a social phenomenon if we do not first see it as what it is?" Now, one way one can imagine the possibility of a social science on the basis of the distinction between facts and values is to restrict social science to causal explanations. But Strauss argues that Weber himself admitted that causal explanations require evaluation. He refers us to Weber's contention that to find the cause of an action of a general or a statesman the political scientist or historian must determine "whether the action concerned was caused by rational consideration of means and ends or by emotional factors" (53). This requires the construction of "the model of a perfectly rational action in the given circumstances," for only then can we determine the extent and nature of the nonrational factors that were responsible for the action in question:

> If the historian shows, by objectively measuring the action of a states-
> man against the model of "rational action in the circumstances," that
> the statesman made one blunder after another, he makes an objective
> value judgment to the effect that the statesman was singularly inept. In
> another case the historian arrives by the same procedure at the equally
> objective value judgment to the effect that a general showed unusual re-
> sourcefulness, resolution, and prudence. It is impossible to understand
> phenomena of this kind without being aware of the standard of judg-
> ment that is inherent in the situation and accepted as a matter of course
> by the actors themselves, and it is impossible not to make use of that
> standard by actually evaluating. (54)

Weber admitted that this procedure implies evaluation, for it forces one "to say that the actor in question made this or that mistake," but argued that such evaluations constitute a "transitional stage in the process of causal explanation" (54). Strauss mockingly observes: "As good children, we are then to forget as soon as possible what, in passing by, we could not help noticing but were not supposed to notice" (54). Weber's suppression of value judgments is the result of his own judgment of the priority of causal explanations to interpretive understanding, for Strauss suggests that Weber regarded the latter not only as transitional to causal explanations but also as incidental to them: "one may wonder whether what Weber regarded as merely incidental or transitional—namely, the insight into the ways of folly and wisdom, of cowardice and bravery, of barbarism and humanity, and so on—is not more worthy of the interest of the historian than any causal explanation along Weberian lines" (54). As Strauss argues later, this value judgment of Weber is based on a view of reality according to which the intelligible is frequently overpowered by what is no longer intelligible or the lower is mostly stronger than the higher (77). Whereas Weber used his heuristic construct only in order to reveal the errors of a statesman and a general, Strauss uses it to reveal both their errors and their prudence (compare Strauss's treatment of the general with Weber's account of the Austrian general Moltke, discussed in Weber 1924, 483, referred to in 54n). In other words, it was Weber's belief that all political action is tragic that led him to prefer causal explanations to interpretive understanding. Does not history offers us examples of excellent generals and statesmen as well as bunglers? Can we not learn from them? Perhaps all political victories are parts of a greater tragedy, but until this is shown we must recognize the possibility of history as a source of political wisdom. By recognizing this possibility, we realize that "the insight into the ways of folly and wisdom, of cowardice and bravery, of barbarism and humanity, and so on" is much more important to the historian than causal explanations along Weberian lines.

VALUE JUDGMENTS AND THE DUTY OF SOCIAL SCIENTISTS

The following is an interpretation of paragraphs 21–23 of Strauss's discussion, which are in fact a response to the question "Is it not the plain duty of the social scientist truthfully and faithfully to present social phenomena?"

While concluding his criticism of Weber's suppression of his value judgments, Strauss begins his response to the question of whether the truthful and faithful presentation of social phenomena is the duty of the social scientist: "As for the question whether the inevitable and unobjectionable value judgments should be expressed or suppressed, *it is really the question of how they should be expressed*, 'where, when, by whom, and toward whom'; it belongs, therefore, before another tribunal than that of the methodology of the social sciences" (54, emphasis added). It is the duty of those who love truth to share it with others, but if telling the truth to some human beings is in the final analysis harmful to them one should express the truth in such a way that those human beings cannot hear it. Esoteric writing conceals the truth only in a manner in which it can be unconcealed by those who honestly seek the truth. Because the issue concerns only the manner of expressing the truth, it belongs before another tribunal.

Having established that it is the duty of the social scientist to present social phenomena truthfully, Strauss considers whether the social scientist can fulfill this duty by avoiding value judgments. According to Strauss, "[s]ocial science could avoid value judgments only by keeping strictly within the limits of a purely historical or 'interpretive' approach" (55). Such an approach requires one to limit oneself to the self-interpretation of one's subjects:

> [the social scientist] would be forbidden to speak of "morality," "religion," "art," "civilization," and so on, when interpreting the thought of peoples or tribes who are unaware of such notions. On the other hand, he would have to accept as morality, religion, art, knowledge, state, etc., whatever claimed to be morality, religion, art, etc. As a matter of fact, there exists a sociology of knowledge according to which everything that pretends to be knowledge—even if it is notorious nonsense—has to be accepted as knowledge by the sociologist. (55)

This approach, however, is not compatible with science, because it "exposes one to the danger of falling victim to every deception and every self-deception of the people that one is studying" (55). Just as a historian cannot but distinguish between a blundering and a prudent general, he cannot accept the self-interpretation of a blundering general. Since groups are not "less liable to deceive themselves than individuals," the social scientist "cannot rest content with the interpretation of a given phenomenon that is accepted by the group within which it occurs" (55). Strauss illustrates this difficulty by examining Weber's well-known discussion of types of legitimate rule. According to Weber, what is alone important in determining whether a leader is charismatic is how he is actually regarded by his followers. Yet as Strauss points out: "Eight lines later, we read: 'Another type [of charismatic leader] is that of Joseph Smith, the founder of Mormonism, who, however, cannot be classified in this way with absolute certainty since there is a possibility that he was a very sophisticated swindler,' i.e., that he merely pretended to have a charisma" (55). Now as Strauss suggests, the translation used in the above passage is actually a mistranslation of Weber's text. According to the German original, Joseph Smith *was* a charismatic leader, despite the fact that he might have been a very sophisticated swindler. It seems that the translator, Talcott Parsons, could not believe that Weber would regard a sophisticated swindler as a charismatic leader. Nonetheless, this mistranslation raises a serious problem, "namely, the problem concerning the difference between genuine and pretended charisma, between genuine prophets and pseudo-prophets, between genuine leaders and successful charlatans" (56), a problem that Weber, despite his aforementioned statement, acknowledged by his use of phrases such as "genuine charisma" and "genuine prophet" (1956, 140–41).

Strauss, however, grants that "the strictly historical approach, which limits itself to understanding people in the way in which they understand themselves, may be very fruitful if kept in its place" (56). To show this place, he begins with the following observation: "Today it is trivial to say that the social scientist ought not to judge societies other than his own by the standards of his society. It is his boast that he does not praise or blame, but understands" (56). But as Strauss suggests, the social scientist of today only makes this boast. One cannot understand without a conceptual framework, and that framework depends on one's frame of reference, one's understanding of what is important and what is unimportant. For social science is not concerned with the study of all facts but with all relevant facts. A social scientist's frame of reference depends on his value judgments, and those of one who does not live alone on Mars are likely to be shaped by his society. Since his frame of reference "is more likely than not to be a mere reflection of the way in which his own society understands itself," he will force other societies "into the Procrustean bed of his conceptual scheme" (56). He will judge other societies by the standards of his own. But to understand other societies as they understood themselves is a necessary task of social science. For although it is true that one cannot understand other societies by limiting oneself to their own self-interpretation, it is also true that one cannot understand them if one does not know their self-interpretation, for "the self-interpretation of a society is an essential element of its being" (56). For instance, Strauss warns that one misunderstands pre-modern societies if one considers them as civilizations. Regarding the notion of Islamic civilization, Abdolkarim Soroush writes:

> Developing an identity or a civilization was never the intention of the prophets. The term *civilization* is a construct of the historians. Moslems, for example, were never aware that they were building or had built a "civilization" until the last century. This is a modern notion. We all know what a boundless and nebulous concept it is and how it can obfuscate judgment. (2000, 24)

Nothing illustrates this obfuscation better than the contemporary Moslem attempt to turn to Islam as a source of social identity in opposition to Western civilization. This attempt is actually a deep submission to the West, for it involves understanding Islam as a civilization. By understanding Islam as a guise for cultural identity, these Moslems have abandoned inadvertently the Islamic understanding of Islam, which is "a repository of truths that point toward the path of worldly and otherworldly salvation" (ibid., 23). Moreover, if a social scientist does not understand societies other than his own, he will not understand his own society, because he will not see what truly distinguishes it from others. He will fail to see what is accidental and what is essential in human society. To return to my earlier example, one cannot understand modern Western society without realizing that it is the only society that understands itself as a civilization, and one cannot know this historical fact and its significance if one does not understand other societies as they understood themselves. Accordingly, Strauss writes that "within the limits of this purely historical and hence merely preparatory or ancillary work, that kind of objectivity which implies the foregoing of evaluations is legitimate and even indispensable, from every point of view [that is, regardless of whether one believes the aim of social science is to test the soundness of doctrines or explain them in sociological or other terms]" (57). This approach must be preparatory and not ancillary, because one cannot, for instance, judge of the soundness of a doctrine "or explain it in sociological or other terms *before* one has understood it, i.e., before one has understood it exactly as its originators understood it" (57; emphasis added). The proper place of this approach is as a preparation to a value judgment or to a causal explanation.

Having made a case for a certain nonevaluating objectivity, Strauss argues that Weber's insistence on his nonevaluating objectivity fails to meet its demands: "It is curious that Weber, who was so fond of that kind of objectivity which requires the forgoing of value judgments, was almost blind in regard to the sphere which may be said to be the home, and the only home, of nonevaluating objectivity" (57). He explains this difficulty by focusing on the parochial character of Weber's conceptual scheme. Although Weber "realized clearly that the conceptual framework which he used was rooted in the social situation of his time" (57), he made no efforts to discover the conceptual framework of his subjects because he believed that social science can never arrive at objective value judgments. To illustrate this Strauss draws our attention to Weber's "three ideal types of legitimacy (traditional, rational, and charismatic)" (57). Despite the parochial origin of this scheme, Weber did not wonder whether his scheme fit "the manner in which, say, the protagonists in the great conflicts recorded in history had conceived of their causes, that is to say, the manner in which they had conceived of the principles of legitimacy" (58).[11] Weber was not "seriously disturbed by the danger that the imposition of his definitely 'dated' scheme might prevent the unbiased understanding of earlier political situations" because he believed that "no conceptual scheme used by social science can be of more than ephemeral validity" (58). To the extent that Weber accepted historicism, he was unable to understand the past historically:

> The goal of the historian of thought is to understand the thought of the past "as it really has been," i.e., to understand it as exactly as possible as it was actually understood by its authors. But the historicist approaches the thought of the past on the basis of the historicist assumption [that the foundations of human thought are laid by specific experiences that are not, as a matter of principle, coeval with human thought as such] which was wholly alien to the thought of the past. He is therefore compelled to attempt to understand the thought of the past better than it understood itself before he has understood it exactly as it understood itself. In one way or other, his presentation will be a questionable mixture of interpretation and critique. (OT, 24)

Although historicism is incompatible with historical objectivity, one cannot ignore the possibility that it is true. Perhaps the only way we can understand earlier thinkers is by understanding them differently than they understood themselves. But historicism cannot show this, for one cannot see this disproportion without understanding earlier thinkers as they understood themselves. Every attempt to show that a historian imposed modern concepts in his statements of earlier views is in fact a confirmation of the possibility of understanding earlier thinkers as they understood themselves. Moreover, if historicism is to be consistent it must maintain that its understanding of the earlier thinkers is not better than their own self-understanding, but historicism cannot maintain this view because historicism itself is a claim that earlier thinkers did not understand themselves adequately. For instance, although Heidegger denies that one can understand a thinker better than he understood himself, Strauss observes that "accord-

---

11. "It is easy to see, for instance, that his distinction of three ideal types of legitimacy (traditional, rational, and charismatic) reflects the situation as it existed in Continental Europe after the French Revolution when the struggle between the residues of the pre-Revolutionary regimes and the Revolutionary regimes was understood as a contest between tradition and reason. The manifest inadequacy of this scheme, which perhaps fitted the situation in the nineteenth century but hardly any other situation, forced Weber to add the charismatic type of legitimacy to the two types imposed on him by his environment" (57).

ing to Heidegger all thinkers prior to him have been oblivious of the true ground of grounds, the fundamental abyss. This assertion implies the claim that in the decisive respect Heidegger understands his great predecessors better than they understood themselves" (*SPPP*, 31).

To avoid any confusion, the issue is not the difficulty but the possibility of understanding earlier thinkers as they understood themselves. The fact that a historian today is likely to approach an old text with different questions than the ones that its author had in mind does not preclude the possibility that at the end of his study he could look at that text with the same questions provided he is willing to accept the author as his guide and not as some prisoner who needs to be tortured to get information out of him. Since those who have come to realize that they lack wisdom are much more likely to seek such guidance, the full understanding of earlier thinkers as they understood themselves can today be actualized only by those who are aware of the impasse of the present-day thought.

Although historicism cannot use historical evidence to deny the possibility of historical objectivity, nonhistoricist thought can use historical evidence to show that the acceptance of historicism has led to historical blunders. Strauss argues that Weber's notion that no conceptual scheme used by social science is of more than ephemeral validity led him to impose modern notions on earlier thought. He gives five examples of Weber's failure to fulfill the duty of the social scientist. He does not choose these examples randomly. These are errors that, once corrected, will cast doubt on the soundness of the very premise that was responsible for them. Accordingly, a brief consideration of each of these errors is appropriate.

The first error: "[Weber] did not hesitate to describe Plato as an 'intellectual,' without for one moment considering the fact that the whole work of Plato may be described as a critique of the notion of 'the intellectual'" (58). Strauss had argued earlier in *Natural Right and History* that historicism is the outcome of the crisis of modern political philosophy. Doubts about the soundness of the principle of modern society became doubts about the possibility of philosophy, because in modern times philosophy was politicized:

> It was this politicization of philosophy that was discerned as the root of
> our troubles by an intellectual who denounced the treason of the intel-
> lectuals. He committed the fatal mistake, however, of ignoring the es-
> sential difference between intellectuals and philosophers. In this case, he
> remained the dupe of the delusion which he denounced. For the politi-
> cization of philosophy consists precisely in this, that the difference be-

tween intellectuals and philosophers—a difference formerly known as
the difference between gentlemen and philosophers, on the one hand,
and the difference between sophists or rhetoricians and philosophers,
on the other—became blurred and finally disappeared. (34)

Plato's or Strauss's critique of the intellectual has nothing to do with what
today is called anti-intellectualism. But what is an intellectual? According
to Strauss, an intellectual is a combination of a sophist and a gentleman. A
sophist is different from a philosopher because "he is concerned with wisdom, not for its own sake, not because he hates the lie in the soul more than
anything else, but for the sake of the honor or the prestige that attends wisdom" (*NRH*, 116). A gentleman is different from a philosopher because he
has "a noble contempt for precision, because [he refuses] to take cogni-
zance of certain aspects of life, and because, in order to live as [a] gentle-
m[a]n, [he] must be well off" (*NRH*, 142). An intellectual would seem to be
someone concerned with wisdom whose concern is motivated by honor
and directed toward "noble" ends which he takes for granted and concerning which he does not seek to have precise knowledge. Such beings are by
no means the worst human beings, but they are the root of our trouble
in the sense that the movement that led to their emergence is also the
movement that is responsible for the contemporary confusion. The error
of Benda would seem to be that while criticizing the politicization of philosophy that characterized the European left and right, he failed to see that
the earlier liberalism that he defended was also a form, and indeed the
original form, of the politicization of philosophy. If Plato's whole work
was devoted to showing the impossibility of the politicization of true philosophy—the impossibility of a political community based on genuine philosophic insights—then one cannot know whether the crisis of modern
philosophy justifies the abandonment of the principles of philosophy unless one first resolves the disagreement between Plato and modern political philosophers.

The second error: "He did not hesitate to consider the dialogue between the Athenians and Melians in Thucydides' *History* as a sufficient basis for asserting that 'in the Hellenic polis of the classical time, a most
naked 'Machiavellianism' was regarded as a matter of course in every respect and as wholly unobjectionable from an ethical point of view.' To say
nothing of other considerations, he did not pause to wonder how Thucydides himself had conceived of that dialogue" (58). Later in his discussion
of Weber, Strauss suggests that the attitude that Weber attributed to the

Greeks was an element of the attitude that gave birth to his moral preference for the irreconcilability of conflicts between ultimate values (65). Had
Weber realized that wise men in the past had found this attitude objectionable, in part because its adherents only hide their own moral views, he
might have discovered the reasons why a strictly moral view is superior to
the blend of morality and amorality that is characteristic of his own attitude.

The third error: "He did not hesitate to write: 'The fact that Egyptian
sages praised obedience, silence, and absence of presumptuousness as godly
virtues, had its source in bureaucratic subordination. In Israel, the source
was the plebeian character of the clientele'" (58). Had Weber realized that
prior to the emergence of philosophy or science all human societies had
one single structure—rule by divine laws, with obedience to those laws
considered to be man's primary duty—he might have considered whether
a proper examination of this moral attitude could lead to a universal answer
to the question of human virtue and the purpose of human society (84–85).

The fourth error: "Similarly, his sociological explanation of Hindu
thought is based on the premise that natural right 'of any kind' presupposes
the natural equality of all men, if not even a blessed state at the beginning
and at the end" (58). Had Weber realized that there were notions of natural right other than modern natural right or the natural right doctrines that
depend on divine providence, neither of which he could accept as knowable
truth, perhaps he would not have accepted the historicist thesis without an
adequate examination of these alternatives.

The fifth error:

> Or, to take what is perhaps the most telling example, when discussing
> the question of what has to be regarded as the essence of a historical
> phenomenon like Calvinism, Weber said: By calling something the es-
> sence of a historical phenomenon, one either means that aspect of the
> phenomenon which one considers to be of permanent value, or else that
> aspect through which it exercised the greatest historical influence. He
> did not even allude to a third possibility, which is, in fact, the first and
> most obvious one, namely, that the essence of Calvinism would have to
> be identified with what Calvin himself regarded as the essence, or as the
> chief characteristic, of his work. (58–59)

This is the most telling example of Weber not understanding his subjects as
they understood themselves because it is obvious that the Calvinists whom
Weber studied identified the essence of Calvinism with what Calvin himself

regarded as the essence of his work, because this blunder influenced Weber's most famous historical essay, and because the other blunders could not be adequately overcome if this one was not corrected first.

THE IRRATIONALITY OF THE REJECTION OF VALUE JUDGMENTS

The following is an interpretation of paragraphs 24–25 of Strauss's discussion, which are in fact a response to the question "Is this not absurd?"

After having shown that it is the duty of the social scientist to present truthfully social phenomena and that this cannot be done by forgoing value judgments, Strauss turns to Weber's most famous historical essay, his study of Protestant ethics and the spirit of capitalism, to show that the rejection of value judgments leads to absurdity. The thesis of that study is that "Calvinist theology was a major cause of the capitalist spirit" (59). Now, Weber acknowledged that the theology that led to the spirit of capitalism was not Calvin's own. As Strauss explains:

> [Weber] contended that Calvinist theology was a major cause of the capitalist spirit. He stressed the fact that the effect was in no way intended by Calvin, that Calvin would have been shocked by it, and—what is more important—that the crucial link in the chain of causation (a peculiar interpretation of the dogma of predestination) was rejected by Calvin but emerged "quite naturally" among the epigones and, above all, among the broad stratum of the general run of Calvinists. (59)

The doctrine that Weber regarded as the cause of the spirit of capitalism is the view that maintains that dedication to one's vocation in the world is a sign of one's salvation. But according to Calvin, any attempt to learn from the conduct of others whether they are chosen or damned is "an unjustifiable attempt to force God's secrets" (Weber 1958, 110). Now, in its consistency with what men divine when they think of god, Calvin's teaching is of much higher rank than the teaching to which Weber traced the spirit of capitalism. As Strauss points out, Weber acknowledged this as well by referring to those who accept that teaching as "epigones and the general run of men" (59), but Weber's methodological principle prevented him from making this value judgment, which Strauss says is fully justified by everyone who has understood the theological doctrine of Calvin, explicit. Had he done so, he would have revised his thesis:

The peculiar interpretation of the dogma of predestination that allegedly led to the emergence of the capitalistic spirit is based on a radical
misunderstanding of Calvin's doctrine or, to use Calvin's own language,
it is a carnal interpretation of a spiritual teaching. The maximum that
Weber could reasonably have claimed to have proved is, then, that a
corruption or degeneration of Calvin's theology led to the emergence of
the capitalist spirit. (60)

Now, Weber did not make this correction of his thesis, because he identified the essence of Calvinism with its historically most influential aspect.
The prohibition against value judgments prevented him from identifying
the essence of Calvinism with the aspect of it that is of permanent value.
But Strauss maintains that that prohibition also *instinctively* led Weber to
avoid identifying the essence of Calvinism with what Calvin himself considered its essence, "for Calvin's self-interpretation would naturally act as a
standard by which to judge objectively the Calvinists who claim to follow
Calvin" (60).[12]

If Weber had made the correction that Strauss suggests, he would have
been led to the question of what was responsible for the corruption or degeneration of Calvin's theology. To answer this question, Strauss suggests
that one must have a more adequate understanding of what the spirit of capitalism is. Weber had correctly "identified the spirit of capitalism with the
view that limitless accumulation of capital and profitable investment of capital is a moral duty," but his "Kantianism" led him to identify moral duty with
"end in itself" and sever every connection between moral duty and the common good. Thus, he introduced into his analysis "a distinction, not warranted by the texts, between the 'ethical' justification of the unlimited accumulation of capital and its 'utilitarian' justification." According to Strauss,
the problem of the genesis of the spirit of capitalism is identical with the
problem of the emergence of the premise that unlimited accumulation of
capital is most conducive to the common good. He argues that the best historical evidence that we have suggests that the emergence of the minor

12. This psychological explanation of Weber's avoidance of Calvin's self-interpretation as a
standard for the essence of Calvinism should be compared to Strauss's contention that Weber connected Calvinism to the spirit of capitalism by "questionable psychological constructs" (61n). According to Weber, the transformation of Calvin's teaching was natural because it is impossible for
ordinary people to live not knowing whether they are saved or not. This may be true for those
who have been raised on the idea that man should control his own destiny, but it is not necessarily
true for those who do not hold this premise. Strauss's psychological explanation of Weber, on the
other hand, is based on Weber's own premise.

premise was due to a revolution in thought that occurred on the plane of purely philosophic or rational or secular thought, a break that was originated by Machiavelli and led to the moral teachings of Bacon and Hobbes (61n).

Now, this correction of a historical thesis is of philosophic importance. If our secular society is the unintended consequence of thoughts of other-worldly men, this experience gives some warrant to think that the ground of history cannot be mastered by man or god. But if our secular society is the consequence of a revolution in thought by secular thinkers who wanted to corrupt the theological tradition and create a new world order, then the course of history is much more intelligible. Strauss's account of modern history weakens the historical evidence in favor of historicism, and by do-ing so it opens us to what Strauss considers to be the real question that an-imates modern history and indeed world history. For if the modern secu-lar world is the result of a conscious attempt by secular thinkers, and if we have reasons to be dissatisfied with the results of this attempt, then we must ask whether this attempt was sound. To ask this question requires one in the first place to reenact the quarrel between the Enlightenment and Or-thodoxy, and more generally between philosophy and divine revelation.

Strauss characterizes Weber's prohibition against value judgements as a "taboo," because it prevents him from presenting the absurdity of vulgar Calvinism for what it is (60). More generally, the rejection of value judg-ments endangers historical objectivity by necessarily leading to two ab-surdities: "In the first place, it prevents one from calling a spade a spade. In the second place, it endangers that kind of objectivity which legitimately requires the forgoing of evaluations, namely, the objectivity of interpreta-tion" (61). According to Weber, to understand the past a historian must avoid value judgments:

> A careful examination of historical works quickly shows that when the
> historian begins to "evaluate," causal analysis almost always ceases—to
> the prejudice of scientific results. He runs the risk, for example, of ex-
> plaining as the result of a 'mistake' or of a 'decline,' what is perhaps the
> consequence of ideals different from his own, and so he fails in his most
> important task, that is, the task of "understanding." (Weber 1949, 33)

Strauss, however, notes that the social scientist who rejects value judg-ments necessarily treats practically all the thought of the past as a result of a mistake. The rejection of value judgments is absurd because it itself is a value judgment—one, moreover, that undermines what it tries to protect:

The historian who takes it for granted that objective value judgments are impossible cannot take very seriously that thought of the past which was based on the assumption that objective value judgments are possible, i.e., practically all thought of earlier generations. Knowing beforehand that the thought was based on a mental delusion, he lacks the necessary incentive for trying to understand the past as it understood itself. (61–62)

Whereas earlier Strauss had reduced Weber's thesis as a moral thesis to nihilism, he now has reduced that thesis as a theoretical thesis to absurdity.

CHAPTER 5

The Problem of Social Science

By reducing Weber's social science to nihilism and absurdity, Strauss has given us sufficient reason to reject that social science, but he has not given us sufficient understanding of the difficulty that led to Weber's thesis. Accordingly, Strauss begins the next section of his argument with the following statement: "Almost all that we have said up to this point was necessary in order to clear away the most important obstacles to an understanding of Weber's central thesis" (62). Strauss distinguishes between Weber's thesis that "there is a variety of values whose demands conflict with one another, and whose conflict cannot be solved by human reason" and the thesis that is at its center (41–42). But what is that central thesis? And how does it generate the peripheral thesis?

The "precise meaning" of Weber's central thesis becomes visible if we examine the limitations of Strauss's criticism of Weber's contention about the origins of capitalism (62). Strauss had argued earlier that Weber's contention should have been that it was not so much Calvinism as "the corruption or degeneration of Calvin's theology [that] led to the emergence of the capitalist spirit," and that Weber failed to make this qualification on account of his prohibition of value judgments (59–60). Strauss now defends Weber by affirming that in fact one may not be able to judge between Calvin and his followers. It is true that one can objectively criticize them given that they "unwittingly destroyed what they intended to preserve" and that even from the point of view of secular thinkers their position is an "impossible position, a halfway house" (62). But this objective value judgment is of "limited significance," for it does not help us judge whether Calvin's followers were better or worse than Calvin: "assuming that Calvinist theology were a bad thing, its corruption was a good thing" (62). If Calvinist theology were a bad thing, vulgar Calvinism would be "preferable to Calvinism proper for the same reason that Sancho Panza may be said to be preferable to Don Quixote" (62). This defense of vulgar Calvinism is in truth its rejection, for its adherents cannot defend it on this ground. Nevertheless, both the rejection and this possible defense are necessary if we are to see the real issue:

> The rejection of vulgar Calvinism is then inevitable from every point of view. But this merely means that only after having rejected vulgar Calvinism is one faced with the real issue: the issue of religion versus irreligion, i.e., of genuine religion versus noble irreligion, as distinguished from the issue of mere sorcery, or mechanical ritualism versus the irreligion of specialists without vision and voluptuaries without heart. (62)

The real issue is not that between Calvin's confused followers and "the irreligion of specialists without vision and voluptuaries without heart" to which they inadvertently contributed. Weber's central thesis is that the conflict between genuine religion and noble irreligion as well as the conflict between religions of the highest rank cannot be resolved by human reason. The irreconcilability of this conflict would render questionable many other apparently objective value judgments. In the first place, Strauss considers Weber's original judgment concerning prostitution, a judgment with which Strauss implicitly agreed. But now he shows why Weber may have thought that his own judgment was not objective:

> It is indeed true that one has already passed a value judgment when speaking of Gretchen and a prostitute. But this value judgment proves to be merely provisional the moment one comes face to face with a radically ascetic position which condemns all sexuality. From this point of view, the open degradation of sexuality through prostitution may appear to be a cleaner thing than the disguise of the true nature of sexuality through sentiment and poetry. (63)[1]

---

1. "Also in the opinion of various Pietistic groups the highest form of Christian marriage is that with the preservation of virginity, the next highest that in which sexual intercourse is only indulged in for the procreation of children, and so on down to those which are contracted for purely erotic or external reasons and which are, from an ethical standpoint, concubinage. On those lower levels a marriage entered into for purely economic reasons is preferred (because after all it is inspired for rational motives) to one with erotic foundations" (Weber 1958, 263).

Similarly, Strauss now shows that the value judgments implied in the preceding section's distinctions between a blundering general and an unusually resourceful one (54–55) and between virtues and vices (51) lose their significance once they are confronted with a position that condemns all sexuality, views war as absolutely evil, and considers all human virtues to be ultimately only splendid vices (63).

This account makes it clear that according to Weber one's perception of social phenomena depends on one's choice of an ultimate value. Whereas earlier Strauss had interpreted Weber's distinction between "reference to values" and "value judgments" as an insistence on neutrality in social science (40), he now suggests that Weber ultimately believed that social science is incompatible with neutrality. The objects of social science are constituted by reference to values, which "presupposes appreciation of values." Because the various values are incompatible, this appreciation of some values necessarily implies the rejection of others: "Only on the basis of such acceptance or rejection of values, of '*ultimate values*,' do the objects of social science come to sight" (64; emphasis added). Social science appears to be neutral only because for all work after the constitution of its objects, and in particular "for the causal analysis of these objects, it must be a matter of indifference whether the student has accepted or rejected the value in question" (64). For instance, a social scientist who did not value political freedom would not study phenomena that are relevant to political freedom, but to understand his work one does not need to value political freedom.

Regardless of whether Weber understood his own position this way, Strauss argues that "Weber's whole notion of the scope and function of the social sciences rests on the allegedly demonstrable premise that the conflict between ultimate values cannot be resolved by human reason" (64). The question is whether this premise "has really been demonstrated or whether it has merely been postulated under the impulse of a specific moral preference" (64). Strauss suspects a moral motive behind Weber's position, for although the proof of Weber's premise would require "an effort of the magnitude of that which went into the conception and elaboration of the *Critique of Pure Reason*" (*WPP*, 22), Weber, "who wrote thousands of pages, devoted hardly more than thirty of them to a thematic discussion of the basis of his whole position" (64). Why was this premise, which had been rejected by "the whole galaxy of political philosophers from Plato to Hegel" (35), so self-evident to Weber?

The moral preference that Strauss considers responsible for Weber's thesis is his preference for the tragic life. To understand the roots of this preference, Strauss follows Weber's suggestion that his thesis is a generalized version of an older and more common view that the conflict between ethics and politics is insoluble: "Political action is sometimes impossible without incurring moral guilt" (64; Weber 1949, 15). Accordingly, Strauss suggests:

> It seems, then, that it was the spirit of "power politics" that begot Weber's position. Nothing is more revealing than the fact that, in a related context when speaking of conflict and peace, Weber put 'peace' in quotation marks, whereas he did not take this precautionary measure when speaking of conflict. Conflict was for Weber an unambiguous thing, but peace was not: peace is phony, but war is real. (64)

By suggesting that Weber postulated his thesis under the impulse of a specific moral preference, Strauss does not suggest that preference is something idiosyncratic.[2] Quite to the contrary, Strauss argues that "Weber's thesis that there is no solution to the conflict between values was a part, or a consequence, of *the comprehensive view* according to which human life is an inescapable conflict" (65; emphasis added). Weber began with the realization that the modern attempt to escape the state of nature, the modern idea of civilization, is a delusion. Reflecting on German peasants and day-laborers in the East who in his view were being driven from their homeland not through political means by a politically superior enemy but through economic means by an "inferior race," Weber wrote: "The somber gravity of the population problem alone is enough to prevent us from being eudaemonists, from imagining that peace and happiness [happiness of mankind] lie waiting in the womb of the future, and from believing that anything other than the hard struggle of man with man can create [win] any elbow-room in this earthly life" (1994, 14). It would seem that human beings can alter the character of serious conflicts but not their existence. In this case, peace and universal happiness are merely delusions: "As far as the dream of peace and human happiness is concerned, the words written over the portal into the unknown future of human history are: 'lasciate ogni speranza'" (1994, 14–15). But Strauss observes that for Weber, the very goal of peace and universal happiness is illegitimate because "it would be the condition of 'the last men who have invented happiness,' against whom Nietzsche had directed his 'devastating criticism'" (65). The recognition of

---

2. Consider Strauss's suggestion that radical historicism is connected with a preference for tragic life (*NRH*, 26n) and his criticism of Carl Schmitt as a whole (*SCR*, 331–51).

such illegitimacy could be the basis of a solution to man's moral problem. As Strauss puts it:

> If peace is incompatible with human life or with a truly human life, the moral problem would seem to allow of a clear solution: the nature of things requires a warrior ethics as the basis of a "power politics" that is guided exclusively by considerations of national interest; or "the most naked Machiavellianism [would have to be] regarded as a matter of course in every respect, and as wholly unobjectionable from an ethical point of view." (65)

This is the position that Weber articulated in his inaugural lecture, "The Nation State and Economic Policy." He rejected peace and universal happiness as the goal of political economy:

> The question which stirs us as we think beyond the grave of our own generation is not the *well-being* human beings will enjoy in the future but what kind of people they will *be*, and it is this same question which underlies all work in political economy. We do not want to breed well-being in people, but rather those characteristics which we think of as constituting the human greatness and nobility of our nature. (1994, 15; emphasis in original)

Political economy is motivated by an altruistic concern for future generations to which it is responsible not only for the kind of economic organizations that it leaves behind but also for the amount of elbow room it has conquered. In short, "the science of political economy is a *political* science. It is a servant of politics, not the day-to-day politics of the persons and classes who happen to be ruling at any given time, but the enduring power-political interests of the nation" (16). Far from being a value-free science, political economy is a science that has the "reason of the state" as its ultimate standard of value (17).

But this view was obviously not Weber's ultimate view. To begin to understand why Weber rejected this position, one must consider in greater depth why Weber regarded the goal of universal happiness as illegitimate. What distinguishes the last men of modern civilization from human beings of all other times and places is their incapacity for self-sacrifice, for being devoted to anything higher than themselves. Unlike Hobbes's state of nature, the comprehensive view of which Weber's view is a part maintains that the conflict between groups, and not between individuals, is inescapable.

So long as political communities are in deadly conflict with each other, they will demand that their members sacrifice their lives for the community. Despite his contention that the goal of utilitarian economics is an illusion, Weber feared that it is possible for man to create peace. If man is unable to eliminate all conflicts, he might be able to eliminate all serious conflicts. By transforming moral-political conflict into economic competition, utilitarian economics could create a situation that no longer demands morality and in which noble natures are at a disadvantage. Accordingly, for Weber, the possibility of morality is tied to the possibility of serious conflicts between groups. The existence of conflict becomes the condition of nobility and hence something that is desired by noble natures. The problem with a warrior ethics is that it leaves the soul of individuals at peace:

> But we would then be confronted with the paradoxical situation that the individual is at peace with himself while the world is ruled by war. The strife-torn world demands a strife-torn individual. The strife would not go to the root of the individual, if he were not forced to negate the very principle of war: he must negate the war from which he cannot escape and to which he must dedicate himself, as evil or sinful. Lest there be peace anywhere, peace must not be simply rejected. It is not sufficient to recognize peace as the necessary breathing time between wars. There must be an absolute duty directing us toward universal peace or universal brotherhood, a duty conflicting with the equally high duty that directs us to participate in "the eternal struggle" for "elbow room" for our nation. Conflict would not be supreme if guilt could be escaped. (65–66)

By understanding the warrior ethics as the solution to man's problem, one places oneself outside the world that fosters nobility. If conflict is the condition of nobility, every solution to the moral problem must be judged as immoral, as ignoble. The warrior ethics can become truly noble if it is accompanied by an ethics that is absolutely antithetical to it, and only an otherworldly ethics can play this role:

> The fact that death and ruin, with their leveling effects, overtake good men and good works, as well as evil ones, could appear to be a depreciation of precisely the supreme values of this world—once the idea of a perpetual duration of time, of an eternal God, and an eternal order has been conceived. In the face of this, values—and precisely the most highly cherished values—have been hallowed as being "timelessly" valid. Hence, the significance of their realization in "culture" has been

stated to be independent of the temporal duration of their concretion. Thereupon the ethical rejection of the empirical world could be further intensified. (Weber 1946, 354)

Weber brings in the otherworldly (timeless) ethics to combat the warrior ethics, but in order for the warrior ethics to hold its own it too must conceive of itself as timeless. Accordingly, Weber speaks of "'the eternal struggle' for 'elbow room' for our nation," although the German nation is hardly eternal. Moreover, in order to defend itself against an otherworldly ethics that condemns its rejection of brotherliness as sinful, the warrior ethics must be conceived as unavoidable. Accordingly, for Weber the highest cultural values "have borne the stigma of a deadly sin, of an unavoidable and specific burden of guilt" (1946, 354). As Strauss observes, Weber did not discuss the question whether "one can speak of guilt, if man is forced to become guilty," because he "needed the necessity of guilt" (66). Since the worldly man has regarded the possession of culture as the highest good, the deepest conflict that Weber affirms is that between a brotherly, otherworldly ethics and "the aristocracy of the intellect": "[Weber] had to combine the anguish bred by atheism (the absence of any redemption, of any solace) with the anguish bred by revealed religion (the oppressive sense of guilt)" (66). Weber "has postulated the insolubility of all value conflicts because his soul craved a universe in which failure, that bastard of forceful sinning accompanied by still more forceful faith, instead of felicity and serenity, was to be the mark of human nobility" (*WPP*, 23).

To show that Weber's rejection of a rational morality was governed by a moral preference for conflict, Strauss argues that even if Weber was right that all values are of the same rank, a social scientist could come up with a reasonable social scheme:

> Now, precisely if this is the case, a social scheme that satisfies the requirements of two values is preferable to one whose scope is more limited. The comprehensive scheme might demand that some of the requirements of each of the two values would have to be sacrificed. In this case the question would arise as to whether the extreme or one-sided schemes are not so good as, or better than, the apparently more comprehensive schemes. To answer that question, one would have to know whether it is at all possible to adopt one of the two values, while unqualifiedly rejecting the other. If it is impossible, some sacrifice of the apparent requirements of the two would be a dictate of reason. (66)

Let us assume that the teaching of the Bible and that of philosophers contradict each other in such a way that the contradiction is irreconcilable. One can still have a reasonably moderate political scheme, if neither of these antagonists can unqualifiedly reject the other. For instance, adherents of the Bible can be shown that they need philosophy to understand and propagate the message of the Bible (*CM*, 1). And adherents of philosophy can be shown the soundness of George Washington's warning against the abolition of or neglect of religion: "[L]et us with caution indulge the supposition that morality can be maintained without religion. Whatever may be conceded to the influence of refined education on minds of peculiar structure, reason and experience forbid us to expect that national morality can prevail in exclusion of religious principle" (quoted in Berns 1985, 13). Weber did not enter into such considerations, nor did he consider whether it is wise to separate social science from the spirit of statesmanship, the spirit that recognizes that extreme solutions to social problems are less sensible than moderate solutions. Although as a practical politician Weber "may have abhorred the spirit of narrow party fanaticism, as a social scientist he approached social problems in a spirit that had nothing in common with the spirit of statesmanship and that could serve no other practical end than to encourage narrow obstinacy." It was Weber's "unshakeable faith in the supremacy of conflict" that "forced him to have at least as high a regard for extremism as for moderate courses" (67).

Now, Strauss's tracing of Weber's thesis partly to a moral preference would be questionable had he not also examined Weber's arguments for his position. Although Weber had not written a comprehensive critique of evaluating reason, he did give, as Strauss puts it, "two or three" or "three or four" proofs for his position (67, 67n), each of which Strauss shows to be inadequate.[3]

---

3. The proof that Strauss limits to a footnote is the conflict between "eroticism and all impersonal or super-personal values" (67n). Strauss observes that the standpoint that permits or fosters erotic relations that are hostile to "everything sacred or good, to every ethical or aesthetic law" (Weber 1949, 17) is not "that of Carmen but that of intellectuals who suffer from specialization or 'professionalization' of life" (67n). Weber wrote: "Under this tension between the erotic sphere and rational everyday life, extramarital sexual life in particular, which had been removed from everyday affairs, could appear as the only tie which still linked man with the natural fountain of all life. For man had now been completely emancipated from the cycle of the old, simple, and organic existence of the peasant" (1946, 346). Strauss draws our attention to Weber's admission that this erotic return to nature is bound up with what Weber called "the systematic preparation of the sexual sphere." Thus, the "intellectual's attempt to escape specialization through eroticism merely leads to specialization in eroticism," and thereby it merely aggravates the ill it was supposed to remedy (67n).

Weber's first proof is that no system of ethics can solve the questions of justice. "Two opposed views are equally legitimate or defensible" (68):

> The implications of the postulate of "justice" cannot be decided unambiguously by any ethic. Whether one, for example—as would correspond most closely with the views expressed by Schmoller—owes much to those who achieve much or whether one should demand much from those who can accomplish much; whether one should, e.g., in the name of justice (other considerations—for instance, that of the necessary "incentive"—being disregarded for the moment) accord great opportunities to those with eminent talents or whether on the contrary (like Babeuf) one should attempt to equalize the injustice of the unequal distribution of mental capacities through the rigorous provision that talented persons, whose talent gives them prestige, must not utilize their better opportunities for their own benefit—these questions cannot be definitely answered. (Weber 1949, 15–16)

Strauss first corrects Weber's "loose" formulation of the problem. The question as presented by Weber is whether one owes much to those who achieve much or one should demand much from such people. But Strauss points out that such people base their claims not on their achievements but on their contributions to society. The question as suggested by Strauss is whether one owes much to those who contribute much or whether one should demand much from such people. That the former is the case is so clear that one can hardly even raise it as a question. Indeed, Strauss points out that Weber acknowledged the strength of this position by the very fact that he did not find it necessary to give an argument for it. As to Weber's argument for the second view, Strauss responds: "Before one could say that this view is tenable, one would have to know whether it makes sense to say that nature committed an injustice by distributing her gifts unequally, whether it is a duty of society to remedy that injustice, and whether envy has a right to be heard" (68).

Although envy does not have a right to be heard, it will necessarily make itself heard. Since anyone concerned with the welfare of society must consider this fact, Strauss leaves open the possibility that Babeuf's view as stated by Weber is as defensible, if not as legitimate, as its alternative. But from this concession it does not follow that one should "incite the adherents of the two opposed views to insist on their opinions with all the obstinacy that they can muster" because such incitement is harmful both to the common good and to justice. Rather, the issue "has to be transferred from the tribunal of ethics to that of convenience or expediency" (69). But Weber excluded discussions of expediency from the discussion of this issue, because he did not reflect on the difference between convenience and expediency. He rejected considerations of expediency because his moral impulse rebelled against anything that smacked of convenience. But one cannot reasonably exclude considerations of expediency from the issue of justice, for there is a "connection between justice and the good of society, and between the good of society and incentives to socially valuable activity" (69). Finally, in defending one-sided positions, Weber excluded his own alleged insight from his assessment of the two parties: "Precisely if Weber were right in asserting that the two opposite views are equally defensible, would social science as an *objective science* have to stigmatize as a crackpot any man who insisted that only one of the views is in accordance with justice" (69; emphasis added).

Weber's second proof was that the conflict between the ethics of intention and the ethics of responsibility is insoluble:

> These [ethical problems that ethics cannot solve on the basis of its own presuppositions] include above all, the basic questions: (a) whether the intrinsic value of ethical conduct—the "pure will" or the "conscience" as it used to be called—is sufficient for its justification, following the maxim of Christian moralists: "The Christian acts rightly and leaves the consequences [success] of his actions to God"; or (b) whether the responsibility for the predictable consequences of the action is to be taken into consideration. All radical revolutionary political attitudes, particularly revolutionary "syndicalism," have their point of departure in the first postulate; all *Realpolitik* in the latter. Both invoke ethical maxims. But these maxims are in eternal conflict—a conflict which cannot be resolved by means of ethics alone. (Weber 1949, 16)

In his formulation of this difficulty, Strauss draws our attention to the difference between "success" and "consequences," a difference that Weber blurs. A Christian, according to the maxim that Weber cites, is indifferent to the success of his actions but not to their consequences. For instance, the maxim suggests that a Christian should not be deterred in pursuing a just cause even though all evidence points to the defeat of that cause. But it does not suggest that in order to gratify his sense of moral self-satisfaction, a Christian should engage in a course of action knowing that it will harm innocent human beings. Second, the ethics of intention cannot possibly be the ethics of a real syndicalist. According to Weber, a convinced syndicalist can rationally reject an argument that shows his action is not likely to be successful and even harmful to the position of the proletariat, because the central concern of a consistent syndicalist must be "to preserve in himself certain attitudes which seem to him to be absolutely valuable and sacred, as well as to induce them in others" (1949, 23–24). Weber even argued that the kingdom of a consistent syndicalist is not of this world (1949, 24). This means that if a syndicalist were consistent "he would cease to be a syndicalist, i.e., a man who is concerned with the liberation of the working class in this world, and by means belonging to this world" (70). Finally, Strauss observes there are two distinct notions of "ethics of intention" in Weber. There is the one that insists that political success should not be achieved through evil and base deeds (Weber 1946, 127), and there is the one that insists that one should disregard the success of one's actions in this world. The first ethics of intention, according to Weber, is not only compatible with the ethics of responsibility but supplements it, and the two of them "in unison constitute a genuine man, a man who *can* have the 'calling for politics'" (ibid.). The second is indeed incompatible with the ethics of responsibility, but that ethics "is a certain interpretation of Christian ethics or, more generally expressed, a strictly otherworldly ethics" (70).[4] Accordingly, Strauss concludes: "What Weber really meant when speaking of the insoluble conflict between the ethics of intention and the ethics of responsibility was, then, that the conflict between this-worldly ethics and otherworldly ethics is insoluble by human reason" (70).

I am now in a position to explain why Strauss spoke of "two or three" and "three or four" proofs. By realizing that the conflict between the ethics of intention and the ethics of responsibility is really the conflict between this-worldly ethics and otherworldly ethics, we realize it is in fact the same conflict as Weber's fourth proof: the conflict between the ethics of resistance to evil and the ethics of nonresistance to evil (*LNRH*, lecture 3.4; see also the reference to *Gesammelte Aufsaetze zur Wissenschaftslehre*, 546, in 70n). We have thus narrowed the list to three issues, but Strauss suggests that there might be only two. This is indeed the case, for the conflict between eroticism and all impersonal or suprapersonal values is not an issue in its own right. It only becomes an issue through dissatisfaction with specialization

---

4. It is doubtful that Weber's interpretation of Christian ethics is the true interpretation, "for why did Jesus demand that one should combine the innocence of doves with the wisdom of serpents?" (*LNRH*, lecture 3.4; see also 70n)

characteristic of modern intellectual life, a dissatisfaction that has its roots in the conflict between this-worldly and otherworldly ethics. Thus, there are only two genuine difficulties: the political conflict about justice and the conflict between biblical morality and this-worldly morality. Weber never proved that the former could not be resolved by human reason. He did not even prove that the latter could not be resolved by human reason: "He merely proved that otherworldly ethics, or rather a certain type of other-worldly ethics, is incompatible with those standards of human excellence or of human dignity which the unassisted human mind discerns" (70–71).

Why was he then "convinced that, on the basis of a strictly this-worldly orientation, no objective norms are possible" (70)? Strauss begins to answer this question by arguing that "one could say, without in the least becoming guilty of irreverence, that the conflict between this-worldly and otherworldly ethics need not be of serious concern to social science. As Weber himself pointed out, social science attempts to understand social life from a this-worldly point of view. Social science is human knowledge of human life. Its light is the natural light. It tries to find rational or reasonable solutions to social problems" (71).[5] Although the insights and solutions of social science "might be questioned on the basis of superhuman knowledge or of divine revelation," social science does not need to take notice of such objections "because they are based on presuppositions which can never be evident to unassisted human reason." By accepting objections based on divine revelation, social science "will transform itself into either Jewish or Christian or Islamic or Buddhistic or some other 'denominational' social science." Moreover, "if genuine insights of social science can be questioned on the basis of revelation, revelation is not merely above reason but against reason" (71). If social science has genuine insights, they cannot possibly be questioned by genuine superhuman knowledge, for such knowledge may exceed human knowledge but cannot contradict it. Finally, it seems that Weber in particular does not have a good reason to take seriously objections made on the basis of divine revelation to the insights of social science, for he maintains that "every belief in revelation is ultimately belief in the absurd" (70, 71). But what is absurd is to take seriously a view that one regards as absurd.[6]

---

5. A reasonable solution is not a rational solution. Whereas a rational solution is one that is demonstrably valid, a reasonable solution is one that can be supported with reasons.

6. Weber supported his view that every belief in revelation is a belief in the absurd with what he called the Augustinian sentence: *Credo non quod, sed quia absurdum est* (1946, 154). But one may wonder whether this sentence is an endorsement of absurdity, for its meaning could be: "I believe an event is a miracle not despite but because it would be impossible otherwise."

Why, then, did Weber take objections to social science on the basis of divine revelation seriously? Social science can disregard objections to its insights that are made on the basis of divine revelation only if the social scientific understanding of the world is "evidently legitimate." But Weber refused to grant this premise, because he "contends that science or philosophy rests, in the last analysis, not on evident premises that are at the disposal of man as man but on faith" (71). By this he did not mean that science is just another way of knowing, for he insisted that science is the only way human beings can know. The problem is, rather, that philosophy or science "is unable to give a clear or certain account of its basis" (72).

In the first place, Weber argued that "science has created this cosmos of natural causality and has seemed unable to answer with *certainty* the question of its own ultimate presupposition" (1946, 355; emphasis added). Strauss explains this suggestion of Weber by way of considering his contention that science lacks knowledge of its own goodness: "*all* our problems are contained in the presupposition that what is yielded by scientific work is important in the sense that it is 'worth being known,'" a presupposition that "cannot be proved by scientific means" (ibid.,143). The goodness of science has become questionable because it can no longer seek its old goals: "The goodness of science or philosophy was no problem as long as one could think that it is 'the way to true being' or to 'true nature' or to 'true happiness'" (72). Genuine metaphysics, genuine physics, and genuine ethics can no longer be conceived as the goals of science. But once science can have "no other goal than to *ascertain* that very limited truth which is accessible to man" (72; emphasis added), one can no longer reasonably insist that science is good. Why? According to Weber, the basis of science is the notion of natural causality, a notion that, according to modern science's own self-understanding, science cannot establish in a demonstrative manner. Since modern science conceives of its concepts as constructions of the mind, Weber did not say that science has discovered that the cosmos is ruled by natural causality but rather that it has created the cosmos of natural causality.[7] Perhaps the goodness of science would not be undermined by the mere admission that science cannot give sufficient reasons for the principle of natural causality. But the situation of science is precarious because there is an alternative principle that is humanly attractive, a

---

7. Consider the following statements by Einstein and Infeld: "Physical concepts are free creations of the human mind, and are not, however it may seem, uniquely determined by the external world." "Without the belief that it is possible to grasp the reality with our theoretical constructions, without the belief in the inner harmony of our world, there could be no science" (quoted in Bruell 1995, 106).

principle that Weber calls "ethical-compensatory causality" (1946, 143). Although the mere existence of an alternative principle might not put the goodness of science in question inasmuch as each person may choose his or her own principle, Weber maintained that "ethical-compensatory causality" is not just an alternative to natural causality but an alternative that attacks it as immoral. To understand this attack, it is useful to consider Maimonides' explication of Aristotle's notion of providence:

> [A]ccording to him, there is no difference between the fall of the leaf and the fall of the stone, on the one hand, or the drowning of the excellent and superior men that were on board the ship, on the other. Similarly, he does not differentiate between an ox that defecates upon a host of ants so that they die, or a building whose foundations are shaken upon all the people at their prayers who are found in it so that they die. And there is no difference, according to him, between a cat coming across a mouse and devouring it or a spider devouring a fly, on the one hand, or a ravenous lion meeting a prophet and devouring him, on the other. (Maimonides 1963, iii.17)

The greatest difficulty, however, is not so much that natural causality denies morality the support that moral human beings seek but that the scientists who create the cosmos of natural causality do so without knowing that causality is the truth about the world. For it seems to me (but perhaps not to Weber) that the adherents of ethical-compensatory causality could not legitimately question the motives of scientists, if the latter were guided by the knowable truth.

In addition to not being able to give a certain account of its basis, science, according to Weber, cannot give a clear account of itself:

> Science has created this cosmos of natural causality and has seemed unable to answer with certainty the question of its own ultimate presuppositions. Nevertheless science, in the name of 'intellectual integrity,' has come forward with the claim of representing the only possible form of a reasoned view of the world. The intellect, like all culture values, has created an aristocracy based on the possession of rational culture and independent of all personal ethical qualities of man. The aristocracy of intellect is hence an unbrotherly aristocracy. Worldly man has regarded this possession of culture as the highest good. In addition to the burden of ethical guilt, however, something has adhered to this cultural value which was bound to depreciate it with still greater finality, namely,

senselessness—if this cultural value is to be judged in terms of its own standards. (1946, 355)

As Strauss explains, despite "this amazing change in the character of science," science continues to be regarded as "valuable in itself." But in this new situation one cannot regard science as valuable in itself without admitting that "one is making a preference which no longer has good or sufficient reasons" (72). Now, one can maintain this stance only by recognizing the principle that preferences do not need good reasons. As a consequence of this recognition, an amazing change in the status of philosophy or science occurs:

> Accordingly, those who regard the quest for truth as valuable in itself may regard such activities as the understanding of the genesis of a doctrine, or the editing of a text—nay, the conjectural correction of any corrupt reading in any manuscript—as ends in themselves: the quest for truth has the same dignity as stamp collecting. Every pursuit, every whim, becomes as defensible or as legitimate as any other. (72)[8]

The devaluation of science, the devaluation of all values, seems to be the consequence of insisting on the intrinsic value of science under new circumstances in which science can no longer aim at its original goals.

But Strauss observes that Weber did not always give science the same status as stamp collecting. He was able to defend science provisionally, because he maintained that science could provide a service to man that, unlike its ability to increase the power of man, is not ambiguous. Although science cannot give us knowledge about the whole, it can give us clarity about the situation of man as man, about the great issues. This clarity is useful to man, because it frees him from delusions and is thereby the foundation of a free life. But Strauss observes that Weber could not maintain this position. Although Weber could say that science is "concerned with knowable truth which is valid regardless of whether we like it or not," he could not say that science is concerned with knowable truth that is valid regardless of whether we seek it or not. According to Weber, "scientific truth is precisely what is valid for all those who seek the truth" (1949, 84). But science cannot possibly free man from delusions if it is not valid for those who do not seek it.

---

8. "And whoever lacks the capacity to put on blinders, so to speak, and to come up to the idea that the fate of his soul depends upon whether or not he makes the correct conjecture at this passage of this manuscript, may as well stay away from science" (Weber 1946, 135).

Strictly speaking, Weber's suggestion is absurd, for if there is a truth that is knowable it is valid for everyone. To explain the difficulty that led Weber to embrace an absurdity, Strauss begins from the point in Weber's thought at which science seems to have triumphed over its adversary. Weber "was inclined to believe that twentieth-century man has eaten of the fruit of the tree of knowledge, or can be free from the delusions which blinded all earlier men: we see the situation of man without delusions; we are disenchanted" (73). This means in the first place Weber was inclined to the view that we have recovered the wisdom of the ancients after "our eyes have been blinded for a thousand years" by Christian ethics, for we (those who have intellectual integrity) now can see again the great issues, the eternal conflict between gods:

> The grandiose rationalism of an ethical and methodical conduct of life which flows from every religious prophecy has dethroned this polytheism in favor of the "one thing that is needful." Faced with the realities of outer and inner life, Christianity has deemed it necessary to make those compromises and relative judgments, which we all know from its history. Today the routines of everyday life challenge religion. Many old gods ascend from their graves: they are disenchanted and hence take the form of impersonal forces. They strive to gain power over our lives and again they resume their eternal struggle with one another. (Weber 1946, 148–49)

But we can see the great issues better than did the ancients, because we are not under the illusion that the great issues are ruled by superhuman beings. The gods of the ancients are in truth impersonal forces. The true situation of man is one without divine guidance, one in which each individual has to choose his own fate by choosing among irreconcilable timeless values.

Strauss, however, observes that Weber could not consistently maintain this belief on account of the influence of historicism:

> But under the influence of historicism, he became doubtful whether one can speak of the situation of man as man or, if one can, whether this situation is not seen differently in different ages in such a manner that, in principle, the view of any age is as legitimate as that of any other. He wondered, therefore, whether what appeared to be the situation of man as man was more than the situation of present-day man, or "the inescapable datum of our historical situation." Hence what originally appeared as freedom from delusions presented itself eventually as hardly more than the questionable premise of our age or as an attitude that will be

superseded, in due time, by an attitude that will be in conformity with
the next epoch. (73)

Under the influence of historicism, Weber became doubtful of the existence of great issues that are coeval with human society and of the superiority of the atheistic understanding of those issues to the polytheistic understanding of them or to their theistic solution. Because atheism appeared
hardly more than the questionable premise of our age, the revival of poly-
theism or of monotheism ceased to appear impossible.

After revealing Weber's wavering between the notion of disenchantment as the truth about the human situation and historicism, Strauss gives
a more precise account of Weber's understanding of the present age: "The
thought of the present age is characterized by disenchantment or unqualified 'this-worldliness,' or irreligion" (73). The age of irreligion is an
age in which man's belief in gods and demons may have survived but in
such a way that they do not have the power of binding a people together.
Accordingly, it is not the same as the age of disenchantment or of unqualified "this-worldliness." Strauss suggests that according to Weber the
thought of the present age is characterized by irreligion. Weber was aware
not only of twentieth-century man's thirst for the divine but also of the
presence of belief in some men. His most considered view, which he confused with disenchantment, is that we live in an irreligious world: "Precisely the ultimate and most sublime values have retreated from public life
either into the transcendental realm of mystic life or into the brotherliness
of direct and personal human relations." Accordingly, he objected to what
he called academic prophecy because it is only capable of producing fanatical sects as opposed to a "genuine community" (Weber 1946, 155).

If we are "irreligious only because fate forces us to be irreligious," the
question emerges whether one should hope for another dispensation by
fate, for a religious revival. Strauss says: "Weber *refused* to bring the sacrifice of the intellect; he did not wait for a religious revival or for prophets
or saviors; and he was not at all certain whether a religious revival would
follow the present age" (73, emphasis added). By "the sacrifice of the intellect" Weber understood both the willingness to accept absurdity and the
willingness to give up one's intellect as one's ultimate guide (1946, 154).
The sacrifice of the intellect that he refused can only be the latter, for if irreligion is "as much and as little delusion as the faiths which prevailed in
the past," there is nothing absurd in waiting for a religious revival. While
refusing to wait for a religious revival, Weber, Strauss suggests, felt an inclination for such a revival. Strauss points to the precise character of that

inclination by distinguishing the inclination for a religious revival from that for prophets or saviors. In Weber's view, only a prophet or a savior can solve man's moral problem, because only a prophet or a savior can tell us which of the warring gods we should serve (ibid., 153). But if one is looking for a solution to the moral problem, there is no reason not to consider seriously, as Strauss himself did, the possibility that prophets or saviors of old could give us the guidance that we need. Weber, however, felt the inclination only for "wholly new prophets," because his concern was for a revival of religion. He felt the inclination for wholly new prophets because he saw that the messages of the prophets of the old have lost their effective power in forming a genuine human community. Weber felt the inclination to wait for a religious revival because "[h]e was certain that all devotion to causes or ideals has its roots in religious faith and, therefore, that the decline of religious faith will ultimately lead to the extinction of all causes or ideals" (73–74).[9] This belief received some support from his historical investigations, which traced modern capitalism and more generally modern rationalism to religious roots, and his observation of the disastrous consequences of the destruction of these roots in his contemporary world. He observed the trivialization of serious human pursuits: "the pursuit of wealth, stripped of its religious and ethical meaning, tends to become associated with purely mundane passions, which often give it the character of sport" (Weber 1958, 182). But dearer to his heart, he observed the effect of irreligion on science: "The rosy blush of [capitalism's] laughing heir, the Enlightenment, seems to be irretrievably fading, and the idea of duty in one's calling prowls about in our lives like the ghost of dead religious beliefs" (ibid.). Because the revival of all ideals and causes depended on a revival of religion, he was inclined to think that a powerful rebirth of old thoughts and ideals must first be preceded by a religious revival. Accordingly, "he tended to see before him the alternative of either complete spiritual emptiness or religious revival" (Strauss 74; compare 42). Faced with these alternatives, Weber thought he was unable to make a rational choice.

According to Strauss, Weber's *belief* that the conflict between values cannot be resolved is the result of his failure to resolve the conflict between his despair at the consequences of "the modern this-worldly experiment" and his attachment to science, in which he was fated to believe. The only way he could justify the value he placed on science was to recognize that value judgments do not need good or sufficient reasons. Given what he saw

---

9. "The Confucian owed nothing to a super-mundane God; therefore, he was never bound to a sacred 'cause' or 'ideal'" (Weber 1951, 236).

as the irreconcilable character of the conflict between science and religion, he was forced to admit that scientific truth is not valid for those who do not seek it. As a result, he maintained on one hand that science is concerned with the knowable truth and on the other that this truth is not valid for those who do not seek it. His attempt to be loyal to science led him to swallow an absurdity. His refusal to bring the sacrifice of the intellect in one sense of the term was itself a sacrifice of the intellect in the deeper and the true sense of the term.

Above I noted Strauss's contention that Weber postulated the insolubility of the conflict between ultimate values under the impulse of a specific moral preference. We have seen this preference at work in his attempts to prove his premise. But according to the account that I have just sketched, Weber's thesis is the consequence of a conflict that he could not resolve but he apparently wanted to resolve. How can we reconcile this contradiction? I suggest that the connection between Weber's moral preference and his thesis is that the former affected his perception of the problem in such a way that the problem in fact became insoluble for him. Weber's preference for the tragic life was an obstacle to doing justice to the theoretical life or the faithful life, for these ways of life are not tragic (*NRH*, 26; *SCR*, 10–11). First, his preference for the tragic life may have prevented him from examining the possibility of a truly human life that is not devoted to causes or ideals, that is, from reconsidering his understanding of the relation between nobility and goodness. Second, Weber's sense that he was fated to believe in science was partly based on his rejection of old prophets and saviors, but this rejection was influenced by his objection to any solution to the moral problem, for such a solution would undermine the tragic character of life.[10] As we shall see, Strauss argues that if Weber had clarified his problem more adequately, he would have considered a serious return to the old faiths.

At any rate, if one grants that every acceptance of divine revelation involves the acceptance of absurdity, and that a truly human life has its roots in religious beliefs, it is impossible to discover a way of life that is both rational and truly human. In short, in order for the conflict to be soluble there must be a common ground between the antagonists, and Weber's conception of the problem denies the existence of such a ground. But there

---

10. Consider the way Weber addressed those who want to return to the old faiths: "To the person who cannot bear the fate of the times like a man, one must say: may he rather return silently, without the usual publicity build-up of renegades, but simply and plainly. The arms of the old churches are opened widely and compassionately for him. After all, they do not make it hard for him" (1946, 155).

is a common ground, because serious unbelievers are concerned with devotion to ideals or causes and intelligent believers are very much concerned with the truth of their faith. Accordingly, one may wonder whether Weber's conception of the problem is correct. We can be certain that all devotion to ideals or causes has its roots in religion, if we assume that modern science is the true science, for if we accept the notion that the real is always individual, a notion of nature that was originally directed against the "supernatural or otherworldly," then one would have to say that all devotion to ideals or causes has its roots in religion (*NRH*, 14). Similarly, if one accepted the modern canons of judgment that were meant to exclude the possibility of religion, then every acceptance of divine revelation would be a sacrifice of the intellect.[11] But there was an idea of science prior to modern science, and that science did not insist on anything like "the modern this-worldly irreligious experiment." Accordingly, Strauss observes that "the crisis of modern life and of modern science does not necessarily make doubtful the idea of science" (74). Thus, to see Weber's doubts about the idea of science more clearly, one must consider Weber's problem in the context of human life as such and science as such. One has "to state in more precise terms what Weber had in mind when he said that science seemed to be unable to give a clear or certain account of itself" (74).

Strauss begins this discussion with the most basic fact about the needs of man: "Man cannot live without light, guidance, knowledge." In the first place, man cannot live without guidance and knowledge: "only through knowledge of good can he find the good that he needs." The question before man is by what light can man acquire that knowledge: "The fundamental question, therefore, is whether men can acquire that knowledge of the good without which they cannot guide their lives individually or collectively by the unaided efforts of their natural powers, or whether they are dependent for that knowledge on Divine revelation" (74). These are the only two alternatives before man: either there are beings superior to man who have chosen to guide man or he has to rely on his own natural powers,

---

11. The difficulty that afflicts Weber's conception of the problem does not seem in Strauss's judgment to be peculiar to Weber, but of anyone who accepts the modern notion of philosophy or science. In an earlier work, Strauss wrote: "Thus at last the 'truth' of the alternative 'orthodoxy' or 'Enlightenment' is revealed as the alternative 'orthodoxy or atheism.' Orthodoxy, with its hostile eye, recognized from early on, from the beginning, that this is the case. Now it is no longer contested even by the enemies of orthodoxy. The situation thus formed, the present situation, appears to be insoluble for the Jew who cannot be orthodox and who must consider purely political Zionism, the only 'solution of the Jewish problem' possible on the basis of atheism, as a resolution that is indeed highly honorable but not, in earnest and in the long run, adequate. *This situation not only appears insoluble but actually is so, as long as we cling to the modern premises.* (PL, 38; emphasis added)

which may or may not have been given to him by superior beings. The alternative between human guidance and divine guidance is the most fundamental alternative, because every important choice presupposes first a choice between these alternatives. Historically, these alternatives have been characteristic of philosophy or science in the original sense of the term (science that seeks knowledge of things as they really are) and the Bible. There is a conflict between these two alternatives, because they proclaim the primacy of opposing ways of living: "a life of obedient love versus a life of free insight" (74). This moral conflict is not accidental. If the light that man needs is available to him through the aid of a superior and benevolent being, the proper attitude for man must be that of obedient love. But if the light that man needs is available to him through his own faculties, his attitude must be that of free inquiry. Since these attitudes cannot be reconciled, one must make a choice, which cannot be evaded by any harmonization or synthesis: "In every attempt at harmonization, in every synthesis however impressive, one of two opposed elements is sacrificed, more or less subtly but in any event surely, to the other: philosophy, which means to be the queen, must be made the handmaid of revelation or vice versa" (74–75). The secularization of biblical morality is not biblical morality, and the harmonization of Aristotelian philosophy with Christian theology is not Aristotelian philosophy. This is not an argument against harmonization or synthesis of philosophy and the Bible, but it is an argument against the view that one can evade the choice between philosophy and the Bible through any harmonization or synthesis.

Now, "a bird's-eye view of the secular struggle between philosophy and theology" shows in a way that "one can hardly avoid the impression" that neither side has really succeeded in refuting the other: "All arguments in favor of revelation seem to be valid only if belief in revelation is presupposed; and all arguments against revelation seem to be valid only if unbelief is presupposed" (75). Moreover, we have no reason to believe that this stalemate is due to incompetence on the part of the representatives of the two views. Rather, it seems to follow from the nature of the issue:

> This state of things would appear to be but natural. Revelation is always
> so uncertain to unassisted reason that it can never compel the assent of
> unassisted reason, and man is so built that he can find his satisfaction,
> his bliss, in free investigation, in articulating the riddle of being. But, on
> the other hand, he yearns so much for a solution of that riddle and human knowledge is always so limited that the need for divine illumination
> cannot be denied and the possibility of revelation cannot be refuted. (75)

There are theoretical and practical reasons that support philosophy and theoretical and practical reasons that support revelation. Now, what appears to be a stalemate is in reality a "state of things that *seems* to decide *irrevocably* against philosophy and in favor of revelation" (75; emphasis added). It certainly decides against philosophy and in favor of revelation for the moment. The inability of revelation to refute philosophy does not put into question the consistency of revelation insofar as revelation's claim on human beings rests on faith. On the other hand, if philosophy cannot reasonably deny the possibility of revelation, it will necessarily contradict itself:

> But to grant that revelation is possible means to grant that philosophy is perhaps not the one thing needful, that philosophy perhaps is something infinitely unimportant. To grant that revelation is possible means to grant that the philosophic life is not necessarily, not evidently, *the* right life. Philosophy, the life devoted to the quest for evident knowledge available to man as man, would itself rest on an unevident, arbitrary, or blind decision. (75)

Moreover, this self-contradiction of philosophy is a confirmation of "the thesis of faith, that there is no possibility of consistency, of a consistent and thoroughly sincere life, without belief in revelation" (74). This self-contradiction of philosophy is a confirmation of the thesis that man will damage his own mind by unbelief. Accordingly, Strauss concludes that "the mere fact that philosophy and revelation cannot refute each other would constitute the refutation of philosophy by revelation" (74). This argument may have little weight for most atheists of today, but it has a lot of weight for scientists or philosophers, that is, for beings who cannot tolerate any inconsistency because reason is their only star and compass.

Two important consequences follow from this account of the situation of philosophy, or science. First, by realizing that "it was the conflict between revelation and philosophy or science in the full sense of the term and the implications of that conflict that led Weber to assert that the idea of science or philosophy suffers from a fatal weakness" (74–75), we understand that science in the original sense of the term is indeed science in the full sense of the term. We realize that the true meaning of science is the attempt to replace opinions about the whole with knowledge about the whole, and that science cannot protect itself by refusing to address metaphysical issues. Second, Strauss's argument gives us new hope that the problem that Weber was struggling with can be solved, for one difficulty that Weber had in solving it was his conviction that every belief in revelation is a belief in absurdity. Strauss's argument not only questions this assumption but reveals more clearly the source of Weber's despair: "[Weber] tried to remain faithful to the cause of autonomous insight, but he despaired when he felt that the sacrifice of the intellect, which is abhorred by science or philosophy, is at the bottom of science or philosophy" (76). By opening the possibility of a return to faith, Strauss's argument opens the path for a more fruitful encounter between philosophy and revelation. Political philosophy can hope to solve this problem only by first showing that it is an indispensable handmaid of theology. This makes intelligible a statement near the beginning of *The City and Man* that at first glance seems to belong to a crank who is stuck in the Middle Ages:

> It is not sufficient for everyone to obey and to listen to the Divine message of the City of Righteousness, the Faithful City. In order to propagate that message among the heathen, nay, in order to understand it as clearly and as fully as is humanly possible, one must also consider to what extent man could discern the outlines of that City if left to himself, to the proper exercise of his own powers. But in our age it is much less urgent to show that political philosophy is the indispensable handmaid of theology than to show that political philosophy is the rightful queen of the social sciences, the sciences of man and of human affairs: even the highest lawcourt in the land is more likely to defer to the contentions of social science than to the Ten Commandments as the words of the living God. (*CM*, 1)

But as this passage also suggests, today it is much more urgent to show that political philosophy is the rightful queen of the social sciences. Strauss's main concern as an educator was to cultivate a serious interest in morality, a concern that is shared by both noble believers and noble unbelievers, for clarity about morality is not only important for understanding the conflict between philosophy and divine revelation but it is also the necessary condition of any genuine social science.

In sum, Weber's social science revolved around three different theses: (1) the conflict between certain timeless values cannot be resolved by human reason; (2) the conflict between philosophy and the Bible cannot be solved by human reason; (3) the conflict between values cannot be resolved by human reason. The second is the central thesis that pushes the first into the third, which is the thesis that led Weber to insist on a "value-free" social science and is tantamount to nihilism. Without the second thesis, the original thesis would not have been reduced to nihilism. The inability of philosophy to deny the possibility of divine revelation is the defeat of philosophy, and for those who are unable or unwilling to defer to divine revelation that defeat amounts to the self-destruction of reason. Yet one may wonder whether the second thesis necessarily leads to nihilism, for great thinkers in the past have wrestled with this conflict without being led into nihilism. As long as man could think that the quarrel between philosophy and revelation could perhaps be solved, that quarrel was "the secret to the vitality of Western Civilization" (*IPP*, 289).

▲   ▲

After stating the reasons for Weber's judgment that the idea of philosophy or science suffers from a fatal weakness, Strauss makes an attempt to "escape" from this trouble:

> Let us hasten back from these awful depths to a superficiality [Weber's writings on the methodology of social sciences] which, while not exactly gay, promises at least a quiet sleep. Having come up to the *surface* again, we are welcomed by about six hundred large pages covered with the smallest possible number of sentences, as well as with the largest possible number of footnotes, and devoted to the methodology of the social sciences. (76; emphasis added)

Strauss yearns for a gay science that promises a quiet sleep, a sleep free from bad dreams. Weber's writings, however, can only promise a quiet sleep, which is sufficient for Strauss. But the return to the surface is not a return to Weber's methodological writings but a return that is made possible by a reflection on those writings.[12] By turning to Weber's methodological writings, we have not "escaped trouble" because Weber's "notion of science, both natural and social, is based on a specific view of reality" (76). Although this view affected his methodological theses, Weber did not thematically investigate this notion of reality because he was much more interested in "the way that reality is transformed by the different types of science" (76–77). According to the view in question, which Weber took

12. By returning to the surface Strauss has in mind a return to an approach to philosophy that was inaugurated by Socrates: "In present-day parlance one can describe the change in question [the change effected by Socrates] as a return to 'common-sense' or to 'the world of common sense.' That to which the question 'What is? points is the *eidos* of a thing, the shape or form or character or 'idea' of a thing. It is no accident that the term *eidos* signifies primarily that which is visible to all without any particular effort or what one might call the 'surface' of the things" (*NRH*, 123).

over from neo-Kantianism, "reality is an infinite and meaningless se-
quence, or a chaos, of unique and infinitely divisible events" (77). But
Strauss maintains that Weber himself could not adhere to this view consistently. Weber admitted that one thing in reality is not infinitely divisible—
the human mind (1949, 72). The indivisibility of the human mind implies
a certain limit and order to human experience. For this reason human experience is more intelligible than natural events (Weber 1975, 125). Weber
"could not deny that there is an articulation of reality that precedes all scientific articulation," because he himself distinguished between concepts of
science and immediate experience, which as experience cannot be chaotic
(ibid., 130). Since according to Weber social science is concerned with social action (action understood as the relation between a human being and
the things handled), Weber himself implied that social science requires the
clarification of the natural world of the social actor (1956, 503). Nonetheless, he did not even attempt a coherent analysis of this articulation and
occupied himself with definitions of ideal types. Weber's neglect of social
reality as it is known in social life was ultimately responsible for "the
glaring disproportion between the scope and definitions of Weber's fundamental assertions [concerning the antagonism between different value
positions] and the complexity of the problems involved" (*LNRH*, lecture
3.4). Moreover, Weber's neglect of social reality as it is known in social life
has profound implications for the problem that Weber was unable to solve.
If one assumes that reality is a chaos of unique and infinitely divisible
events, one would be more apt to think that all devotion to ideals or causes
must have otherworldly roots. It leads one to assume in advance that "the
lower is mostly stronger than the higher" (77). Above all, this view of reality is one expression of the modern premise that the real is always individual. If one accepts this premise as characteristic of science, there is no
common ground between science and divine revelation, for this premise at
the outset rejects the idea of devotion. But if concern with ideals and causes
is a natural concern of both believers and unbelievers, then there is hope
that by clarifying those ideals or causes one could settle the conflict between belief and unbelief. Accordingly, Strauss argues that in order to understand the character of the conflict between fundamental alternatives
and to determine whether the conflict is soluble, one must develop a comprehensive analysis of social reality as "it is known to 'common sense,'" that
is, as we know it in actual life (77–78).

Weber's resistance to the suggestion that social science must be based
on an analysis of social reality as it is experienced in social life has its roots
in "the spirit of a tradition of three centuries" according to which "'com-

mon sense' is a hybrid, begotten by the absolutely subjective world of the individual's sensations and the truly objective world progressively discovered by science" (78). The founders of this view still regarded the modern scientific understanding as the perfection of the natural understanding. Because the victory of the new philosophy was decided by the victory of the new physics, modern natural science, as opposed to modern philosophy, came "to be regarded as the perfection of man's natural understanding of the natural world" (78–79). But "the discovery of non-Euclidean geometry and its use in physics" rendered this view implausible (*IPP,* 266). Now, if the scientific understanding of the world emerges by way of a radical modification of the natural understanding, the latter understanding is the presupposition of science. Accordingly, it became clear—especially to Edmund Husserl—that "the analysis of science and of the world of science presupposes the analysis of the natural understanding, the natural world, or the world of common sense" (79). Given that not too long before the emergence of phenomenology modern natural science was considered the perfection of man's natural understanding, it is understandable that Husserl was concerned with the natural articulation of objects of theory. But it became clear—especially to Martin Heidegger—that "the natural world, the world in which we live and act, is not the object or the product of a theoretical attitude; it is a world of 'things' or 'affairs' which we handle" (79). But Strauss observes that "[A]s long as we identify the natural world or prescientific world with the world in which we live, we are dealing with an abstraction. The world in which we live is already a product of science. To say nothing of technology, the world in which we live is free from ghosts, witches, and so on, with which, but for the existence of science, it would abound" (79). The world in which we live is not natural not chiefly because of technology but because our own minds are no longer simply natural. To recover genuine liberty, one must first recover one's primary bondage, the world that is not free from ghosts, witches, and so on. This recovery requires historical studies (79–80), but it also requires something more, for it does not suffice to see that before the emergence of philosophy or science people believed this and were troubled by that. We must recover the natural world for ourselves, and this can only be done if one sees through a philosophic critique that the apparent liberation of the present is in fact a kind of bondage and that the original bondage is something more than mere bondage because it is our only access to the primary issues.

PART III

The majority, therefore, lives in perpetual adoration of itself; only foreigners or experience can make certain truths reach the ears of the Americans.

Tocqueville

CHAPTER 6

Strauss's Polemic against the New Political Science

In my discussion of Strauss's critique of Weber, I have followed Strauss's argument that the actualization of a genuine social science requires a clarification of social reality as it is known to "common sense" and that Weber did not attempt such a clarification on account of the influence of a "tradition of three centuries" that rejected the cognitive value of the common-sense understanding of the world (*NRH*, 78). In order to test the truth of Strauss's suggestion more fully, I turn to the most thoroughgoing attempt to establish political science through a break with prescientific understanding of political life.[1]

Leo Strauss's thematic reflections on the scientific approach to the study of politics occur in an epilogue to *Essays on the Scientific Studies of Politics*, a work that in addition to Strauss's essay includes four essays written by his former students and a preface by the editor, Herbert Storing. Strauss's essay is so polemical that it provoked a ferocious response by John Schaar and Sheldon Wolin (1963), a response all the more remarkable given that one of its authors was already a left-wing critic of the new political science and indeed in a few years became one of the leaders of "the post-behavioral revolution."

---

1. Bentley expresses this break very clearly: "We have in this world many lawyers who know nothing of lawmaking. They play their part, and their learning is justified by their work. We have many law-makers who know nothing of law. They too play their part and their wisdom — though they may not be able to give it verbal expression — is none the less real. But the *practical lore* of neither of these types of men is scientific knowledge of society. Nor by putting their two *lores* together do we make an advance. It is they themselves we must study and know, for what they are, for what they represent" (Bentley 1967, 164; emphasis added).

Despite Wolin and Schaar's contention that the five essays in the volume are "of such uniform texture that it might have been written by one hand" (1963, 126), there is a difference in texture between Strauss's essays and those of his students. Certainly, both Storing and Strauss were aware of it. As the title of Strauss's essay indicates, it is not the epilogue to the volume but "An Epilogue." Similarly, in response to Wolin and Schaar's criticism Storing writes: "the uniformity of texture which the critics find (and find so objectionable) in the volume is, I report at the risk of some editorial loss of face, exaggerated" (Storing 1963, 151). Storing most likely had Strauss in mind, who after all was the contributor most immune to editorial pressure. The essays written by his students are ultimately critical of the authors whom they study, but they obviously take their authors with great seriousness and are guided by them even in arriving at their criticism of them. Although Wolin and Schaar contend that the book is "so often unfair to its subjects that it has provoked our considerable indignation," at least some of its subjects do not agree. Harold Lasswell describes Horowitz's criticism of him as "a conscientious, competent, and often valuable statement," and he judges the book as a whole as one of two "especially well informed" works in the "anti-behavioral literature" (1963, 165–166; the other work is Crick 1959). Similarly, Herbert Simon is reputed to have said that he would rather be criticized by Storing than defended by Wolin. Strauss's essay, on the other hand, seems to be a *tour de force* spanking of the new political science. And his rhetoric had apparently disastrous effects. It contributed to the whole volume being neglected by adherents of the new political science; it aroused the indignation of even some of the critics of that science and colored their reading of the other essays (see Havard 1984, 55); it probably made it even more difficult for Strauss's students to receive appointments in many political science departments; it probably strengthened the opposition to him within his own department, an opposition that eventually forced Strauss to leave the University of Chicago.[2] Yet, Strauss did not seem to think that his rhetoric was questionable, for he republished the essay in substantially the same form.[3]

Strauss's rhetoric in this essay is not characteristic of his writings in

---

2. Compare David Easton's respectful acknowledgment of Strauss in *The Political System* (1953, ix) with his implied condemnation of Strauss in his presidential address (1968). Consider also Cropsey's account of the circumstances that led to Strauss's departure (Cropsey 1999, 39–40).

3. It was republished in *LAM*. In the second version, the original nineteen paragraphs are divided into thirty-six paragraphs, the footnotes that referred to the other essays in the volume are eliminated, and one typographical error is corrected. I will generally refer to the second version because it is more commonly available.

general (compare *NRH*, 7–8). Even in this essay he reminds us of the classical view that the task of a political scientist is to settle disputes that arise among citizens, to become an impartial judge. Yet Strauss here presents himself as a partisan, as one of "those intransigent opponents of the new political science," one of those "who reject the new political science root and branch" (*LAM*, 204). Why does he do this? One possibility is that he hated the new political science for moral and political reasons. He certainly criticized it for fostering permissive egalitarianism and for being soft on communism. Yet although we may regard these criticisms as sincere, they do not explain Strauss's bellicose approach. A better explanation is provided by Strauss's own statement that he "criticized the new political science above all because of its lack of reflection or its narrowness" (Strauss 1963b, 153).[4] I regard this statement as definitive, and it explains why in general he is so critical of positivism; but it requires explication, for there are other dogmatic positions that Strauss does not attack in the same way. Moreover, the treatment of positivism in "An Epilogue" is more polemical than his other treatments, for example, that found in *Natural Right and History* (7–8).

But what is the precise character of this rhetoric? It seems to revolve around the question of the value of the new political science to liberal democracy. Now, Strauss did seem to think that the new political science was bad for liberal democracy, but here we are concerned with the manner in which he expresses his objection. For instance, in discussing a step toward new universals that may have been made by the new political science, a step that denies the qualitative difference between liberal democracy and communism, Strauss writes:

> Yet we cannot forever remain blind to the fact that what claims to be a purely scientific or theoretical enterprise has grave political consequences—consequences which are so little accidental that *they appeal for their own sake* to the new political scientists: everyone knows what follows from the demonstration, which presupposes the begging of all important questions, that there is only a difference of degree between

4. Consider the difference in Strauss's treatment of Alexandre Kojève, who was openly an atheist, a Stalinist, and one whose thought, in Strauss's words, produces "an amazingly lax morality" (*WPP*, 111). To be sure, he criticizes Kojève, but not before distinguishing him from "the many who today are unabashed atheists and more than Byzantine flatterers of tyrants for the same reason for which they would have been addicted to the grossest superstitions, both religious and legal, had they lived in an earlier age" (*WPP*, 104). Strauss was a friend of Kojève, not despite his thought, but because of it, that is, because his thought was based on philosophic reflection.

liberal democracy and Communism in regard to coercion and freedom. (*LAM*, 215; emphasis added)[5]

Now, Strauss is correct that the denial of qualitative difference between regimes is characteristic of the new political science and that it appealed to the new political scientists because they believed it would lessen the tension between liberal democracy and communism, but Strauss's statement could easily be interpreted to mean that the new political scientists are not loyal to liberal democracy. He allows his statement to express a view that he does not share: "It goes without saying that while our social scientist may be confused, he is very far from being disloyal and from lacking integrity" (*WPP*, 20). The second example of Strauss's rhetoric is his seemingly most intemperate comment, the final paragraph of the essay. After arguing that the new political science is part of the crisis of liberal democracy because it is unable to defend liberal democracy from its enemies, Strauss writes:

> Only a great fool would call the new political science diabolic: it has no attributes peculiar to fallen angels. It is not even Machiavellian, for Machiavelli's teaching was graceful, subtle, and colorful. Nor is it Neronian. Nevertheless, one may say of it that it fiddles while Rome burns. It is excused by two facts: it does not know that it fiddles, and it does not know that Rome burns. (*LAM*, 223)

The contempt that exudes from this paragraph hides the fact that at its very center is an important exculpation of the new political science. It is not Neronian: it did not burn Rome and it is not indifferent to the suffering of Rome. That is to say, the new political science is a part or a product of the crisis of the West, but it is not responsible for that crisis. Strauss both reveals and hides this thought. Strauss's rhetoric is ultimately philosophic because it deliberately exposes its false insinuations to careful readers. But what good can come out of an accusation against the new political science?

To answer this question we have to consider those for whom he is writing his essay. He indicates his audience by identifying the kind of men the new political science should want to win over. He wishes "to win the sym-

---

5. Strauss's characterization of this step was meant to explain the underlying motive that animates the new political science and the political problems that will necessarily afflict it. I am not aware of any political scientist who formulated the issue the way Strauss presents it. Strauss gives no citation to support it and almost begs his readers to demand such a citation, for his comment was the first of four steps toward a new kind of universal and the only one of them that is not supported by a footnote ("An Epilogue," *LAM* 319–20).

pathy of the best men of the coming generation—those youths who possess the intellectual and the moral qualities which prevent men from simply following authorities, to say nothing of fashions" (*LAM*, 204). It seems that Strauss thought that rhetoric is necessary for helping the best men of the coming generation to free themselves from the authority of the new political science.

Indeed, the very first theme of Strauss's essay concerns the conditions of freedom of thought:

> It [the new political science] wields very great authority in the West,
> above all in this country. It controls whole departments of political sci-
> ence in great and in large universities. It is supported by foundations of
> immense wealth with unbounded faith and unbelievably large grants. In
> spite of this one runs little risk in taking issue with it. For its devotees
> are fettered by something like a Hippocratic oath to subordinate all con-
> siderations of safety, income, and deference to concern with the truth.
> The difficulty lies elsewhere. It is not easy to free one's mind from the
> impact of any apparently beneficent authority, for such freeing requires
> that one step outside of the circle warmed and charmed by the authority
> to be questioned. (*LAM*, 203)

Freedom of speech is neither a sufficient nor a necessary condition of freedom of mind, for coercion does not necessarily suppress the minds of those whose tongues have been tied, whereas what can suppress their minds is their belief that an apparently beneficent authority is in fact truly beneficent, a belief that authorities characteristically generate in the circles in which they govern. Accordingly, to see whether an apparently beneficent authority is truly beneficent, one must step outside of the circle warmed and charmed by that authority. Now, the new political science exists within the larger circle of liberal democracy. Being a part of this circle, it is influenced by it, by its insistence on freedom of speech, and by its understanding that this freedom is a condition of the discovery of the truth. But it is also at odds with liberal democracy because it denies that any compelling case can be made for freedom of speech: "The new antidote to wilfulness [*sic*] is propaganda. If the mass will be free of chains of iron, it must accept its chains of silver. If it will not love, honour and obey, it must not expect to escape seduction" (Lasswell 1927, 222). As Strauss's example indicates, liberal democracy is more powerful than the new political science. Accordingly, the new political scientists in their actions contradict their science's implicit claim that safety, income, and deference are more important motives than love of truth and the right to express one's thoughts.[6] In order to free themselves from contradiction, the new political scientists must first step into the circle of liberal democracy. They must see their amoral political science from the moral point of view of democracy. They must see not only that their science is objectionable but also that it is worthy of condemnation from that point of view. Strauss's accusation against the new political science is an indispensable step for its young adherents, to see their own situation, the situation of human beings who as citizens of a democracy are devoted to democracy but who as scholars regard "democracy and nondemocracy . . . as postulates to which the individual may or may not add a declaration of personal preference" (Lasswell 1963, 156).

The accusation of Strauss reminds the adherents of the new political science that their science is an authority operating within democracy. And as such it must accept the principles of democracy. It "owes an account of itself to those who are subjected, or are to be subjected, to it" (*LAM*, 203). The new political science has to show its superiority to the old:

> Precisely if the new political science constitutes the mature approach to political things, it presupposes the experience of the failure of earlier approaches. We ourselves no longer have that experience: "George" has had it for us. Yet to leave it at that is unbecoming of men of science; men of science cannot leave it at hearsay or at vague remembrances. To this one might reply that the resistances to the new political science have not entirely vanished: the old Adam is still alive. But precisely because this is so, the new political science, being a rational enterprise, must be able to lead the old Adam by a perfectly lucid, coherent, and sound argument from his desert which he mistakes for a paradise to its own green pastures. (*LAM*, 204)

Although obligation to democracy compels the new political science to confront the old, its own concern for truth compels it to be satisfied only with a victory that is genuine. It cannot be satisfied with the historical "defeat" of the old; it must show to itself that the change from the old to the new was a change for the better. But since the representatives of the old are still alive, it must show them that they are mistaken by a perfectly lucid, co-

---

6. The expression "safety, income, and deference" is from Lasswell. He sometimes has expanded the list, but as Horowitz has argued, these motives are fundamental for Lasswell. For instance, "Lasswell lists rectitude as a subdivision of the value 'deference'" (Horowitz 1962, 258–61).

herent, and sound argument. In order to avoid the begging of important questions, that argument must begin with the premises accepted by the opponents of the new political science. It must show to those who do not speak its language that it is the true science, and to do so "it must cease to demand from us, in the posture of a noncommissioned officer, a clean and unmediated break with our previous habits, that is, with our common sense; it must supply us with a ladder by which we can ascend, in full clarity as to what we are doing, from common sense to science" (*LAM*, 204).

By showing what is necessary in order to prove the superiority of the new political science to the old, Strauss has given the youths who possess the intellectual and moral qualities that prevent men from simply following authorities, some of whom may have been his own students, a ladder by which they can ascend in full clarity to science, a ladder whose first rung is liberal democracy. Those who are to climb this ladder need not be young in age but they must be young in heart, for such ladders can only be climbed by those who dare to take intellectual risks.

CHAPTER 7

The New Political Science

Given the diversity of views that is characteristic of the adherents of the new political science, in what sense can one speak of it as if it were a single school of thought? Is not the expression "the scientific study of politics" too broad to be meaningful? The authors of *Essays on the Scientific Studies of Politics* were not unaware of these difficulties. As Storing explains, they "did not begin by trying to define 'the scientific study of politics,' or by considering whether or in what sense it is proper to speak of 'the' scientific study of politics. Important as these questions are, they belong properly at the conclusion rather than the beginning of our investigation" (1962, v). It was Strauss's task, to the extent that his essay is a kind of conclusion to the volume, to answer these questions. Strauss's answer is not based on the average opinion of those who consider themselves adherents of the new political science. He focuses his attention on "the handful of opinion leaders, the men responsible for the breakthroughs on the top" and not on "the many who drive on the highways projected by the former" (*LAM*, 203). Now, even among the leading advocates of the scientific study of politics there are important disagreements, but these disagreements rest on a more fundamental agreement. These opinion leaders themselves, it seems, drive on highways projected by opinion leaders of an even higher order. In sum, according to Strauss, there is a basic political and scientific notion that underlies the diversity of its leading adherents.

Strauss, however, for reasons that are not immediately clear, gives two accounts of the new political science: political (paragraph 3) and theoreti-

cal (paragraph 5).[1] The first finds the common element among the new political scientists in their politics and the second in their adherence to a general notion of science. The first account is political also because it is animated
by a political concern, that is, by the concern for the state of the profession
of political science "as it stands now"; it views the profession from a political
perspective and accordingly divides it into political camps (friends, enemies,
and those with divided loyalties); and it culminates in a political act: an act of
self-defense that takes the form of counterattack against a strong opponent.
In contrast, the second account is not concerned with the here and now;
it views the new political science in a theoretical perspective; and it is free
from any polemics. Whereas the first account is ambiguous, the second is
a response to a demand "to avoid ambiguities, irrelevancies, and beatings
around the bush," that is, to a demand to state as precisely as possible "*the
fundamental difference*" between the two sciences (emphasis added).

THE POLITICAL PRESENTATION OF THE NEW POLITICAL SCIENCE

The political presentation is confined to one short paragraph that begins
with the suggestion that to understand the new political science, one
must understand a phenomenon that is not limited to political science,
for "the fairly recent change within political science has its parallels in
other social sciences." Yet political science, as the oldest social science,
provides a privileged perspective for understanding this change in the
social sciences in general. Although political science may be the least advanced of the social sciences, the very fact that it is "a carrier of old traditions which resist innovation" allows it to reveal more clearly the character of the innovation, for one cannot understand a change without
knowing what preceded it, and the remnants of the old thought have
survived in political science more than in any other social science.[2]
These remnants manifest themselves in its themes: "Political science as

1. In the version of the essay published in *LAM*, the political account is in the fourth paragraph and the theoretical account is divided into paragraphs 6–10. All unspecified quotations
from Strauss in this chapter are to these paragraphs as they appear in *LAM* and to the paragraph
that connects them.
2. Strauss's suggestion that the character of the new political science can be seen most easily
by comparing it to what it rejects is confirmed by the following observation of Robert Dahl: "Perhaps the most striking characteristic of the 'behavioral approach' in political science is the ambiguity of the term itself. . . . [It] is like the Loch Ness monster: one can say with considerable confidence what it is not, but it is difficult to say what it is. I judge that the monster of Loch Ness is not

we find it now consists of more heterogeneous parts than any other social science. 'Public law' and 'international law' were established themes
centuries before 'politics and parties' and 'international relations,' nay,
sociology, emerged." As the names of the old and the new themes indicate, the new themes presuppose a critique of the importance of law and
of the public. This critique, Strauss suggests, has political implications:

> If we look around us, we may observe that the political science profes-
> sion contains a strong minority of the right, consisting of the strict
> adherents of the new political science or the "behavioralists," a small
> minority of the left, consisting of those who reject the new political sci-
> ence root and branch, and a center consisting of old-fashioned political
> scientists, men who are concerned with understanding political things
> without being much concerned with "methodological" questions but
> many of whom seem to have given custody of their "methodological"
> conscience to the strict adherents of the new political science and who
> thus continue their old-fashioned practice with a somewhat uneasy con-
> science.

The strict adherents of the new political science are few but they are
strong. Both their strength and its source reveal themselves in the power
that they exercise over the old-fashioned political scientists. The source of
their strength is the power of the scientific method. In contrast, the old-
fashioned political scientists are many but they are weak. They are weak
because of the weakness of the tradition. But they remain the center of the
profession, because they are primarily concerned with the subject of political science: political things. In contrast to the old-fashioned political scientists, those who reject the new political science root and branch have
more than a tangential concern for methodology. As to their strength, the
strength of his own camp, Strauss is silent. He only refers to their size: they
are small. But why does Strauss call strict adherents the right wing of the
profession and their opponents the left wing?

> It may seem strange that I called the strict adherents of the new political
> science the right wing and their intransigent opponents the left wing,

---

Moby Dick, nor my daughter's goldfish that disappeared down the drain some ten years ago, nor
even a misplaced American eight heading for the Henley Regatta. In the same spirit, I judge that
the behavioral approach is not that of the speculative philosopher, the historian, the legalist, or
the moralist" (Dahl 1961, 763)

seeing that the former are liberals almost to a man and the latter are in the odor of conservatism. Yet since I have heard the intransigent opponents of the new political science described as unorthodox I inferred that the new political science is the orthodoxy in the profession, and the natural place of an orthodoxy is on the right.

Here Strauss corrects his earlier suggestion that "one runs little risk in taking issue" with the new political science (*LAM*, 203). This is not surprising because if one cannot justify the goodness of truth, it is doubtful that one can prefer love of truth to other considerations that claim to be important. But it is not necessarily the new political scientists' concern for safety, income, or deference that leads them to criticize their opponents as unorthodox, but their political concerns. The strict adherents are "liberals almost to a man." Strauss implies that there is a connection between the devaluation of law and the public, adherence to the scientific method in political science, and being a kind of liberal. Their opponents, on the other hand, are not conservatives but they are in "the odor of conservatism." In choosing a phrase that reminds one of "the odor of sanctity," Strauss implies that the decisive political difference between the liberalism of the new political science and the conservatism of the old concerns their attitude toward religion and not, say, toward the free market. Having revealed the size or strength of the opponents and their flags, he deflects a blow against his own camp back onto his enemy: the new political science is the right wing of the profession, a new orthodoxy. Strauss's attack reveals the source of his strength: the power of the principle of contradiction. According to Strauss, then, the new political science is characterized by a kind of liberalism, which participates in what it believes it loathes in its opponents.

THE THEORETICAL ACCOUNT OF THE NEW POLITICAL SCIENCE

Strauss subjects the preceding account of the new political science to a criticism by a kind of political scientist not mentioned in the preceding taxonomy of the profession: "A *rigorous* adherent of the new political science" (emphasis added). Such an adherent subordinates the political implication of that science to "the only important issue, that issue being the soundness of the new political science." Strauss, however, argues that the concern for soundness demands turning one's attention toward, not away from, the old political science, for "to state that issue is to bring out the fundamental difference between the new political science and the old." But in order to state this difference as precisely as possible, one should begin by comparing the new political science not with the old political science of the immediate past but with "the 'original' of the old, that is, with Aristotelian political science," because, having been influenced by the general scientific revolution that occurred in the seventeenth century, the old political science of the immediate past had already moved very far "in the direction of the new" (*LAM*, 207). In order to see the issue between the old and the new political science, one must compare the new political science, understood as the consistent development of "the revolution which occurred in the seventeenth century," with Aristotelian political science, for that revolution was primarily a revolution against Aristotle.

Strauss arrives at an understanding of the new political science through a series of contrasts. In each step, he presents first an Aristotelian view and then the rejection of that view by the new political science. As he shows how each Aristotelian view is rejected, he also shows how the implications of that view are also rejected. He begins with Aristotle's and the new political science's views about the character and division of the sciences and excavates the foundations of these views. Strauss's exposition of Aristotle is not meant to be an adequate account of his thought, to say nothing of classical political philosophy in general: "Plainly, these remarks were not meant to be more than a rough sketch serving the purpose of bringing out as clearly as possible the characteristics of the new political science" (Strauss 1963b, 154). Accordingly, I shall interpret his comments in order to bring out the characteristics of the new political science.

The Separation of Political Science from Political Philosophy

The most obvious difference between the Aristotelian political science and the new political science is that the former raises philosophical questions and the latter avoids them. Strauss begins the exposition of this difference with the following statement: "For Aristotle, political science is identical with political philosophy because science is identical with philosophy." But given that science is primarily the possession of knowledge of beings and philosophy is the quest for wisdom (knowledge of the whole), how can science be identical with philosophy? Aristotle's identification of philosophy and science is based on an understanding of philosophy which maintains that to understand the whole does not mean primarily to understand the origins of the whole but to understand "the articulation of the whole" (*NRH*, 122–23). Philosophy is knowledge of all the beings. To understand the articulation of the whole, one must understand the parts of the whole (the results of sciences) and the joints that connect the parts (the principles of sciences). Because one cannot have knowledge of the whole without knowledge of its parts, and because one cannot have full knowledge of the parts without at least some knowledge of the whole, philosophy and science are identical.

The division and the order of sciences are governed by the character of the beings and the affairs that they study:

> Science or philosophy consists of two kinds, theoretical and practical
> or political; theoretical science is subdivided into mathematics, physics
> (natural science), and metaphysics; practical science is subdivided into
> ethics, economics (management of the household), and political science
> in the narrower sense; logic does not belong to philosophy or science
> proper, but is as it were the prelude to philosophy or science.

Logic does not belong to philosophy or science proper because it is concerned not with any being in particular but with the proper approach to the study of beings. The distinction between theoretical and practical inquiries is based on the different characteristics of the things investigated: theoretical science is concerned with knowledge of beings and practical science with deliberation regarding actions. There is an order within each of the divisions because sciences are distinct but not separate from each other. The sciences are distinct because they deal with different classes of beings that have their own principles and therefore are for the most part intelligible on their own terms. They are not separate because they study beings that are parts of larger wholes. Thus, the mathematical things cannot be separated from the natural things but they can be understood in abstraction from them, and natural things cannot be separated from the whole but they can for the most part be understood in abstraction from it. Metaphysics is the highest theoretical science, because it deals with knowledge of the first causes and principles of things, which knowledge allows one to know why a thing is the way it is to the highest degree. Similarly, just as man is distinct from but part of the household and the household is distinct from but part of the political community, so ethics, economics, and politics are distinct but related sciences. Political science is more important than economics because the good of a political community is more comprehensive than the good of a household, and economics (household management that is not limited to the pursuit of pecuniary interest) is more important than ethics because the good of a household is more comprehensive than that of an individual.[3] Accordingly, politics is not only a distinct practical science but also sovereign over other practical sciences. Metaphysics is higher than political science because unchanging first principles are more important than ephemeral human affairs. But political science is a queen within her own realm, the realm of human affairs. Since there is a rank ordering of human affairs, political science is necessarily normative. In short, political science is identical with political philosophy because political science is "the all-embracing study of human affairs" (*WPP,* 17).

The new political science, on the other hand, is based on a notion of science that denies the identity of philosophy and science, the division between theoretical and practical sciences, the rank ordering of sciences of human affairs, and the normative claims of political science. Whereas in presenting Aristotle's view of science Strauss relies on Aristotle's own account, he discovers the new political science's view of science by discussing the genesis of that view. The separation of science from philosophy is the unintended consequence of a revolution made in the seventeenth century by thinkers who, like Aristotle, regarded philosophy and science to be identical (Strauss 1964b, 94): "This revolution was primarily not the victory of science over metaphysics, but what one may call the victory of the new philosophy or science over Aristotelian philosophy or science." The revolutionaries did not intend to replace Aristotle's science with a metaphysically neutral one. They wanted to replace Aristotle's false philosophy or science with the true philosophy or science, but their attempt led to the victory of science over metaphysics, at least partly because it "was not equally successful in all its parts. Its most successful part was physics (and mathematics)." Unlike every previous physics, the new mathematico-mechanical physics did not take its bearing by the character of natural beings but by an order that originated in the human mind. Despite this, the new physics was originally metaphysical, because it assumed that its mathematical constructs corresponded to the nature of reality. This notion of the new physics eventually gave way to another notion, elaborated first by Newton, that maintained that physics does not need to depend on any hypothesis about the ultimate reality: "The victory of the new physics led to the emergence of a physics which seemed to be as metaphysically neutral as, say, mathematics, medicine, or the art of shoe-

---

3. Strauss suggests that the relation of the practical sciences to each other is more complicated than the relation of the theoretical sciences to each other. In his discussion of the transformation of Aristotle's notion of science in modern times, he implies that for Aristotle economics depends on ethics while being inferior in dignity to politics. This leaves undetermined the relation between ethics and politics, that is, the rank order of the good of the man and the good of the city.

making." Strauss does say that the physics that emerged out of the new physics only seemed to be metaphysically neutral because by continuing to exclude, say, Aristotelian notions of the universe, its implicitly maintained universe is of a particular kind.[4]

But the emergence of an apparently metaphysically neutral physics has profound implications for sciences in general and social sciences in particular, because this physics is seen as the model of all genuine sciences. First, science becomes independent of philosophy. Second, science becomes an authority for philosophy, given that the latter is believed to lack genuine knowledge. Accordingly, science transforms the character of philosophy by defining its scope and limits. Finally, since the natural sciences were sciences "that are admittedly in existence and not mere desiderata," their practice becomes an authority for the social sciences:

> It [the emergence of a metaphysically neutral physics] paved the way for
> an economic science that is independent of ethics, for sociology as the
> study of non-political associations as not inferior in dignity to the politi-
> cal association, and, last but not least, for the separation of political sci-
> ence from political philosophy as well as the separation of economics
> and sociology from political science.

The new economics is no longer an ethical science but a positive science that articulates laws of observable economic behavior. It may be prescriptive insofar as it can distinguish between efficient and inefficient solutions, but it cannot claim that efficiency is the most important value. Its results, according to itself, do not depend on any claims regarding the true human good or the true morality. The new apparently metaphysically neutral science implies a pluralistic world and therefore undermines the old rank ordering among social sciences. Political science becomes the study of one field among others and not intrinsically superior to them. And once political science ceases to claim to comprehend all human affairs, it ceases to be normative, and thus becomes separate from political philosophy. In this way,

4. It suffices to refer to two metaphysical presuppositions of this science: "First, the real world in which man lives is no longer regarded as a world of substances possessed of as many ultimate qualities as can be experienced in them, but has become a world of atoms (now electrons), equipped with none but mathematical characteristics and moving according to laws fully statable in mathematical form. Second, explanations in terms of forms and final causes of events, both in this world, and in the less independent realm of mind, have been definitely set aside in favor of explanations in terms of their simplest elements, the latter related temporally as efficient causes, and being mechanically treatable motions of bodies wherever it is possible to regard them" (Burtt 1999, 303).

political science becomes the narrow study of "one aspect of his [man's] total behavior, and by no means a very important aspect" (Eulau 1963, 19).

The Dependence of Political Science on "Scientific" Psychology

Unlike Aristotelian political science, the new political science tends to be
interdisciplinary in the sense that it relies on other sciences of human behavior, and especially on psychology. According to Strauss, this is a consequence of the rejection of the distinction between practical and theoretical
sciences.

The Aristotelian distinction implies that "human action has principles
of its own which are known independently of theoretical sciences." We do
not need to analyze the human soul to know what the ends of our action
should be, because we have a natural awareness of those ends, of the noble
and the good. This sense is the necessary condition for man "seeking and
finding appropriate means for his ends, or for his becoming practically wise
or prudent." Practical wisdom or prudence is the virtue that one finds in
an enlightened statesman. However impressive it is, it falls somewhat short,
because it does not have a clear understanding of the ends of man.

> Practical science in contradistinction to practical wisdom itself sets forth
> coherently the principles of action and the general rules of prudence
> ("proverbial wisdom"). Practical science raises questions that within
> practical or political experience, or at any rate on the basis of such expe-
> rience, reveal themselves to be the most important questions and that
> are not stated, let alone answered, with sufficient clarity by practical wis-
> dom itself.

Practical wisdom does not have a coherent understanding of man's natural
ends because it is incapable of clearly raising certain questions, the raising
of which is necessary for understanding the natural order of human ends.
Such questions—for instance, What is virtue?—are not questions that
within practical or political experience reveal themselves to be the most
important questions, for if they were it would be inexplicable why practical wisdom has difficulty stating them. They must, then, be questions that
on the basis of practical or political experience reveal themselves as the most
important questions. Moreover, these questions reveal their importance on
the basis not of the experience of any kind of action but of noble and just
actions. Accordingly, Aristotle's practical science is based on political experience. If genuine knowledge of the ends of action is available on the

basis of reflections on political experience, theoretical sciences are not necessary for guiding our affairs: the sphere governed by prudence is self-sufficient. But why does Strauss speak of the sphere governed by prudence? Should he not have said "the sphere governed by practical science"? Practical science cannot govern the sphere in question because something in that sphere is impervious to its wisdom. For ultimately practical wisdom cannot give a coherent account of the principles of actions, because such an account leads to the transcendence of "the dimension of political life," to the realization "that the ultimate aim of political life cannot be reached by political life, but by a life devoted to contemplation, to philosophy" (*WPP*, 91). In this respect, the sphere governed by prudence is closed to knowledge about the whole.[5] While not depending on theoretical science, practical science culminates in the view that the theoretical life is the best human life, a view that theoretical sciences cannot adequately establish on their own. Although prudence ultimately lacks coherence, it is "sufficiently consistent for all practical purposes" (*NRH*, 157). Accordingly, Aristotle sought to protect it against false doctrines about the whole. To defend prudence, Aristotle had to employ his own theoretical arguments. But, according to Strauss, "the theory defending prudence is, however, misunderstood if it is taken to be the basis of prudence," for that theory is not in complete agreement with prudence.[6]

Strauss suggests that the break with the Aristotelian notion of practical sciences was based partly on an agreement with Aristotle's understanding of the relation between the sphere of prudence and theoretical sciences: "This complication—the fact that the sphere of prudence is, as it were, only *de jure* but not *de facto* wholly independent of theoretical science—makes

---

5. The distinction between practical wisdom, which sees the principles of action in twilight, and practical science, which coherently articulates the principles of action, points to the fundamental ambiguity of the Aristotelian notion of practical science (*NRH*, 156). Whereas practical wisdom maintains that the demand for exactness in political matters is unreasonable, practical science leads to a coherent account of the principles of action. Whereas the young may lack the experience necessary for practical wisdom, practical science is available to the young, and indeed it is available only to those who are young at heart. Strauss's discussion of Maimonides' statement on political science is an interpretation of a work that was written in his "early youth," at the age of sixteen (*WPP*, 155–69).

6. For instance, to prevent the corrosive effects of a theoretical view according to which a political community is not fundamentally different from a household, Aristotle argues that political life is different from other associations because it is the natural end of all human associations. But as Wayne Ambler has shown, Aristotle, in his theoretical discussion of household management, presents the movement from the family to the city as a movement away from nature (1985, 487–502). Aristotle's understanding of the naturalness of the city as well as his understanding of nature is much more complicated than the account in the beginning of his *Politics* suggests.

understandable, although it does not by itself justify, the view underlying the new political science according to which no awareness inherent in practice, and in general no natural awareness, is genuine knowledge, or, in other words, only 'scientific' knowledge is genuine knowledge." Aristotle and the seventeenth-century founders of the view in question agree that prudence is not genuine knowledge. But Aristotle argued that political experience can be the basis of genuine knowledge. The seventeenth-century thinkers, who originated the view in question, seemed to have rejected Aristotle because they thought that "within prescientific political thought genuine knowledge of political things is inseparable from prejudices or superstitions; hence one cannot get rid of the spurious elements in prescientific political thought except by breaking altogether with prescientific thought" (*LAM*, 213). In other words, they believed that Aristotle could not defend prudence from what they believed to be superstition. His theory as well as any other theory that was available to them was insufficient given that they would have to combat a teaching regarding human virtues and vices that was based on an account of the origins of things that apparently could not be refuted either by demonstrative reasoning or dialectics:

> The tenets that the world is the creation of the omnipotent God, that miracles are therefore possible in it, that man is in need of revelation, cannot be refuted by experience or by the principle of contradiction; for neither does experience speak against the guidance of the world and of man by an unfathomable God, nor does the concept of an unfathomable God contain a contradiction within itself. (*PL*, 31)

Since they thought the old approach could not meet this new challenge, they took a new path that required a break with common sense:

> Thus, if one wished to refute orthodoxy, there remained no other way but to attempt to prove that the world and life are perfectly intelligible without the assumption of an unfathomable God. That is, the refutation of orthodoxy required the success of a system. Man had to establish himself theoretically and practically as master of the world and master of his life; the world created by him had to erase the world merely 'given' to him; then orthodoxy would be more than refuted—it would be "outlived." (*PL*, 32)

Philosophy or science, they reasoned, could give a clear and certain account of itself if one could show that the world is intelligible without the assumption of an unfathomable God and that the problems of political life could be solved in such a way that man's yearning for that God would dry up.

The new political science is then based on an inherited thesis that was meant to respond to a problem that the new political science itself has ceased to recognize as a problem. Nonetheless, it is necessarily a carrier of the implications of that thesis. The view that only scientific knowledge is genuine knowledge leads to the denial of the possibility of practical sciences proper, which are based on the legitimacy of practical experience. Since the need for useful sciences survives, practical sciences are replaced by applied sciences, which are preceded by the theoretical sciences in time and order.[7] This change has important implications for sciences dealing with human affairs and for political science in particular:

> It implies above all that the sciences dealing with human affairs are es-
> sentially dependent on theoretical sciences—especially on psychology,
> which in the Aristotelian scheme is the highest theme of physics, not to
> say that it constitutes the transition from physics to metaphysics—or
> become themselves theoretical sciences to be supplemented by such ap-
> plied sciences as the policy sciences or the sciences of social engineer-
> ing. The new political science is *then* no longer based on political expe-
> rience but on *what is called* scientific psychology. (emphasis added)

Sciences dealing with human affairs will become either applied sciences dependent on theoretical sciences such as psychology or independent theoretical sciences supplemented by applied sciences that guide political decision-making or the construction of society. Regardless of whether it is a theoretical or an applied science, political science, according to this view, must be based on a scientific psychology. The reason seems to be that what makes political entities beings with properties of their own is their moral

---

7. If we disregard the important distinction between making and acting, which distinction Aristotle emphasized chiefly because action can be pursued for its own sake, then the view in question can be said to lead to the primacy of practice. The seventeenth-century thinkers who first articulated the view that only scientific knowledge is genuine knowledge were aware of this consequence: "For [new notions in physics] opened my eyes to the possibility of gaining knowledge which would be very useful to life, and of discovering a practical philosophy which might replace the speculative philosophy taught in schools" (Descartes 1988, 47). In his discussion of Hobbes in *NRH*, Strauss argues that mathematical physics, which rests on a synthesis of Platonism (mathematics) and Epicureanism (materialism), implies the primacy of practice: "The abandonment of the primacy of contemplation or theory in favor of the primacy of practice is the *necessary consequence* of the abandonment of the plane on which Platonism and Epicureanism had carried on their struggle. For the synthesis of Platonism and Epicureanism *stands or falls* with the view that to understand is to make" (*NRH*, 177n; emphasis added).

character, a character that the scientific constructs do not acknowledge. Political entities must be understood in terms of the individuals who make them, but this requires an understanding of what moves those individuals: "The political behavior of the individual person is the central and crucial empirical datum of the behavioral approaches to politics" (Eulau 1963, 14). Strauss raises doubts about whether any psychology that does not properly understand the influence of morality on individuals can be a true psychology. Accordingly, he concludes: "The new political science is *then* no longer based on political experience but on *what is called* scientific psychology" (emphasis added).

The Use of an Extensive Technical Vocabulary

It is well known that the new political science recasts political concepts in a language that is different from that of political life, whereas Aristotelian political science begins with that language. According to Strauss, this difference is a consequence of their respective perspectives, their different attitudes toward the awareness that is inherent in practice.

Aristotle's political science is based on political experience, because it maintains that "the awareness of the principles of action shows itself primarily to a higher degree in public or authoritative speech, particularly in law and legislation, rather than in merely private speech." This awareness reveals itself more clearly in speech than in deed, because what one praises and blames reveals one's unalloyed aspirations, whereas one's mute deeds are "always equivocal" regarding one's aspirations (*PPH*, 144–45), although they may reveal the most effectual motives. Public or authoritative speech reveals that sense to a higher degree than private speech, because the public good appears to be more comprehensive than the good of an individual or because that which orders other activities must be accompanied by an opinion regarding the highest good of man, that good which is pursued for its own sake. Since it begins with the recognition of the supremacy of politics, Aristotelian political science "views political things in the perspective of the citizen." Thus, it does not regard law and legislation as objects at which we look with detachment. Now, it would seem that there is no such thing as the perspective of the citizen; we are citizens of particular societies with particular regimes. But the attachment of an Aristotelian political scientist to his political community is not one that ultimately fosters partisanship. Since one cannot be attached to one's political community without wishing its citizens to live in peace, the highest duty of a good citizen is to settle the most fundamental political controversies, and therefore to become an umpire. According to the Aristotelian view, one cannot settle these controversies by simply siding with one of the parties but only by reaching a perspective that "encompasses the partisan perspectives," and one can reach that perspective only if one "possesses a more comprehensive and clearer grasp of man's natural ends and their natural order than do the partisans."

Instead of looking at political things from the perspective of a citizen, the new political science looks at political things "from without, in the perspective of the neutral observer, in the same perspective in which one would look at triangles or fish, although or because it may wish to become 'manipulative'; it views human beings as an engineer would view materials for building bridges." The perspective of the neutral observer is different in kind from that of the impartial judge. To look at political things from the perspective of the neutral observer is to refuse to take sides with respect to the goodness or badness of laws and regimes. In contrast, an impartial judge is a mediator, and a mediator never altogether loses interest in what is at issue between parties and the relative merits of the parties. To look at political things from the perspective of the neutral observer is perfectly consistent with the desire to manipulate political things, and it may even be its necessary condition, for one does not manipulate things that have a claim on one. As long as one regards justice and nobility as what they claim to be, one seeks to be true to them and not to manipulate them. There are, however, two different ways of being a neutral observer, for one does not look at triangles from the same perspective with which one looks at fish. To understand this difference, let us consider another of Strauss's articulations of the difference between the perspectives of classical political philosophy and those of present-day social science:

> Thus the attitude of classical political philosophy toward political things
> was always akin to that of the enlightened statesman; it was not the atti-
> tude of the detached observer who looks at political things in the way
> in which a zoologist looks at the big fishes swallowing the small ones, or
> that of the "social engineer" who thinks in terms of manipulating or con-
> ditioning rather than in terms of education or liberation, or that of a
> prophet who believes he knows the future. (*WPP*, 90)

The perspective from which one looks at triangles is very much like that of the social engineer or the prophet, because one can think of triangles as if they are our own constructs and, given that they are fully knowable, we can predict the character of all future triangles. Strauss implies that the new political science looks at political things from the same perspective from which one would look at triangles, because he maintains that "it views human beings as an engineer would view materials for building bridges." Human beings are materials for the construction of political things. The new political science "views" human beings whereas it only "looks at" political things, that is, it pays more attention to the behavior of men than to laws and legislation, because human beings are more fundamental than political things.

The different perspectives of Aristotelian political science and the new political science affect their respective languages. Since the former views political things from the same perspective as the citizen, its language is identical with that of the political man: "it hardly uses a term which did not originate in the market place and is not in common use there." It is not simply identical with that of political man; it does occasionally use terms that did not originate in the marketplace and are not in common use there. The difference between the languages of the two kinds of political science consists in this: whereas the Aristotelian political science introduces new terms only insofar as they become necessary to remedy the shortcomings of the language of political men, shortcomings that reveal themselves by looking at political things from the same perspective as citizens but with greater attention, the new political science uses a technical vocabulary from the outset. Since it looks at political things from the perspective of the neutral observer, it replaces political terms with terms that can be scientifically verified in accordance with its rules. It replaces commonsense terms with terms that are susceptible to mathematical operations. Whereas Aristotelian political science refines and corrects the moral judgments inherent in political life, the new political science avoids such judgments and, in particular, replaces evaluative expressions found in political life (tyranny) with new scientific terms (authoritarianism).

The Value-Free Character of Political Science

Whereas the new political science is descriptive, Aristotelian political science is both prescriptive and descriptive. It necessarily evaluates political things because the knowledge in which it culminates has the character of categorical advice and exhortation. It has the character of categorical advice because it is knowledge of the hierarchy of man's natural ends. It has the character of exhortation because an adequate understanding of man's natural ends leads one to take an active interest in the welfare of others, that is, to become public-spirited. Since it arrives at this knowledge by working through the contradictions of various opinions about the good and the noble, it has the character of an ascent that has a culmination. The new political science, on the other hand, "conceives of principles of actions as 'values' which are merely 'subjective'; the knowledge it conveys has the character of prediction and only secondarily that of hypothetical advice." The new political science cannot conceive of principles of actions as objective, because the knowledge it conveys is strictly theoretical. But this theoretical knowledge can be the basis for giving hypothetical advice in such forms as the following: "In order to produce such and such a state of affairs, such and such must be done" (Simon 1945, 248). Since the knowledge it conveys has the character of prediction, which is always susceptible to refutation by reality, the new political science has no end, no culmination.

The Denial of the Common Good

The new political science denies the existence of the common good. Strauss traces this view to the denial of the view maintained by Aristotelian political science that the political community is a genuine whole.

Aristotelian political science culminates in a knowledge that has the character of exhortation, because it conceives of man as "a being *sui generis*, with a dignity of its own: man is the rational and political animal." According to Aristotle, man is not unique in being political. Bees share this quality. But man is the only animal that has reason (*Politics* 1253a-7-10). Man is a being *sui generis* because he is the rational animal. Yet to show the intimate connection between man's rational and political characters, Strauss does not turn to Aristotle's well-known discussion of this theme in book I of the *Politics* but to some comments of a well-known Aristotelian, Friedrich Nietzsche. This peculiar approach is not without reason, for Strauss wants to articulate the understanding of man that is presupposed in Aristotle's practical science, and Nietzsche's critique of liberalism is helpful in bringing to light these presuppositions: "Man is the only being that can be concerned with self-respect; man can respect himself because he can despise himself; he is 'the beast with red cheeks,' the only being possessing a sense of shame. His dignity is then based on his awareness of what he ought to be or how he should live." Strauss uncovers the presuppositions of Aristotelian political science by beginning with the modern notion of man's worth, the notion of self-respect. As Nietzsche points out, the possibility of self-respect presupposes that of self-contempt: "Whoever despises himself still respects himself as one who despises" (1967a, #78). He presents Nietzsche's observation that man is "the beast with red cheeks" as evidence for the judgment that man is the only being with a sense of shame. Now, shame presupposes morality, an awareness of how one should live. But morality presupposes an awareness of how one ought to be, for we should live in such a way that we become what we ought to be. Now, this awareness cannot be clarified without the use of reason. Accordingly, the dignity of man is essentially connected with his capacity for morality, a capacity made possible because he is a rational being. Now, if man has a dignity of his own, so does political life: "Since there is a necessary connection between morality (how a man should live) and law, there is a necessary connection between the dignity of man and the dignity of the political order: the political is *sui generis* and cannot be understood as derivative from the subpolitical." To live a good life, one must live with others, and one cannot live with others well without laws. The purpose of law is not merely to help us get along with others, or to facilitate our private wishes, but to help us live the life that we should live. Law restrains those passions and desires that are contrary to morality. Law is not so much a tool for protecting morality as a form of morality, its authoritative form.

Strauss argues that the Aristotelian notion of the dignity of man and of the public order depends on a thesis about the nature of man and ultimately on a thesis about beings: "The presupposition of all this is that man is radically distinguished from non-man, from brutes as well as from gods" (see *Politics* 1253a27-29). Now, Strauss maintains that "this presupposition is ratified by common sense, by the citizen's understanding of things; when the citizen demands or rejects, say, 'freedom from want for all,' he does not mean freedom from want for tigers, rats, or lice." Even this extremely liberal political slogan acknowledges the essential difference and rank ordering among beings, for Strauss's example reveals not only that citizens distinguish men from animals but that they make distinctions of rank among animals. Citizens as citizens have a respect for tigers that they do not accord to lice, even though tigers are more dangerous to men. Now, the presupposition that man is radically distinguished from non-man, from brutes as well as from gods, "points to a more fundamental presupposition according to which the whole consists of essentially different parts." According to the second presupposition, the world is composed of beings that have natures, qualities that are necessarily coeval with particular species, and beings can have natures only if they are parts of the whole—the world. Strauss does not say that the first presupposition, which is ratified by the citizen's understanding, is based on this more fundamental presupposition. He says the former points to the latter, because common sense that is not affected by philosophy is unaware of the notion of nature and of the whole (*NRH*, 81). To be sure, we naturally see beings that are radically different from each other, but do we naturally assume that these differences are governed by a necessity? We naturally see ourselves belonging to earth, but do we naturally see heaven and earth as parts of a whole? This more fundamental thesis is a clarification of the citizen's understanding of things. Aristotle's political science is not based on a cosmology but points to a cosmology. It is so little based on cosmology that one can say that the clarification of political experience prepares one for the study of the cosmos.

Whereas Aristotle's political science points to a fundamental presupposition about beings, the new political science begins with a fundamental premise about beings: "there are no essential or irreducible differences: there are only differences of degree; in particular there is only a difference of degree between men and brutes or between men and robots."[8] This is because the new political science is the result of the application of a universal logic to political affairs. Although that logic does not understand itself as a metaphysics, it in effect is a metaphysics because it denies the existence of essential or irreducible differences, not to mention that it implicitly denies the existence of god. Strauss points to the implication of the hidden ontology of the logic in question:

> In other words, according to the new political science, or the universal science of which the new political science is a part, to understand a thing means to understand it in terms of its genesis or its conditions and hence, humanly speaking, to understand the higher in terms of the lower: the human in terms of the subhuman, the rational in terms of the subrational, the political in terms of the subpolitical.

If there are no irreducible differences, there is no reason to treat of wholes as genuine wholes. In fact, the logic underlying the new political science dictates that one must understand complex things in light of their simple elements, for if to understand is to make, one can only understand (master) the beings that one has not made by resolving them into their parts and then reconstructing them. For humans, the meaning of this logic is that one must understand the high in terms of the low. Since there is no essential difference between human beings and beasts, one must understand the

---

8. Harold Lasswell, in his presidential address to the American Political Science Association, raised the question: "And at what point do we accept the incorporation of relatively *self-perpetuating* and mutually influencing 'super-machines' or 'ex-robots' as beings entitled to the policies expressed in the Universal Declaration [of Human Rights]?" (1956, 976; emphasis added.)

human in terms of the subhuman, say, human decisionmaking in light of the behavior of rats. If there are no essential differences between human beings and beasts, the distinctly human quality of reason must be understood in terms of subrational factors. Accordingly, the new political science is based on psychological theories (behaviorism, psychoanalysis, and so on) that tend to understand reason as a modification of subrational qualities. If the political community is not a genuine whole, one must understand it in light of subpolitical things. Accordingly, not only do sociology and economics become separated from political science, but the sociological and economic approaches to the study of politics come to dominate political science. If the political community is not a genuine whole, the new political science must deny "that the common good is something that is." Accordingly, on account of the influence of the new political science, "in mainstream political science the existence of a common good is probably more often denied than asserted" (Lindblom 1982, 10 n. 4).

In following Strauss's characterization, I must point out that adherents of the new political science often acknowledge that political entities, like political institutions, influence individual behavior. To this extent, they do not necessarily reduce the political to the subpolitical, but Strauss's point is that the logic underlying the new political science pushes them toward this reduction. For instance, the insistence that "institutions can and must be analyzed in terms of the behavior of their molecular units" implies that these units have fundamental characteristics that are independent of their particular political structures and that these characteristics ultimately determine the character of those institutions (Eulau 1963, 15). The issue is this: Does the old political science lose something of importance by not understanding political things in terms of individual behavior? Or does the new political science lose something of importance by not understanding political things on their own terms?

CONCLUSION

Strauss's theoretical discussion of the nature of the new political science gives us an inkling why two presentations—one political and one theoretical—were necessary. The two presentations reflect the two approaches to political science. Whereas Aristotelian political science begins with the surface, with the awareness inherent in practice, and moves toward first principles by clarifying that surface, the new political science begins with the first principles. An exposition of the new political science by an Aristotelian political scientist will necessarily use both approaches, because beginning with the surface means beginning with the self-understanding of one's subject. Accordingly, Strauss introduces the theoretical exposition with a dialogue with a rigorous adherent of the new political science. The two discussions are complementary inasmuch as the theoretical presentation sheds light on suggestions made in the political presentation. Since the new political science is based on scientific principles that implicitly deny the existence of god and of the common good, of views that place a restraint on individuality or diversity, it is not surprising that the new political science favors a liberalism that tends not to place moral demands on citizens. It goes without saying that the liberalism of the new political science is much more morally lax than the original forms of liberalism, which did not deny the existence of the common good. Since the awareness that is inherent in practice points in the first place to the supremacy of law and morality (hence to the view that human happiness requires a community in which one part, that which embodies to a higher degree what is best in man, rules over the other parts) and to beings higher than man, the old political science favors a kind of conservatism. Strauss's conservatism, one based on classical political philosophy, is different from the European conservatism of the nineteenth century in that it respects religion without rejecting reason or science (*LAM*, viii–ix). It is different from the American economic conservatism of the twentieth century in that it is wary of an increasingly powerful state or of a big society that may suppress small societies without believing that wealth or technology can cure the deepest evils or that private activity in principle has greater dignity than public service (*CM*, 6, 49; *LAM*, 272). It seems that it was Strauss's respect for public service that made him, among other things, so attractive to the neo-conservatives.

Strauss's theoretical discussion of the nature of the new political science also suggests that underlying the diversity of the new political scientists there is a single notion of science, which is responsible for the general characteristics of the new political science. He suggests that the separation of this science from political philosophy is the consequence of its being modeled after a metaphysically neutral physics; its dependence on other social sciences and ultimately on a scientific psychology is the consequence of the view that only scientific understanding is genuine understanding; its use of an extensive technical vocabulary is the consequence of its looking at political things from the perspective of the neutral observer; its non-evaluative character is the consequence of the theoretical character of its knowledge; its denial of the existence of the common good is the consequence of its assumption that there are no irreducible differences.

Moreover, Strauss suggests that four of these scientific premises—the metaphysically neutral character of science, the adoption of the perspective of the neutral observer (the social engineer), the hypothetical character of scientific knowledge, and the denial of the existence of irreducible differences—are the consequences of a decision made in the seventeenth century according to which only scientific understanding is genuine understanding. It is not surprising, then, that only in his discussion of this view does Strauss raise the question of the soundness of the new political science.

Strauss's characterization of the basic premises of the new political science does not by itself imply an objection to those premises. But it does raise objections to two great thinkers who had profound influence on the new political science. Thomas Hobbes was the first thinker who tried to establish political science on the principles of modern natural science. In his study of Hobbes, Strauss has argued that the fundamental insight of Hobbes's political science was based on reflections on moral matters and not on natural science and that natural science was brought in only after he had conceived of the ideals of modern civilization. Unlike the new political science, Hobbes's is philosophic; it is based on political experience; it is public-spirited; it is evaluative; and it does insist on a fundamental difference between men and beasts (*WPP*, 176n). But his attempt to base that science on modern natural science puts in question all of these characteristics of his science. As Strauss puts it, "[t]o the extent to which Hobbes attempts to replace that 'common sense' understanding [man's understanding of himself] by a scientific understanding of man, he endangers his political science as a normative science and prepares the 'value free' political science of our time" (*WPP*, 181). The break with commonsense understanding was originally motivated by a desire to protect valid moral-political judgments from certain religious views, but it culminates in the belief that all moral-political judgments are subjective. The second great thinker who influenced the new political science is Nietzsche, who more emphatically than anyone else has argued that science must free itself from moral judgments. As we have seen, Strauss uses Nietzsche's characterization of man as a beast with red cheeks in order to explain the Aristotelian view that there is an essential difference between human beings and other animals. But Nietzsche presented that statement in a context that suggests that there is no fundamental difference between man and beast (*Thus Spake Zarathustra* [1954], "On the pitying"). According to him, man is the beast with red cheeks, because he had been ashamed too often. We may question the wisdom of Nietzsche or his decision to wage his unforgettable war against human degradation on the basis of a denial of the essential difference between good and evil and between the human and the subhuman.

CHAPTER 8

The Revolt against the Old Political Science

If the new political science constituted the mature approach to political things, it would be able to demonstrate the soundness of its revolt against the old political science. According to the new, the old paid too much attention to the Ought and not enough to the Is, and its notions and techniques are not applicable to our new society (paragraph 6; paragraphs 11–13 in *LAM*). In addition to these substantive objections, the old political science is rejected because it is not scientific or empirical (paragraphs 7–10; paragraphs 14–20 in *LAM*).[1] In sum, the revolt against the old is based on the argument that only a scientific-empiricist political science can understand social-political realities in such a way that it can meet the demands of a fully modern society.

SUBSTANTIVE OBJECTIONS

The new political science's contention that the old was blind to political things was primarily directed against the political science that immediately preceded the new, one that "had already moved very far from Aristotelian political science in the general direction of the new political science." That political science "was accused of paying too great attention to the law or to the Ought and of paying too little attention to the Is or to the actual behavior of men. For instance, it seemed to be exclusively concerned with the

---

1. All unspecified references in this chapter are to these sections in *LAM*, 207–13.

legal arrangements regarding universal suffrage and its justification and not to consider at all how the universal right to vote is exercised; yet democracy, as it is, is characterized by the manner in which that right is exercised." Strauss grants that a protest against a merely legalistic political science is justified and that "not so long ago there was a political science which was narrowly legalistic—which, for example, took the written constitution of the U.S.S.R. very seriously." But he denies that this is a sufficient reason for rejecting the old political science as such, because this error "had been corrected as it were in advance, by an older political science, the political science of Montesquieu, of Machiavelli, or of Aristotle himself." The organizing notion of Aristotle's political science, the regime, or *politeia*, is not a legalistic notion:

> The *politeia* is more fundamental than any laws; it is the source of all laws. The *politeia* is rather the factual distribution of power within the community than what constitutional law stipulates in regard to political power. The *politeia* may be defined by laws, but it need not be. The laws regarding a *politeia* may be deceptive, unintentionally and even intentionally, as to the true character of the *politeia*. (*NRH*, 136)[2]

Politeia refers to both the factual distribution of power within the community and the norms that are legislated to the community by its rulers. It is accompanied by a general view of the priorities of the community. Aristotle's political science, and more generally classical political science, corrects the errors of legalists not by paying less attention to the laws or to the Ought but by interpreting them with a greater care than mere legalists are likely to do.

Second, by turning their attention away from the Ought, the new political scientists expose themselves to "the danger of disregarding the important things known to those legalists":

> "[V]oting behavior" as it is now studied would be impossible if there were not in the first place a universal right to vote, and this right, even if not exercised by a large minority for very long periods, must be taken

---

2. To illustrate this last point, Strauss refers to Xenophon's account of the Persian regime prior to Cyrus's empire: The old Persia appeared to be democracy, because all Persians were allowed to send their children to common schools of justice, attendance at which was required for holding political office. Xenophon, however, points out that for the most part only the rich sent their children to these schools, because the poor could not maintain their children without having them work. What appeared to be democracy was, according to Xenophon, in fact an oligarchy (*Cyropaidia* i.2.15; referred to in *NRH*, 137n).

into consideration in any long-range prediction since it may be exercised by all in future elections taking place in unprecedented and therefore particularly interesting circumstances. That right is an essential in-
gredient of democratic "behavior," for it partly explains "behavior" in
democracies (for instance, the prevention by force or fraud of certain
people from voting).

Since in politics the Ought is one of the causes of the Is, the tendency of
the new political scientists to turn their attention away from the Ought is
likely to lead to a truncated understanding of the Is. Now, the right to vote
can affect behavior in the sense that it allows for the possibility that everyone will vote, a possibility that may be actualized in the future when the
masses are enlightened or up in arms, or it can affect behavior by leading
some people to use force or fraud to prevent others from voting. In other
words, optimism about democratic enlightenment is not the only reason
that leads one to acknowledge the importance of legal rights for an understanding of democratic behavior. The new political science is in danger of
forgetting this importance, because while not denying the existence of the
moral-legal component of behavior, it relegates it "to the background, to
'the habit background.'"[3] Since human "behavior" is driven by a sense of
what ought to be done, the relegation of the moral-legal component to the
background amounts to putting "the cart before the horse."

Finally, Strauss indicates the priority of the Ought to the Is by his very
characterization of the new political science's objection to the old as an accusation. The complaint of the new political scientists that the old were
paying too much attention to the Ought and not enough to the Is was itself a moral-political protest. The old political science's focus on political
institutions prevented it from addressing democratic wants: "we certainly
should find that the relatively perfect adjustment of any society was a function not of some absolutely and independently stated characteristics of political structure, but instead, of underlying group conditions, of situations
and disturbances of situations, due to factors far down beneath the political level" (Bentley 1967, 459). Accordingly, Merriam tended to regard the

---

3. The expression "habit background" is Arthur Bentley's: "There are 'rules of the game'
in existence, which form the background of the group activity. There is no savage tribe so low but
that it has rules of the game, which are respected and enforced. I hardly need to add [see his own
reference to "low"] that a large part of this habitual activity is commonly discussed in terms of
moral factors. The habit background may usefully be taken into the reckoning as summing up a
lot of conditions under which groups operate, but reliance on it is apt to check investigation where
investigation is needed, or even become the occasion for the introduction of much unnecessary
mysticism" (Bentley 1967, 218).

old political science's concern with justification of institutions as "transparent rationalizations of those who have or seek power" (Merriam 1925, 100). As Lasswell argues in his account of the origin of the new political science, its insistence on the Is is an attempt to respond to Marxist criticism of democracy:

> There were two replies to the Marxist indictment—to ignore the facts or to restudy them. In America the "individualistic" attitude was to deny the facts, to affirm the substantial identity between democratic values and the existing state of affairs. To liberals, and particularly to middle western liberals, certain facts were all too conspicuous. By assembling them, they hoped to bring reality into closer conformity with doctrine. In intellectual circles hope of reform, not certainty of revolution, was the dominant view of the future. In such a setting democratic values were not in question. (1942, 27)

Lasswell here is defending these liberals for not questioning democratic values, but the very fact that their insistence on the Is was fueled by an Ought is reason enough to question their judgment that in political affairs the Is is more important than the Ought. By not examining their own interpretation of democratic values, the new political scientists repeated the mistake of the legalists. Whereas a legalist may believe that the Soviet Union was a democracy on account of its constitution, the new political scientists' denial of qualitative differences between regimes leads them to think that the Soviet Union is not fundamentally different from Western democracies (*LAM*, 215).

The second example that Strauss gives of the new political science's contention that the old political science was blinded by an excessive focus on the Ought concerns its failure to see the need for propaganda: "To illuminate the mechanisms of propaganda is to reveal the secret springs of social action, and to expose to the most searching criticism our prevailing dogmas of sovereignty, of democracy, of honesty, and of the sanctity of individual opinion" (Lasswell 1927, 222). According to Lasswell, social scientists must in the first place become propagandists for social science and then use propaganda to make society receptive to their policies. Strauss grants some merit to this discovery, for he does admit that the democratic orthodoxy of the immediate past had an unfounded belief in the rationality of the masses (*LAM*, 223). But he suggests that the error was corrected in advance by an older political science, for the alleged discovery was nothing but a partial rediscovery of the need for vulgar rhetoric. Moreover, what obscured this need was not Aristotle's understanding of human rationality but that of the modern enlightenment, for that "need . . . had become somewhat obscured from a few generations which were comforted by faith in universal enlightenment as the inevitable by-product of the diffusion of science, which in its turn was thought to be the inevitable by-product of science." Strauss does not explain why the discovery of the need for propaganda is only a partial rediscovery of the need for vulgar rhetoric, but I suggest the following interpretation. The purpose of vulgar rhetoric is to move people toward what is higher through due consideration of their lower but more powerful desires and the opinions generated by those desires. The full discovery of the need for vulgar rhetoric requires the recognition of the vulgarity of the ends of the vulgar. Lasswell's understanding of propaganda, however, accepts the ends of the vulgar, for his propaganda is in the service of a kind of liberalism that accepts safety, income, and deference as the values that need to be protected. Lasswell is in the grip of the masses that he is trying to manipulate or of the thinkers who contributed to giving the masses their ends, because he has not thematically reflected on the ends of political life, on the Ought.

Strauss ends his discussion of the new political science's accusation that the old political science paid too much attention to the Ought and not enough to the Is with the following comment: "Generally, one may wonder whether the new political science has brought to light anything of political importance which intelligent political practitioners with a deep knowledge of history, nay, intelligent and educated journalists, to say nothing of the old political science at its best, did not know at least as well beforehand." This statement has appalled many adherents of the new political science without inducing them to respond to it.

The new political science's main substantive objection, however, is that the old political science may have been helpful in understanding older societies but it cannot help us understand our radically new society. Our new society requires a new political science:

> The politics of the new world into which we are coming must correspond with the rest of its life. It cannot be a thing apart, surviving from a pre-scientific period. Politics must reckon with a new world in which time and space are fundamentally altered; a new world of universal leisure; a new world of universal education; a nontraditional state of mind; a world of scientific methods and results; a race of beings master of

nature's forces in greater measure than before dreamed possible; the participation of the bulk of the community in its fundamental conclusions. (Merriam 1925, 101)

For the same reason Bentley objects to "a dead political science" that is concerned with the most external characteristics of governing institutions:

> It loves to classify governments by incidental attributes, and when all is said and done it cannot classify them much better now than by lifting up bodily Aristotle's monarchies, aristocracies, and democracies, which he found significant for Greek institutions, and using them for measurements of all sorts and conditions of modern government. And since nobody can be very sure but that the United States is really a monarchy under the classification or England really a democracy, the classification is not entitled to great respect. Nor do the classifications that make the fundamental distinction that between despotism and republics fare much better. (1967, 162)

The same reason underlies Eulau's paradoxical argument that the behavioral approach is a continuation of the tradition of classical theorists because it rejects the careful reading of their works:

> A good deal depends on what one means by continuity. If one means continued textual exegesis of the classics as if they were sacred writings, the behavioral persuasion does, in fact, make a radical break with political theory. But if by continuity one means, as I think one should, the application of modes of thought and techniques of inquiry appropriate to one's own time to the problems of the time, then the behavioral persuasion is a direct and genuine descendent of the classical tradition. (1963, 8)

Strauss begins his examination of this objection by first considering the new political science's own response to our unprecedented political situation: "the unprecedented political situation calls for an unprecedented political science, *perhaps* for a judicious mating of dialectical materialism and psychoanalysis to be consummated on a bed supplied by logical positivism" (emphasis added). The mating of dialectical materialism and psychoanalysis is a reference to the thought of Harold Lasswell, who is generally considered to be the leading representative of the new political science. As Strauss's use of "perhaps" indicates, Lasswell did not conceive of his combination in the way Strauss presents it. But since this combination is not a synthesis but an eclectic combination of incompatible positions, one may ask what allows Lasswell to insist on it. In answering this question, Strauss points to the role of logical positivism, for one way of combining Marxism and psychoanalysis is "by claiming to transform their dogmatic and incompatible assertions into hypotheses while forgetting that claim most of the time" (Strauss 1963b, 153). Strauss articulates this bedroom scene in the following way:

> Just as classical physics had to be superseded by nuclear physics so that the atomic age could come in via the atomic bomb, the old political science has to be superseded by a sort of nuclear political science so that we may be enabled to cope with the extreme dangers threatening atomic man; the equivalent in political science of the nuclei is *probably* the most minute events in the smallest groups of humans if not in the life of infants; the small groups in question are certainly not of the kind exemplified by the small group which Lenin gathered around himself in Switzerland during World War I. (emphasis added)

Logical positivism, which regards modern natural science as authoritative, leads the new political science to understand the complex political phenomena in light of its simplest parts. These parts, the political nuclei, are provided by the group approach, which is a relic of Marxist attempts to account for political life through class conflict, and by psychoanalysis's attempt to explain human troubles through examination of childhood events. Under the influence of logical positivism, these nuclei are understood as probable hypotheses. Now, whereas Freud denied that psychoanalysis can solve social problems because there can be no solution to those problems on account of the individualistic nature of man, and Marx argued that social problems can only be solved through political means (a political revolution), their combination leads to the belief that the dangers threatening nuclear man can be solved without political means. This is because the new political science's nuclei are subpolitical. Unlike the group around Lenin, the small groups that the new political science studies are nonpolitical; they are groups without a political leader. But this approach faces an insuperable difficulty:

> In making this comparison we are not oblivious of the fact that the nuclear physicists show a greater respect for classical physics than the nuclear political scientists show for classical politics. Nor do we forget that, while the nuclei proper are simply prior to macrophysical phenomena, the "political" nuclei, which are meant to supply explanations for

the political things proper, are already molded, nay, constituted by
the political order or the regime within which they occur: an American
small group is not a Russian small group.

Modeling political science after natural science is possible only if one forgets that political things shape subpolitical things. Strauss says "forget" because this is something that everyone knows. I illustrate his point by considering Eulau's explanation of the original use of psychological theories by
the new political science: "[The behavioral approach's] interdisciplinary
orientation stems, at least initially, from the very simple assumption that
man's political behavior is only one aspect of his total behavior, and by no
means a very important aspect" (1963, 19). Now, a Spartan would not have
said that man's political behavior is not a very important aspect of man's total behavior. Eulau can treat this assumption as unproblematic because he
lives in a society that regards private matters as more important than political matters, or rather, because he does not investigate whether his liberal
values are the correct ones.[4] If Eulau's explanation of the reliance of the
new political science on psychological and sociological theories is sound,
then one would have to say that this reliance was guided by the political
opinions of a segment of the political order that it refused to investigate in
political terms.

Having considered the new political science's response to our unprecedented situation, Strauss argues that the old political science is not
obsolete provided our situation is still a political situation. In the first
place, he shows that our situation is still a political situation. A political situation is one in which there are a number of societies that cannot live
together, in contradistinction to uneasily coexisting, because their pre-
ponderant parts are dedicated to incompatible ends.[5] Since a political situation is characterized by the existence of friends and enemies, and since

---

4. As to the question of why the new political scientists have so much less respect for the
old political scientists than nuclear physicists have for classical physicists, it seems that in the former case the opposition is political. Since the new political scientists are not always conscious of
this, they cannot always treat their disagreement as a disagreement regarding political matters. Instead of debating the opponents of behavioralism, Eulau recommends that they be sent to psycho-
analysts: "Why such resistance occurs is a matter of interest to the sociologist of knowledge, and
how it might be overcome is a task for psychoanalyst" (1963, 32).

5. Despite their apparent agreement regarding the ends of human society, liberal democracy
and communism are qualitatively different regimes because their disagreement about the means is
at bottom a moral disagreement: "For some time it seemed sufficient to say that while the Western movement agrees with Communism regarding the goal—the universal prosperous society of
free and equal men and women—it disagrees with it regarding the means: for Communism, the

enemies are reluctant to share their plans, statesmen must make their decisions by relying partly on guesses. As long as we live in a political situation, precise prediction of political events is impossible. According to Strauss, inherent in modernity is a tendency to transform man's situation into a nonpolitical situation, but this tendency has only led to a new political situation:

> The new political science which is so eager to predict is, as it admits, as unable to predict the outcome of the unprecedented conflict peculiar to our age as the crudest soothsayer of the most benighted tribe. In former times people thought the outcome of serious conflicts is unpredictable because one cannot know how long this or that outstanding leader in war or counsel will live, or how the opposed armies will act in the test of the battle, [the comma is added in *LAM*] or similar things. We have been brought to believe that chance can be controlled or does not seriously affect the fate of societies. Yet the science which is said to have rendered possible the control of chance has itself become the refuge of chance: man's fate depends now more than ever on science or technology, hence on discoveries or inventions, hence on events whose precise occurrence is by their very nature not predictable.

As the reference to soothsayers reminds us, one other factor that led many people in the past to think that the result of human conflicts is unpredictable was their belief that god or gods rule over the world. The attempt to conquer chance was an attempt to free mankind from this belief by showing him that he can be master of his own fate. But this attempt has only led to new reliance on chance, on unpredictable scientific and technological discoveries. Finally, Strauss argues that the new political scientists could not have been interested in our situation if they really thought it was unprecedented: "A simply unprecedented political situation would be a situation of no political interest, that is, not a political situation."

After showing that our situation remains and will be for the foreseeable future a political situation, Strauss defends the old political science

---

end, the common good of the whole human race, being the most sacred thing, justifies any means; whatever hinders the achievement of that end is devilish. The murder of Lumumba was described by a Communist as a reprehensible murder, by which he implied that there can be irreprehensible murders, like the murder of Nagy. It came to be seen that there is not only a difference of degree but of kind between the Western movement and Communism, and this difference was seen to concern morality, the choice of means" (*CM*, 5).

from the charge that it is obsolete: "Now, if the essential character of all political situations was grasped by the old political science, there seems to be no reason why it must be superseded by a new political science." Just as one can know the necessary characteristics of triangles without observing every triangle, the old political science may have understood the necessary characteristics of all political situations without experiencing all possible political situations. For an examination of Strauss's claim that the old political science grasped the essential character of all political situations one has to turn to Strauss's discussion of classical political philosophers (one place to start is his essay on Plato in *CM*). But in showing the mere possibility that they did, he shows here the inadequacy of the claim that our unprecedented political situation necessarily calls for a new political science. Moreover, Strauss maintains:

> In case the new political science should tend to understand political things in nonpolitical terms, the old political science, wise to many ages, would even be superior to the new political science in helping us to find our bearings in our unprecedented situation in spite or rather because of the fact that only the new political science can boast of being the child of the atomic age.

If political science understands political things in nonpolitical terms, it will fail to see the political disagreements that shape the perspectives of different regimes. In implicitly imposing its own perspective on others, such a political science is apt to misunderstand the particular political situation. In response to Schaar and Wolin's protest against this statement, Strauss writes: "I believe indeed that Aristotelian political science is more likely to free us from certain well known delusions regarding disarmament than is the new political science" (Strauss 1963b, 154). For instance, in his presidential address to the American Political Science Association, Quincy Wright wrote:

> There is only too much reason to anticipate that concerted and effective efforts to assure that the United States would be in a position to win if a war should break out will encourage equally concerted efforts on the part of the advisors of the Soviet Union to make sure that the Soviet Union will win. The consequence is likely to be a war in which both will lose. I do not mean by this to dissuade political scientists from a reasonable interest in national defense. I certainly do not want the United States to lose if a war should occur. The question is, however, whether

as political scientists we should not place prime emphasis upon means
whereby the political struggle can be moderated and developed in such a
way that neither side will lose. (1950, 7)

In the spirit of a realistic political science, Wright recommends a general
education in political science: "It is my experience that such an education
tends to develop a spirit of moderation and to qualify the natural human
disposition toward doctrinairism and intolerance. It is hard to see how a
political scientist can be either a Nazi or a Communist" (1950, 7–8). Instead of preparing our military for war, it seems, we should have sent political scientists to the Soviet Union to transform Soviet politicians into
relativistic liberals. This advice is in fact more reasonable than the view
underlying Wright's assumption that Stalin and his advisors would have
voluntarily followed our lead in not preparing every means that would as-
sure victory in the case of a war, a view that seems to assume that they were
already liberals like Wright himself.

Methodological Objections

Strauss begins this discussion with the assertion that "one will never understand the new political science if one does not start from that reason advanced on its behalf, which has nothing whatever to do with any true or alleged blindness of the old political science to any political things as such."
That reason is a notion of science according to which all awareness of political things that is not scientific is cognitively worthless. Since the old political science is based on the nonscientific awareness of political things,
"serious criticism of the old political science is a waste of time, for we know
in advance that it could only have been a pseudo-science." Most statements
of the old political science cannot be turned into operational hypotheses
that can be scientifically verified. Accordingly, Robert Dahl rejects "traditional political theories" because "it is usually impossible to say with any
high degree of precision what would constitute a fair test of a political theory; and even if a fair test could be formulated, it would normally be impossible to summarize the information required for such a test" (1958–59,
95). But even when the adherents of the new political science do "sometimes engage in apparent criticism" of the old, Strauss maintains, they are
unable to understand the criticized "doctrines in their own terms," because
they look at the old political science through the lenses of their own notion
of science.

Strauss bridges this communication gap by working through an ambiguity inherent in the new political science's understanding of science: "What science is, is supposed to be known from the practice of the other sciences, of sciences that are admittedly in existence and not merely desiderata, and the clearest example of such sciences are the natural sciences. What science is, is supposed to be known, above all, from the science of science, that is, logic." The new political science's understanding of science is determined by the practice of genuine sciences, but that practice is known through logic. But the problem is that this logic, according to its own understanding of science, is not a science. The natural sciences are said to be genuine sciences because there is an agreement among their practitioners regarding their fundamental principles and basic conclusions, but among professors of philosophy there is no agreement that logical positivism—as opposed to Aristotelian or Kantian or Hegelian logic—is the true logic. If we are to respect the specialization of sciences dictated by the new notion of science, the fact that the logic in question "is controversial among the people who must be supposed to be competent to judge in such matters" is sufficient reason for the political scientist to realize that not only can he not regard that logic as a standard but that he himself is not competent to judge its soundness as a logical theory. But he is competent to test it by its fruits in his field: the political scientist "is competent to judge whether his understanding of political things as political things is helped or hindered by the new political science that is derived from the logic in question." Indeed, the demand that political scientists should comply with logical positivism is not a scientific demand according to logical positivism: "[The political scientist] is perfectly justified in regarding as an imposition the demand that he comply with 'logical positivism' or else plead guilty to being a 'metaphysician.' He is perfectly justified in regarding this epithet as not 'objective,' because it is terrifying and unintelligible like the war cries of savages." Since according to logical positivism all emotive and normative judgments are meaningless, the demand that scientists should comply with logical positivism is, according to the principles of logical positivism, meaningless. The new notion of science cannot be the standard for the political scientist; the standard must be the political things themselves.

But what makes the new political science attractive to many political scientists is precisely that it seems to insist more emphatically on the importance of focusing one's attention on observable political phenomena. Now, Strauss characterizes the demand to proceed empirically as a demand of common sense, a demand that is also recognized by "the essentialism" of the old political science: "No one in his senses ever dreamt that he could know anything, say, of American government as such or of the present political situation as such except by looking at American government or at the present political situation." If every political scientist recognizes the legitimacy of the demand to proceed empirically, then the issue between the old and the new political science is which of these sciences meets this demand, or what is reasonable in it, more adequately.

According to Strauss, the incarnation of the empirical spirit is the man from Missouri, the "show me" state:

> The incarnation of the empirical spirit is the man from Missouri, who has to be shown. For he *knows* that he, as well as everyone else who is of sound mind and whose sight is not defective, can see things and people as they are with his eyes and that he is capable of knowing how his neighbors feel; he takes it for *granted* that he lives with other human beings of all descriptions in the same world and that because they are all human beings, they all understand one another somehow; he *knows* that if this were not so, political life would be altogether impossible. If someone would offer him speculations based on extrasensory perception, he would turn his back more or less politely. (emphasis added)

This statement is an articulation of the presuppositions of the demand to proceed empirically. The demand to be shown would be unreasonable if one's eyes could not see things and people as they are, if other healthy human beings did not have the same senses, and if one could not know the feelings of human beings with whom one is in contact. According to Strauss, the man from Missouri knows that these premises are true. But the presupposition of these presuppositions is that the diversity of human beings is bound by a common nature and that all human beings live in the same world. According to Strauss, the man from Missouri does not know these fundamental presuppositions but takes them for granted, because he knows that if "it were not so, political life would be altogether impossible." Finally, the demand to proceed empirically assumes that no human being has extrasensory perceptions, for it would be unreasonable to insist that extrasensory perceptions be verified by one's senses.

The old political science is truly empirical because it accepts these presuppositions of empirical knowledge:

> It did not claim to know better or differently than [the man from Missouri] such things as that the Democratic and Republican parties are now, and have been for some time, the preponderant parties in this

country, and that there are presidential elections every fourth year. By admitting [that] facts of this kind are known independently of political science, it admitted that empirical knowledge is not necessarily scientific knowledge or that a statement can be true and *known* to be true without being scientific, and above all, that political science stands or falls by the truth of the prescientific *awareness* of political things. (emphasis added)

Although Aristotelian political science is based on empirical knowledge, it also corrects or deepens it. According to Aristotle, empirical knowledge is not necessarily scientific knowledge, for to possess empirical knowledge is to know that a thing is, but to possess scientific knowledge is to know the why of a thing (*Metaphysics* 981a24–27). The old political science accepts the man from Missouri's knowledge that there are presidential elections every fourth year but it in principle can explain why such things are the way they are. Moreover, by speaking of the prescientific awareness of political things, instead of the prescientific knowledge of political things, Strauss suggests that the cognitive status of prescientific understanding varies from thing to thing. No one in his senses confuses a monkey with a man, but many people confuse an unjust action with a just one. Aristotelian political science corrects the prescientific grasp of political things by clarifying it.

Empiricism, however, begins with a certain doubt about the truth of empirical statements: "Yet one may raise the question as to how one can be *certain* of the truth of empirical statements which are prescientific" (emphasis added). How can we be certain that there is such a thing as human nature and that we live in a world with an unchanging structure? To establish the certainty of empirical statements that are prescientific, one needs an explanation of how our perceiving of things and people is possible—an epistemology. Accordingly, Strauss distinguishes an empiricist statement from an empirical statement. An empirical statement is one that is based on experience, which is the grasp of things that arises from repeated perception of them. An empiricist statement is one that is based on the explicit assumption of a specific epistemology. But the problem with epistemology is that it presupposes what it purports to establish, for "our perceiving of things and people is more manifest and more reliable" than "any explanation of how our perceiving of things and people is possible." Accordingly, the prescientific understanding of things as things remains the standard for epistemology even while it is trying to articulate a standard by which to judge this understanding:

If a logical positivist tries to give an account of "a thing" or a formula for "a thing" in terms of mere sense data and their composition, he is looking, and bids us to look, at the previously grasped "thing"; the previously grasped "thing" is the standard by which we judge of his formula. If an epistemology—for example, solipsism—manifestly fails to give an account of how empirical statements as meant can be true, it fails to carry conviction.

The very attempt to escape from the "fundamental reliance that underlies or pervades empirical statements" confirms the necessity of that reliance. The awareness of that reliance is tantamount to the recognition of "the fundamental riddle." We can only accept the evidence of our senses on faith because we do not know what being is. What Strauss finds objectionable in the epistemology of logical positivism is that it obscures the existence of this riddle by denying the meaning of metaphysical assertions. But the denial of this riddle amounts to a solution of the riddle, for it leads one in effect to disregard and hence to reject the possibilities that might cast doubt on the legitimacy of the clear and distinct account of the world. Indeed, Strauss argues that one can legitimately reject logical positivism's practical imperatives:

> But no man needs to be ashamed to admit that he does not possess a solution to the fundamental riddle. Surely, no man ought to let himself be bullied into the acceptance of an alleged solution—for the denial of the existence of a riddle is a kind of solution of the riddle—by the threat that if he fails to do so he is a "metaphysician." To sustain our weaker brethren against that threat one might tell them the belief accepted by the empiricists, according to which science is in principle susceptible of infinite progress, is itself tantamount to the belief that being is irretrievably mysterious.

In order for science to exist, its objects must be accessible to human reason. But since, according to contemporary empiricists, the object of science "reveals itself in an infinite process, one can say with at least equal right that it is radically mysterious" (Strauss 1961, 154; see also Weber 1946, 138–40). The science that sought to establish the certainty of the clear and distinct account of the world has itself become the refuge of mystery.

To show the difficulty that afflicts epistemology, Strauss exhorts us to "try to restate the issue." This is tantamount to an attempt to establish empiricism empirically. He only tries to restate the issue, because it is not possible to establish empiricism empirically, but seeing this impossibility reveals the fundamental difficulty of epistemology. He begins with empiricism's criticism of the man from Missouri:

> A simple observation seems to be sufficient to show that the man from Missouri is "naive": he does not see things with his eyes; what he sees with his eyes are only colors, shapes, and the like; he would perceive things, in contradistinction to sense data, only if he possessed "extrasensory perception"; his claim—the claim of common sense—implies that there is "extrasensory perception." What is true of "things" is true of "patterns," at any rate of those patterns which students of politics from time to time claim to "perceive."

The man from Missouri is naive because he is not aware of his own views: on one hand he denies the existence of extrasensory perception and on the other he asserts it. Strauss, however, pays a not altogether ironic compliment to this perplexed man: "We must leave the man from Missouri scratching his head; by being silent, he remains in his own way a philosopher." Empiricists, however, "do not leave it at scratching their heads," that is, they are not satisfied with being philosophers. Instead, they resolve the perplexity of the man from Missouri by maintaining that our perceptions of "things" are really constructions of the mind made from sense data. They distinguish between scientific (conscious) constructs, which understand things in terms of "functional relations between different series of events," and commonsense (unconscious) constructs, which refer to "things possessing qualities." Whereas commonsense constructs are subjective, the scientific constructs are objective, in every respect the same—not indeed for everyone—but for everyone who chooses to construct them in the scientific fashion (for the vagueness of scientific constructs in political science see *LAM* 217).[6] Now, the difference between scientific understanding and commonsense understanding is especially profound when one is studying human beings, "for at least some of the properties which we ascribe to

---

6. The modern notion of science is at the heart of the transformation of the meaning of the words "subjective" and "objective." Originally, "subjective" referred to the essential being of a thing and "objective" referred to what is true only in relation to the mind of the knower. The modern notion of science practically reverses the meaning of these terms so that "objective" comes to refer to what is external to the mind of the knower. But it is external only in the sense that others can have the same exact concepts.

things are sensually perceived, whereas the soul's actions, passions, or states can never become sense data." More precisely, actions and passions of the soul do have visible manifestations. What can never become sense data are the states of the soul such as virtues and vices (Aristotle, *Nicomachean Ethics* 1105b-19–1106a-13). Accordingly, an empiricist political science suffers from more profound difficulties than an empiricist economics or sociology, because political communities are based on agreements regarding the just and the noble (ibid.; see *CM*, 13n). Since an empiricist political science cannot even recognize just and noble actions, it cannot be helpful for the *deeper* understanding of them, for seeing what is not visible to political experience and political understanding. It necessarily reduces noble and just actions to passions as they manifest themselves in sense data.

But one cannot reduce the political to the subpolitical without first seeing the political. Accordingly, Strauss argues that the new political science comes into being through an attempted break with common sense, a break that cannot consistently be carried out. He proves this more generally by observing that "empiricism cannot be established empiricistically: it is not known through sense data that the only possible objects of perception are sense data." Moreover, one cannot establish empiricism empirically:

> [T]he relation of eyes to colors or shapes is established through the same kind of perception through which we perceive things as things rather than sense data or constructs. In other words, sense data as sense data become known only through an act of abstraction or disregard which presupposes the legitimacy of our primary awareness of things as things and of people as people.

According to empiricism, human eyes can only see simple perceptions such as color or shapes. It is the mind that constructs complex perceptions ("things") out of these perceptions. But the human eye does not see shapes as a simple perception, for shapes are always accompanied by color. The understanding of sense data as consisting of colors and shapes presupposes the legitimacy of complex perceptions, which legitimacy empiricism disregards. By showing that empiricism in fact rests on the understanding of things that empiricism renders doubtful, Strauss shows that "the only way of overcoming the naiveté of the man from Missouri is in the first place to admit that that naiveté cannot be avoided in any way or that there is no possible human thought which is not in the last analysis dependent on the legitimacy of that naiveté and the awareness or the knowledge going with it."

Strauss ends his discussion with a consideration of "the most massive or the crudest reason to which empiricism owes much of its attractiveness," a reason that he says "we must not disregard," perhaps because to disregard it is to disregard the context within which empiricism exists. This reason is the desire to fight superstition or prejudice. According to Strauss, some adherents of the new political science may not deny that prescientific thought about just and noble actions contains genuine knowledge, but because they believe that genuine knowledge is inseparable from superstition or prejudice, they choose to act on the assumption that prescientific thought does not have the character of knowledge. If the prescientific understanding of political things is inseparable from superstition or prejudice, then a clean break with prescientific understanding is necessary, for "by trusting common sense one is in danger of bringing back the whole kingdom of darkness with Thomas Aquinas at its head."

The old political science's approach to the difficulty in question is very different: "The old political science was not unaware of the imperfections of political opinion, but it did not believe that the remedy lies in the total rejection of common-sense understanding as such." Whereas the new political science believed that there was genuine but tainted knowledge in political opinion, the old believed that political opinions are crude but revealing. Accordingly, it sought to clarify political opinion: "It was critical in the original sense, that is, discerning, regarding political opinions." It was not critical in the sense of following the rules of the scientific method, rules that were meant to combat the claims of divine revelation, but it was critical in the sense of separating the truth and falsity of specifically political opinions.[7] But since much of the appeal of superstition lies in confused political opinions, clarity about political opinions helps one, with the aid of natural science, to free oneself from superstition: "it was aware that the errors regarding witches were found out without the benefit of empiricism." Strauss ends his discussion of the old political science's response to superstition with two sentences that at first seem to be utterly unconnected with that theme:

> It was aware that judgments or maxims which were justified by the un-
> contested experience of decades, and even of centuries or millenniums,

7. "Plato, as it were, says: Take any opinion about right, however fantastic or 'primitive,' that you please, you can be certain prior to having investigated it that it points beyond itself, that the people who cherish the opinion in question contradict that very opinion somehow and thus are forced to go beyond it in the direction of the one true view of justice, provided that a philosopher arises among them" (*NRH*, 125).

may have to be revised because of unforeseen changes; it knew, in the words of Burke, "that the generality of people are fifty years, at least, behind hand in their politics." Accordingly, the old political science was concerned with political improvement by political means as distinguished from social engineering; it knew that those political means include revolutions and wars, since there may be foreign regimes (Hitler Germany is the orthodox example) that are dangerous to the free survival of this country, regimes that would be expected to transform themselves gradually into good neighbors only by the criminally foolish.

If the empiricist attempt to defeat superstition requires the construction not only of perfectly lucid concepts but of a society that is based on those concepts, then the most massive reason for attraction to empiricism is in fact the reason for the mass society. Accordingly, Strauss criticizes the new political science's concern with social engineering on the basis of the new political science's insistence that unforeseen circumstances may require radical revisions of one's judgments or maxims. And as the reference to Burke indicates, the old political science was aware of the danger of strict reliance on old books. But precisely because the old political science did not think that man can free himself from the possibility of unforeseen changes, it "was concerned with political improvement by political means as distinguished from social engineering." For the idea of social engineering presupposes that by controlling chance man can put an end to unforeseen circumstances. Since the old political science did not reduce the political to the subpolitical, it could recognize foreign regimes that are dangerous, and since it sought to address political problems by political means it was willing to use such means as war or revolutions to oppose those regimes. Clearly, the unorthodox example, the example that Strauss as an unorthodox member of the political science profession had in mind, is the Soviet Union. Since an empiricist political science necessarily reduces the political to the subpolitical, and since it seeks to address political problems through social engineering, it is incapable of meeting the threat of Soviet Union with political means.

In short, Strauss has shown that the revolt against the old political science was unjustified. The old political science is more empirical than the new political science, and it is more able to meet the demands of the day. Moreover, one may even wonder whether, in light of developments in the twentieth century, the seventeenth-century founders of empiricism, being highly rational beings, would have revised their opinion about the goodness of their project. The attempt to solve the theological question by

erecting the City of Man on the ruins of the City of God led to the unforeseen emergence of explicitly atheistic political orders that instead of
being the home of freedom were its enemies and of an empiricist political
science that could not see the threats to liberal democracy posed by these
regimes.[8]

8. Although after the war the new political scientists hated anything that smacked of Hitler,
the new political science hardly recognized his danger. In a book originally written in Berlin in
1932, Merriam wrote: "Without undertaking the role of prophet, just disclaimed, it is perhaps appropriate to say that I myself look forward to fundamental changes in the political, the industrial,
the religious, the scientific order, changes that will shatter many of the present-day and historic
power structures beyond recognition and remake them in new forms that will be terrifying to
those who love the *status quo*, either because it deals gently with them or because they fear the in-
security of change" (Merriam 1950, 325). According to Merriam, it seems that only class interest
and an irrational fear of change would lead one to reject the new political structures, whatever
they may be.

CHAPTER 9

The New Political Science and Liberal Democracy

In the concluding section of his discussion of the new political science Strauss considers "whether there is not a necessary connection between value-free social science and liberalism, although liberalism is not, as goes without saying, value-free," a connection that may explain "the very frequent 'personal' union of liberalism and value-free social science" (*LAM*, x). He seems to discover this connection in the mutual influence of two consequences of the new political science:

> In the first place, the new political science is constantly compelled
> to borrow from common-sense knowledge, thus unwittingly testifying
> to the truth that there is genuine prescientific knowledge of political
> things. Second, the logic on which the new political science is based
> may provide sufficient criteria of exactness; it does not provide objective
> criteria of relevance.

Since the logic underlying the new political science lacks objective criteria of relevance, it finds guidance "by surreptitious recourse to common sense" and by that logic's criteria of exactness. The new political science's attachment to a peculiar interpretation of liberal democracy is the consequence of the combined effect of these two sources of guidance.

THE NEW POLITICAL SCIENCE'S CRITERIA OF RELEVANCE

The old political science's criteria of relevance are those that are inherent in the prescientific understanding of political things, because it recognizes that "intelligent and informed citizens distinguish soundly between important and unimportant political matters" (*LAM*, 214). Strauss qualifies this assertion by the suggestion that political men may not be adequately aware of "the principles of preference which supply the criteria of relevance in regard to political things" (*LAM*, 214; Strauss 1963b, 154), because different regimes look up to different things, and the criteria of relevance of political men are derived from their own regime. An adequate understanding of the principles of preference can be obtained only by settling the dispute among different regimes: "The qualitatively different regimes, or kinds of regimes, and the qualitatively different purposes constituting and legitimating them, by revealing themselves as the most important political things, supply the key to the understanding of all political things and the basis of the reasoned distinction between important and unimportant political things" (*LAM*, 214). But even the question of the best regime emerges through reflections based on political life, that is, on the conflict between societies with different regimes. Although the old political science recognizes the importance of technical things and politically neutral things, it subordinates these questions to those that are politically controversial. The needs of a society to feed and defend itself are vital, but the questions regarding these matters are not questions that in principle rend a society apart. Since even the highest theme of the old political science is based on reflections on the most important political debates, Strauss characterizes its perspective in the following way: "what is most important for political science is identical with what is most important politically. To illustrate this by the present-day example, for the old-fashioned political scientists today, the most important concern is the Cold War, or the qualitative difference which amounts to a conflict, between liberal democracy and Communism" (*LAM*, 214).[1]

By abandoning the criteria of relevance that are inherent in political understanding, the new political science begins with no orientation toward political things: "It is confronted by a chaotic mass of data into which it

---

1. One may object that the things that are most important are not political but private matters. Almost every politician today is in the habit of saying that their family is more important than their office. But this view of the relation between public and private matters is a consequence of a particular political order. Moreover, even the constitution of the family is affected by the political order. For instance, the principle of the family is non-democratic, but families living in a democracy are willy-nilly transformed by the democratic principle. Indeed, the principle of a regime penetrates into the soul of its citizens: "The regimes and their principles pervade the societies throughout, in the sense that there are no recesses of privacy which are simply impervious to that pervasion, as is indicated by such expressions, coined by the new political science, as 'the democratic personality'" (*LAM*, 214).

must bring an order alien to those data and originating in the demands of political science as a science anxious to comply with the demands of logical positivism" (*LAM*, 214–15). Since logical positivism does not have objective criteria of relevance, the new political science is likely to search for new kinds of universals on the basis of its criteria of exactness. In the first place, the universals of the old political science (the various regimes and their purposes) must be rejected, because by blending facts and values they cannot be considered objective. In the second place, the very assumption that there are no natural wholes guides the search for the new kind of universal. For if there are no natural wholes, qualitatively different things can be understood in terms of the quantity of their homogeneous elements. Referring to his collaborators' interpretations of the works of Bentley, Lasswell, and Simon, Strauss constructs an orderly search for a new kind of universal. But he begins with a step that apparently precedes all the other steps: the reduction of the political to politically neutral things. He then discusses the reduction of the political things to the sociological groups, of these groups to theories of personality, and of these theories to the behavior of animals.

In each step, he shows the political irrelevance of the new universal and how the new universal is unable to fulfill its own intention. For instance, the motive to understand different regimes in terms of what is present in all regimes (coercion and freedom) is to avoid the value judgments that are inherent in the notion of regimes. Strauss, however, shows that this step alienates the political scientist from important political issues: "What is important for us as political scientists is not the politically important" (*LAM*, 215). And it does so without really freeing itself from the Ought, because the admission that there are no qualitative differences between liberal democracy and Communism has "grave political consequences—consequences which are so little accidental that they appeal for their own sake to the new political scientists" (*LAM*, 215).[2] Second, Bentley rejects the old political science's focus on regimes because it leads to "a formal study of the most external characteristics of governing institutions" or because it leads one to "lose all sight of the content of the process in some trick point about the form" (Bentley 1967, 162). But Strauss observes that the attempt to

---

2. It seems that one of the differences between twentieth-century liberalism and conservatism is that the former is more apt to be concerned with goods that are not politically controversial: "Here and now a man who is in favor of the war on poverty and opposed to the war in Vietnam is generally regarded as doubtlessly a liberal, and a man who is in favor of the war in Vietnam and opposed to the war on poverty is generally regarded as doubtlessly a conservative" (*LAM*, vii).

understand political societies in terms of groups in general "is in fact a formalism unrivaled in any scholasticism of the past" (*LAM*, 215). The reduction of the political to the sociological leads to formalism because it disregards the distinctively political features of political associations, namely, that they are associations composed of rulers and ruled: "All peculiarities of political societies, and still more of the political societies with which we are concerned as citizens, become unrecognizable if restated in terms of the vague generalities which hold of every conceivable group" (*LAM*, 215). Third, Strauss does not dwell on the reduction of the sociological to the psychological except to point out the distance it creates between political science and political life: "we know nothing of the political wisdom or folly of a statesman until we know everything about the degree of affection which he received from his parents, if any" (*LAM*, 216). Finally, Simon seeks to illuminate human rational decisionmaking by a mathematical model that in his view is more appropriate for the behavior of a rat than a human being (see Storing 1963, 113–15). The purpose of this model is to show that we should "be skeptical in postulating for humans, or other organisms, elaborate mechanisms for choosing among diverse ends" (quoted in ibid., 114). Although we may have much in common with rats, it is doubtful that their behavior can be a model of human rational decisionmaking, because human reason is connected with our capacity for speech and our awareness of the relation between mental symbols and external objects, which necessarily give human decisionmaking a complexity that is wanting in the behavior of rats. In other words, there is something absurd in Simon's attempt to understand human rationality through the behavior of an animal that is incapable of speech: "We do not doubt that we can observe, if we try hard enough, the overt behavior of humans as we observe the overt behavior of rats. But we ought not to forget that in the case of rats we are limited to observing overt behavior because they do not talk, and they do not talk because they have nothing to say or because they have no inwardness" (*LAM*, 216). The reduction of the complex to the simple is a movement from the surface to the depth, but the simple things to which political things are reduced are the actions of beings that have no inwardness, no depth.

After following the new political science's search for universals, Strauss abruptly returns to the surface: "Yet to return from these depths to the surface, an *important* example of the formalism in question is supplied by the well-known theory regarding the principles of legitimacy which substitutes formal characteristics (traditional, rational, charismatic) for the substantive principles which are precisely the purposes to which the various regimes are dedicated and by which they are legitimated" (*LAM*, 216; emphasis added). The very phrase "let us return from these depths to the surface" reminds one of the memorable paragraph in his discussion of Weber that begins with the phrase, "But let us hasten back from these *awful* depths to a superficiality which . . ." (*NRH*, 76; emphasis added). Our impression that Strauss wants to compare the new political science with Weber's is confirmed by his mentioning of Weber's principles of legitimacy, which are accepted by the new political science. Indeed, the very first step toward new universals, which Strauss did not identify with any particular author, is one consequence of Weber's definition of the state as an association that has a monopoly over the legitimate uses of violence, a definition that was necessary in order to avoid a definition in terms of the various ends of states (Weber 1946, 78). Both Weber's social science and the new political science are value-free, and thus they both reject the notion of regimes. But here ends their similarity. Unlike the universals of the new political science, Weber's universals are important because they remind one of important political conflicts, in particular, of the conflict between conservatives and revolutionaries in the aftermath of the French Revolution. In contrast:

> There is an amazing disproportion between the apparent breadth of the goal (say, a general theory of social change) and the true pettiness of the researches undertaken in order to achieve that goal (say, a change in a hospital when one head nurse is replaced by another). This is no accident. Since we lack objective criteria of relevance, we have no reason to be more interested in *a world-shaking revolution* which affects directly or indirectly all men than in the most trifling "social changes." (*LAM*, 216; emphasis added)

Although Weber's principles of legitimacy were parochial insofar as they reflected "the situation as it existed in Continental Europe after the French revolution" (*NRH*, 57), they were of much wider scope than the universals of the new political science. This difference between Weber and the new political science is a consequence of their different understanding of universals: "The universals for which the new political science seeks are 'laws of human behavior'; those laws are to be discovered by means of 'empirical' research" (*LAM*, 216). Weber, on the other hand, denied that laws of human behavior are proper goals of social science. He denied that social science should accept the goals of natural science, because he insisted that social science must deal with important problems. Moreover, he understood empirical research in a way that did not preclude him from studying in an intensive manner societies in the past. In contrast:

[T]he most cherished techniques of "empirical" research in the social sciences can be applied only to human beings now in countries in which the government tolerates research of this kind. The new political science is therefore constantly tempted (and as a rule does not resist the temptation) to absolutize the relative or peculiar, that is, to be parochial. We have read statements about "the revolutionary" or "the conservative" which did not even claim to have any basis other than observations made in the United States at the present moment. (*LAM*, 216–17)

Now, one may object that the new political science is not in a fundamentally different situation than, say, Aristotle's political science, for Aristotle's investigations too are limited to particular societies. The difference is that Aristotle's reflections are based on examination of political societies with different regimes: Persia, Sparta, Athens, Crete, and so on. Above all, Aristotle reflects on societies that would not have tolerated him. But the techniques of the new political science are applicable only in societies that tolerate such researches, and such societies are not only constituted by a particular regime but by a *peculiar* regime, the only regime that was meant to protect scientific inquiry. Since the observations about "the revolutionary" or "the conservative" are made through lenses shaped by a peculiar regime, one may suspect that they cannot even be fully true regarding "the revolutionary" or "the conservative" in that regime. By favoring data that are only available in present-day liberal democratic societies, the very universals of the new political science foster a liberal democratic parochialism.

Digression on Religion

Strauss interrupts his main argument with a discussion that he introduces in the following manner: "At the risk of some repetition we *must* say a few words about the language of the new political science" (*LAM*, 217; emphasis added).[3] He risks repeating not what he has said about the language of the new political science, for he has hardly said anything about it, but what he has said about the concepts of the new political science. His discussion of the language of the new political science supplements his earlier

---

3. The only other consideration that Strauss introduces with the verb "must" is his discussion of "the massive or crudest reason to which empiricism owes much of its attractiveness" (*LAM*, 213). Both discussions deal with the new political science's rejection of religion. To understand the new political science, Strauss implies, one must focus on that rejection.

statement that its logical criteria of exactness lead to utterly formal notions with a consideration that shows that these criteria can also lead to vulgar notions. The new political science rejects the language used by political men because it is believed to be ambiguous and imprecise. But Strauss argues that this rejection is unwarranted: "Political life would be altogether impossible if its language were unqualifiedly vague; that language is capable of the utmost unambiguity and precision as in a declaration of war or in an order given to a firing squad." Political language is capable of precision when it is necessary: "If available distinctions like that between war, peace, and armistice prove to be insufficient, political life finds, without the benefit of political science, the right new expression (Cold War as distinguished from Hot or Shooting War) which designates the new phenomenon with unfailing precision." The vagueness of political language is not truly vagueness, because it "it corresponds to the complexity of political life" and because "it is nourished by political experience with political things in a great variety of circumstances" (*LAM*, 217). Since political language reveals its own inadequacy in the cases in question, and since it is a language nourished by long experience, it provides the starting point for the discovery of genuinely unambiguous and precise universals. In contrast, the wholesale rejection of that language leads to an "irredeemable vagueness":

> The thinking men who are regarded as the classic interpreters of power, Thucydides and Machiavelli, did not need these expressions ["power" or "power relations"]; these expressions as now used originate, not in political life, but in the academic reaction to the understanding of political life in terms of law alone: these expressions signify nothing but that academic reaction. (*LAM*, 217)

Hobbes and a number of thinkers who followed after him did use the term "power" as an important part of their political theory. Strauss, however, seems to distinguish between their use of "power," which was a deliberate attempt to reduce different motives to one, and the use of that term by the new political science, which signifies in a vague manner forces that are not moral or legal. Since there is almost no content to this notion of power, one cannot overcome its vagueness by unpacking its meaning. The language of political life, however, is suggestive: "Political language does not claim to be perfectly clear and distinct; it does not claim that it is based on a full understanding of the things which it designates unambiguously enough; it is suggestive; it leaves those things in the penumbra in which they come to sight." In contrast, "the purge effected by 'scientific' definitions of those things has the character of sterilization" (*LAM*, 217). Although the terms of the new political science are provisional in the sense that "they are meant to imply hypotheses about political life," that language is constructed so that it "channels research in such directions that the 'data' which might reveal the inadequacy of the hypothesis never turn up" (*LAM*, 218). Strauss illustrates the difference between the two languages by comparing "conscience" with "Super-Ego":

> When one speaks of "conscience" one does not claim that one has fathomed the phenomenon indicated by that term. But when the new political scientist speaks of the "Super-Ego," he is certain that anything meant by "conscience" which is not covered by the "Super-Ego" is a superstition. As a consequence, he cannot distinguish between a bad conscience, which may induce a man to devote the rest of his life to compensating another man to the best of his powers for an irreparable damage, and "guilt feelings," which one ought to get rid of as fast and as cheaply as possible. (*LAM*, 218)

The use of "Super-Ego" presupposes a rejection of divine beings as well as of the genuine character of the experience of guilt.[4] The notion of conscience may indeed imply both of those things, but it is open to evidence against them in a way that that the notion of "Super-Ego" is not open to their opposites. Strauss supplements this example with one that illustrates the effect of a psychological term on one's understanding of political phenomena: "Similarly, [the new political scientist] is certain to have understood the trust which induces people to vote for a candidate for high office by speaking of the 'father image'; he does not have to inquire whether and to what extent the candidate in question deserves that trust—a trust different from the trust which children have in their father" (*LAM*, 218). The notion of "father image" automatically leads one to assume that people's trust in politicians is something childish, ignoring the possibility that a people may trust a politician because they have reckoned that he is trustworthy. As Strauss's examples indicate, the dogmatic implications of the

---

4. According to Strauss, classical philosophers did not have a word for "conscience," which is a term of Christian origin (*NRH*, 163). The above discussion suggests that terms of biblical origin do not present the same difficulty as modern scientific terms. According to Strauss, we have fallen into an unnatural cave "less because of the tradition itself than of the tradition of polemics against the tradition" (*PL*, 136).

language of the new political science tend to weaken the claims of what is high. Accordingly, he concludes that "to the extent to which the new political science is not formalistic, it is vulgarian. This vulgarianism shows itself particularly in the 'value-free' manner in which it uses and thus debases terms that originally were meant only for indicating things of a noble character—terms like 'culture,' 'personality,' 'values,' 'charismatic,' and 'civilization'" (*LAM*, 218). Here Strauss is again comparing the new political science to Weber's social science. Whereas Weber regarded culture as a social cultivation of our higher faculties, the new political science regards culture as a pattern of conduct common to any human group; whereas according to Weber one can become a personality through a devotion to a cause, the new political science assumes that everyone has a personality; whereas Weber distinguished values from desires, the new political science conflates them; whereas Weber referred to charisma as a sacred quality possessed by a leader, the new political science treats charisma as any quality that makes a leader well liked; whereas Weber distinguished civilization and barbarism, the new political science makes no such distinction.

But given that both Weber's social science and the new political science are value-free, why did Weber still maintain a distinction between high and low? Strauss traces the difference between the new political science and Weber's social science to their different attitudes toward religion. Weber insisted that human reason cannot resolve conflicts between values because he believed that science was unable to meet the challenge of religion. The new political science has inherited Weber's thesis but it is utterly oblivious to the problem that is responsible for that thesis: "The new science uses sociological or psychological theories regarding religion, which exclude, *without considering it,* the possibility that religion rests ultimately on God's revealing Himself to man; hence those theories are mere hypotheses which can never be confirmed. Those theories are in fact the hidden basis of the new political science" (*LAM*, 218; emphasis added). Not logical positivism but the atheistic sociological or psychological theories that it allows to be accepted in a dogmatic manner are the true basis of the new political science. Strauss does not claim that the new political scientists are necessarily atheists, for some of them may not even be aware of the atheistic character of the theories that they use. The new political scientists, he argues, use, for instance, Freud's or Marx's theories regarding religion without considering the alternative to them. Accordingly, the atheism of the new political science, whether it be implicit or explicit, is necessarily dogmatic. In contrast, Strauss maintains that

Max Weber, who had perhaps as great an influence on the new political science as Marx, Freud and logical positivism—although he was surely as little a new political scientist as Marx and Freud—took the possibility of revelation seriously; hence his writings, even and especially those dealing with science as such, possess a depth and a claim to respect which, I believe, I have properly recognized; I venture to say that this particular open-mindedness was ultimately the reason why he was not a new political scientist. (Strauss, "Replies to Schaar and Wolin," 153)

Strauss describes the dogmatic atheism of the new political science as "the most important example of the dogmatism to which we have alluded" because this dogmatism affects the very status of it as a science or because the choice between human guidance and divine guidance is the most fundamental of human choices.

Now, Strauss admits that there are some adherents of the new political science who are aware of their atheism and who insist that atheism should be the basis of their science because otherwise they would violate the demands of intellectual honesty. In response to them, Strauss writes:

We gladly grant that other things being equal, a frank atheist is a better man than an alleged theist who conceives of God as a symbol. But we must add that intellectual honesty is not enough. Intellectual honesty is not love of truth. Intellectual honesty, a kind of self-denial, has taken the place of love of truth because truth has come to be believed to be repulsive, and one cannot love the repulsive. Yet just as our opponents refuse respect to unreasoned belief, we on our part, with at least equal right, must refuse respect to unreasoned unbelief; honesty with oneself regarding one's unbelief is in itself not more than unreasoned unbelief, probably accompanied by a vague confidence that the issue of unbelief versus belief has long since been settled once and for all. (*LAM*, 218–19)

Strauss, of course, does not object to intellectual honesty. He only maintains that it is not a sufficient basis for science. Science must be established on knowable truths, and if atheism is not knowable it cannot be the basis of science. Since atheism based on intellectual honesty is probably accompanied by a vague confidence that the issue of unbelief versus belief has been settled, the first step toward science would be to see whether that confidence is warranted, that is, whether this issue in fact has long been settled. Finally, Strauss suggests that science cannot be defended if it cannot show that the truth that it discovers is good for man.

Strauss ends this digression with the following sentence: "It is hardly necessary to add that the dogmatic exclusion of religious awareness proper renders questionable all *long-range predictions* concerning the future of societies" (*LAM*, 219; emphasis added). This statement reminds one of Strauss's earlier suggestion that the universal right to vote "must be taken into consideration in any *long-range predictions* since it may be exercised by all in future elections taking place in unprecedented and therefore particularly interesting circumstances" (*LAM*, 208; emphasis added). No long-range prediction of the future of societies can be adequate if it neglects the religious and moral-legal awareness of human beings. Since Weber did not neglect these matters, his reflection on the future of Western society has a certain plausibility. I am, of course, referring to his observation of the alternative between "spiritual renewal ('wholly new prophets or a powerful renaissance of old thoughts or ideals')" and "'mechanized petrifaction, varnished by a kind of convulsive sense of self-importance,' i.e., the extinction of every human possibility but that of 'specialists without spirit or vision and voluptuaries without heart'" (*NRH*, 42).

In the previous section, we followed Strauss's suggestion that the new political science has a tendency of absolutizing the experience that is found in a peculiar society. This digression brings to our attention the notion that the peculiarity of modern liberal society consists in its attempt to transform religion into a private matter. I conclude that the new political science's use of psychological or sociological theories regarding religion, which exclude, without consideration, the possibility that religion rests ultimately on God's revealing himself to man, is the most important reason why it as a rule cannot resist the temptation of absolutizing the peculiar situation of a society that allows for free investigation.

THE NEW POLITICAL SCIENCE'S ATTEMPTED BREAK WITH COMMON SENSE

The reduction of the political to the subpolitical implies the denial of the existence of the common good. Both that reduction and this denial are consequences of the denial of the existence of genuine wholes by the logic underlying the new political science. But, according to Strauss, "the consistent denial of the common good is as impossible as every other consistent manifestation of the break with the common sense" (*LAM*, 219). Since human beings cannot live well without living in a society, and what defines a society is a certain view of the common good, anyone who explicitly denies the existence of the common good is apt to contradict that denial. In

particular, the new political science's rejection of the common good necessarily leads it to another notion of the common good: "The empiricists
who reject the notion of wholes are compelled to speak sooner or later of
such things as 'the open society,' which is their definition of the good society" (*LAM*, 219). The alternative to this admission of a common good
would seem to be the contention of the "group politics" approach, which
allows for the existence of substantive group interests but not a substantive
public interest. Besides being unable to give adequate reasons for denying
to the country what it grants to the group, this approach culminates in the
same notion of the common good as the "open society" because it "surreptitiously reintroduces the common good in the form of 'the rules of the
game' with which all conflicting groups are supposed to comply because
those rules, reasonably fair to every group, can reasonably be admitted by
every group" (*LAM*, 219). This notion of the common good amounts to
the admission of the open society as the good society, for "the rules of the
game" are rules that do not suppress any group.

According to Strauss, the consistent denial of a common good requires
a radical individualism. The new political science, in fact, asserts such individualism. According to it, there cannot be a common good if the objective in question is not approved by all members of society: "even if an objective is to the interest of all, but not believed by all to be the interest of
all, it is not to the public interest: everyone is by nature the sole judge of
what is his interest" (*LAM*, 219–20). Now, Strauss observes: "This premise is not the discovery or invention of the new political science; it was
stated with the greatest vigor by Hobbes" (*LAM*, 220). Yet Hobbes saw that
the destructive character of radical individualism points to a new understanding of the common good: "Hobbes still saw that his premise entails
the war of everybody against everybody and hence drew the conclusion
that everyone must cease to be the sole judge of what is his interest if there
is to be human life; the individual's reason must give way to the public reason" (*LAM*, 220). Rejecting any notion of natural right, the new political
science rejects the possibility of public reason. The government may be a
broker of interests, but it cannot be a rational broker. The only kind of rationality that is legitimate is instrumental rationality, that of the new political science:

> The true public reason is the new political science which judges in a
> universally valid, or objective, manner of what is to the interest of each,
> for it shows to everyone what means he must choose in order to attain
> his attainable ends, whatever those ends may be. It has been shown ear-

lier in this volume what becomes of the new political science, or of the only kind of rationality which the new political science still admits, if its Hobbesian premise is not conveniently forgotten: the new form of public reason goes the way of the old. (*LAM*, 220)

The passages to which Strauss refers bring out the despotic, and even the tyrannical, character of the new political science. As Storing wrote: "The tendency of Simon's hard teaching is not liberal democracy—or even a Leviathan that, though absolute, is protective of natural rights of each individual—but a tyranny in which government becomes the means of harnessing all but one man to the gratification of that one" (1962, 108–9). This is a necessary consequence of a radical individualism that rejects all natural right teachings. Although Lasswell hoped that the psychoanalytocracy of the future would be composed of men of rectitude, Horowitz pointed out that Lasswell had "no basis for understanding rectitude except as a form of self-seeking" (1962, 299).

The question becomes, Why does the new political science tend to forget its Hobbesian premise? By answering this question, one will understand why the new political science prefers democracy to tyranny. The new political science conveniently forgets its radical individualism because it understands the denial of the common good not as a consequence of that individualism but "as a *direct* consequence of the distinction between facts and values according to which only factual judgments, not value judgments, can be true or objective" (*LAM*, 220; emphasis added). This distinction requires from a scientist an attitude of neutrality toward various regimes: "Whereas acting man has necessarily chosen values, the new political scientist as pure spectator is not committed to any values; in particular, he is neutral in the conflict between liberal democracy and its enemies" (*LAM*, 220). Yet this neutrality turns into a commitment to liberal democracy, for this distinction seems to allow for rationally preferring certain values to others. Since "the traditional value systems . . . claimed to be derived from facts—from divine revelation or from similar sources," the distinction between facts and values amounts to "a refutation of the traditional value systems as originally meant." The rejection of a traditional value system's own self-interpretation is likely to lead to the rejection of that value system: a morality that denies that the Bible was revealed by God will almost certainly not be the same morality as one that recognizes the Bible as revealed by God. At any rate, the distinction between facts and values implies that men can posit values without relying on false or at least unevident assertions regarding what is. Men can posit these values as their preferences, which are not strictly speaking opinions and hence cannot be true or false. Accordingly, it is possible to have a rational society based on the true understanding of values. Since according to the distinction in question all values are equal before the tribunal of reason, "the rational society will be egalitarian or democratic and permissive or liberal" (*LAM*, 220). By leveling all values, the distinction between facts and values rationally justifies the preference for liberal democracy.

The new political science's distinction between facts and values is self-contradictory. On one hand, it denies that one can reasonably derive values from facts. On the other, that very distinction, which is a factual distinction, provides the basis for a rational justification of liberal democracy. This contradiction leads Strauss to wonder whether the distinction between facts and values or the assertion that no Ought can be derived from an Is is well founded. Since this is a factual assertion about the human situation, Strauss articulates its understanding of that situation. Those who accept this distinction generally deny that there is a "one-to-one relation between value *a* and the Is A" and maintain that "man possesses a certain latitude" in choosing from various values (*LAM*, 221). Yet this fact about man provides a basis for judging human beings: "A man lacking this latitude—for example, a man for whom every stimulus is a value or who cannot help giving in to every desire—is a defective man, a man with whom something is wrong." Moreover, a theory that equates values with desires or mere preferences fails to grasp the human situation articulated by this relativism: "The fact that someone desires something does not make that something his value; he may successfully fight his desire, or if his desire overpowers him, he may blame himself for this as for a failure on his part; only choice, in contradistinction to mere desire, makes something a man's value. The distinction between desire and choice is a distinction among facts" (*LAM*, 221). Strauss now shows that this relativistic understanding of man undermines both modern natural right and the permissive egalitarianism that is supported by the relativism of the new political science:

> Man is then understood as a being which differs from all other known beings because he posits values; this positing is taken to be a fact. In accordance with this, the new political science denies that man has natural ends—ends toward which he is by nature inclined; it denies more specifically the premise of modern natural right according to which self-preservation is the most important natural end: man can choose death in preference to life, not in a given situation, out of despair, but simply: he can posit death as his value. (*LAM*, 221)

This view implies a formal ethics that necessarily rejects values corresponding to mere desires. Accordingly, Strauss concludes that "the 'relativism' accepted by the new political science according to which values are nothing but objects of desire is based on an insufficient analysis of the Is, that is, of the pertinent Is, and furthermore that one's opinion regarding the character of the Is settles one's opinion regarding the character of the Ought" (*LAM*, 221–22).

Strauss has thus shown that the more intolerant relativism of Max Weber is factually superior to the relativism of the new political science.[5] Now, as I have suggested, the relativism of the new political science supports the permissive egalitarian interpretation of liberal democracy:

> [I]f a man is of the opinion that as a matter of fact all desires are of equal
> dignity, since we know of no factual consideration which would entitle
> us to assign different dignities to different desires, he cannot but be of
> the opinion, unless he is prepared to become guilty of gross arbitrari
> ness, that all desires ought to be treated as equal within the limits of the
> possible, and this opinion is what is meant by permissive egalitarianism.
> (*LAM*, 222)

Since this relativism is based on an insufficient analysis of man, why does the new political science choose it instead of Weber's relativism?

According to Strauss, the democratism of the new political science is the consequence of values embodied in its methodology, which in fact is not value-free. The "techniques of research which are believed to guarantee the maximum of objectivity" put a higher value on the study of things that occur frequently now in democratic societies than on the study of things that have occurred rarely in the past in all sorts of societies: "neither those in their graves nor those behind the Curtains can respond to questionnaires or interviews" (*LAM*, 222). Studying beings that are all shaped by the same regime, these techniques prevent one from reflecting on the regime itself: "Democracy is then the tacit presupposition of the data; it does not have to become a theme; it can easily be forgotten: the wood is forgotten for the trees; the laws of human behavior are in fact laws of the behavior of human beings more or less molded by democracy; man is tacitly identified with the democratic man" (*LAM*, 222). Moreover, the

---

5. As we have seen, Weber's relativism does lead to nihilism, but it does so on account of a difficulty of which the new political science is hardly aware.

methodology of the new political science puts a premium "on observations which can be made with the utmost frequency and therefore by people of the meanest capacities" than on observations that can be made rarely because they can be made only by people of the greatest capacities: "It therefore frequently culminates in observations made by people who are not intelligent about people who are not intelligent" (*LAM*, 222).

Not only is the new political science unable "to see democracy or to hold a mirror to democracy," its value-free notions strengthen the most dangerous proclivities of democracy:

> By teaching in effect the equality of all desires, it teaches in effect that there is nothing of which a man ought to be ashamed; by destroying the possibilities of self-contempt, it destroys with the best of intentions the possibility of self-respect. By teaching the equality of all values, by denying that there are things which are intrinsically high and others which are intrinsically low as well as by denying that there is an essential difference between men and brutes, it unwittingly contributes to the victory of the gutter. (*LAM*, 222)

But how could a political science that began with a wholesale critique of democracy become so democratized?

> Yet the same new political science came into being through the revolt against what one may call the democratic orthodoxy of the immediate past. It had learned certain lessons which were hard for that orthodoxy to swallow regarding the irrationality of the masses and the necessity of elites; *if it had been wise*, it would have learned those lessons from the galaxy of antidemocratic thinkers of the remote past. (*LAM*, 223; emphasis added)

Strauss suggests that the new political science learned the lesson about the irrationality of masses and the necessity of elites from antidemocratic thinkers of the recent past—from Nietzsche in particular. But what was wrong with Nietzsche as an educator? Whereas the antidemocratic writers of the remote past criticized democracy on behalf of morality, Nietzsche's criticism of democracy was accompanied by a criticism of morality in general. Accordingly, the earlier writers would help their readers consider the moral claims of democracy, which in turn would lead them to consider the very complex pros and cons of democracy. Nietzsche's approach leads his readers to reject the moral claims of democracy with contempt, but since there is some merit to these claims they reassert themselves. In other words, the new political science did not learn but only believed that it had learned that no compelling case can be made for liberal democracy. Lacking the compelling power of knowledge, Nietzsche's lessons proved to be too hard for the new political science to swallow:

> But it succeeded in reconciling those doubts with the unfaltering commitment to liberal democracy by the simple device of declaring that no value judgments, including those supporting liberal democracy, are rational and hence that an ironclad argument in favor of liberal democracy ought in reason not to be expected. The very complex pros and cons regarding liberal democracy have thus become entirely obliterated by the poorest formalism. The crisis of liberal democracy has become concealed by a ritual which calls itself methodology or logic. (*LAM*, 223)

Insofar as Nietzsche's critique of morality laid the basis for the denial of knowledge of values, it contributed to neutralizing his own criticism of democracy.

Since the distinction between facts and values allows the new political science to put aside its own doubts about liberal democracy, Strauss speaks of it as an "almost willful blindness to the crisis of liberal democracy" and suggests that it itself is part of that crisis (*LAM*, 223). On one hand, the distinction between facts and values allows for unfaltering commitment to liberal democracy, and on the other, it prevents political scientists from having anything "to say against those who unhesitatingly prefer surrender, that is, the abandonment of liberal democracy, to war" (*LAM*, 223). More generally, it is part of the crisis of liberal democracy because it shows to those who have come to have doubts about liberal democracy that its intellectual authorities are utterly incapable of addressing its shortcomings.

Strauss ends his discussion with an apparently fiery paragraph that I have already mentioned. The new political science is not evil: "Only a great fool would call the new political science diabolical: it has no attributes peculiar to fallen angels" (*LAM*, 223). Whereas the devil turned against a moral teaching, the new political science fell away from an immoral one (*WPP*, 20). It is not Machiavellian because its drab and uniform denial of the truth of value judgments cannot be confused with Machiavelli's "graceful, subtle and colorful" critique of morality. It is not Neronian because it does not share Nero's indifference to the suffering of his country: "Nevertheless, one may say of it that it fiddles while Rome burns. It is excused by two facts: it does not know that it fiddles, and it does not know that Rome burns" (*LAM*, 223). It does not know that it fiddles because it lacks an adequate criterion for judging important and unimportant matters, and for that very reason it does not know that Rome burns.

This final judgment by Strauss, or his view that today we face a threat to the "whole western heritage which is at least as great and even greater than that which threatened Mediterranean civilization around 300 of the Christian era" (Strauss 1995a, 307), is apt to be controversial. Only those who have understood the meaning of that heritage are in a position to know whether there is such a threat. Yet, its existence is often denied by those who are not interested in that heritage or think that the meaning of the heritage reveals itself through a cursory and facile reading of its seminal texts. Our study of the noble but unsuccessful attempt of Max Weber to preserve the idea of science has helped us see the threat to what we have inherited from classical antiquity. The threat to our biblical heritage or the fact "that the land of philistines is perhaps nearer than it ever was" is more obvious (*LAM*, 202). Elaborating on some comments by Nietzsche, Strauss articulates this combined threat:

> The reading of the morning prayer had been replaced by the reading
> of the morning paper: not every day the same thing, the same reminder
> of man's absolute duty and exalted destiny, but every day something new
> with no reminder of duty and exalted destiny. Specialization, knowing
> more and more about less and less, practical impossibility of concentra-
> tion upon the very few essential things upon which men's wholeness en-
> tirely depends—this specialization compensated by sham universality,
> by the stimulation of all kinds of interests and curiosities without true
> passion, the danger of universal philistinism and creeping conformism.
> (Strauss 1995a, 307)

CONCLUDING REMARKS

I have examined Leo Strauss's contribution to the scientific study of politics without inquiring into his account of the political science that seems in his judgment to be truly scientific—the classical political science. Nonetheless, my study of his critique of modern social science points to certain principles for a political science that is concerned with wise action.

1. *The aim of political science is the discovery of valid political judgments through the clarification of our understanding of human excellence.* This task, of course, requires clear thinking about the consequences of particular political actions, but this clear thinking is not possible without knowledge of moral and political principles that allow us to judge these consequences. Accordingly, political science must shift its focus from the measurement of public opinion to the clarification of public opinion. This requires a fundamental shift in the habits of mind of political scientists. It requires more emphasis on the art of logic, and in particular on the art of dialectical reasoning, and less on methodology. Since in spite of relativism we have moral and political convictions that we believe to be sound, and since many of our fellow citizens do not share some of these convictions, it is our duty as social scientists and citizens to understand the basis of such disagreements so that we can replace our opinions about moral principles with knowledge. We are much more likely to understand our political situation by relentlessly thinking through substantive disagreements, for instance, between liberals and conservatives in terms accepted by them than by building grand but hypothetical theoretical constructs (such as Hobbes's state of nature, Rawls's original position, or Habermas's deduction of egalitarian politics from the character of language).

2. *A political science that does not thematically reflect on the need for human excellence or virtue is apt to suffer shipwreck.* First, it is neither possible nor desirable to eliminate the human desire for excellence or virtue. Second, despite the constitutional means that have been used to protect our regime, a democracy is ultimately only as good or as bad as the character of its people. The people are a mixture of human beings of various intellectual and moral qualities, and the character of this mixture varies in different times and places: a democratic community can be admirable or despicable. By correcting visionary expectations regarding the electorate or the democratic process, we can see clearly the most important task of a democratic statesman, which is to educate the public sentiment so that what is best in the people sets the tone of the society.

3. *In arriving at its political judgments political science should in general prefer the perspective of the morally serious man to those of sophisticated amoralists.* Those who dismiss morality generally tend to misunderstand themselves, and having misunderstood themselves they are less capable of making sound judgments. The example of those who in denying the validity of a moral doctrine find themselves unknowingly in the grip of some version of it is a sobering lesson regarding the dangers of pseudo-sophistication. By showing the superiority of the moral man to the sophisticated, we have come to understand Werner Dannhauser's observation that Strauss has taught us that in order to become wise, we must first become naïve again (Dannhauser 1973–74, 636–42).

4. *In every study, however limited, the political scientist must keep in mind the question of the whole political order.* Whatever may be the case in the natural world, the political regime is a whole that influences its parts. By being mindful of the effect of political wholes on their parts, I have pointed to a different kind of specialization, one that never loses sight of the connection between the political thing that is being studied and the regime of which it is part. In this way, we can resolve the problem caused by the conflict between the requirements of knowledge (hence, specialization) and those of political relevance, a problem that has afflicted the profession of political science for some time. This focus also allows us to look at the new political science's reservations about what it calls anecdotal evidence. Such reservations are justified inasmuch as there is truth to the adage that one swallow does not make a spring. But observations made by great thinkers should not be dismissed because they do not emerge from empirical studies. Since individual events carry the stamp of the whole, those who have reflected on the whole can see the evidence presented by indi-

vidual events much more clearly than others. The observations of a Nietzsche or a Tocqueville are much more adequate than observations based on
the techniques of the new political science, which in themselves cannot distinguish the important from the unimportant.

5. *Political science must show a decent respect for the opinions of the rest of
mankind, including the opinions of the dead.* Although the main concern of
politics is to solve the problems of our day, we cannot understand those
problems adequately if our vision is restricted to our own age. Accordingly,
political science must be based on a comprehensive reflection on politics,
and for this task the great works of political philosophy and political history are indispensable. The new political science's concern for precision or
objectivity has led it to restrict its attention to a small segment of human
history. But in the study of politics exactness that is bought at the price of
a narrowing of vision is a kind of imprecision. We have seen that the empirical research favored by scientific relativism necessarily, if surreptitiously, absolutizes the perspective of the liberal secular society. More generally, belief in the idea of progress, in the historical relativity of all values,
in the impossibility of objective value judgments, or in the equality of all
cultures implies a rejection of the opinions of almost every society that has
ever existed. To respect an opinion is to take seriously its claim to be true
and to accept or reject it on the basis of a consideration of the reasons ad-
duced in its favor.

▲ ▲

This study is also a necessary step toward understanding Strauss's contribution to political science as a theoretical pursuit. The goal of political science is knowledge not of universally valid laws of political behavior but of
the universal structure of politics, that is, of permanent political problems.
Moreover, the possibility of political science depends on the resolution of
a difficulty that in our time has rendered questionable the legitimacy of all
theoretical pursits. This difficulty is the problem of relativism.

In this study, I have both recovered the problem of social science relativism as our own problem and freed us from modern social science's formulation of that problem. We have seen that it was Weber's inability to
solve the conflict between philosophy and divine revelation that led him to
deny that human reason can solve the conflict between values in general.
We have seen that the conflict between philosophy and divine revelation
was connected in Weber's mind with the conflict between the aristocracy of
the intellect and brotherliness, on the one hand, and the conflict between

attachment to science and devotion to ideals or causes, on the other. The root cause of modern relativism is a problem that has three parts: god versus nature, aristocracy versus democracy, and contemplation versus devotion. In other words, modern relativism is the result of the awareness of the failure of the modern political philosophers to solve what Strauss, following Spinoza, has called "the theological-political problem."

But the very relativism that is caused by this complex problem tends to obscure these substantive perplexities. The belief that value judgments cannot—and therefore need not—have objective foundations paradoxically allows social scientists to be wholeheartedly attached to democracy, science, and a kind of liberal morality. As Strauss puts it bluntly but precisely:

> When [the scientific social scientist] says that democracy is a value which is not evidently superior to the opposite value, he does not mean that he is impressed by the alternative which he rejects, or that his heart or his mind is torn between alternatives which in themselves are equally attractive. His "ethical neutrality" is so far from being nihilism or a road to nihilism that it is not more than an alibi for thoughtlessness and vulgarity: by saying that democracy and truth are values, he says in effect that one does not have to think about the reasons why these things are good, and that he may bow as well as anyone else to the values that are adopted and respected by his society. (*WPP*, 20)

Max Weber, whose heart and mind were torn by substantive perplexities of the greatest consequence, is the exact opposite of such social scientists. Yet, there is something wrong with an expression of a problem that obscures that problem. Indeed, we have seen that Weber's thesis that human reason is incapable of solving the conflict of values is not the logical consequence of the conflict between philosophy and revelation but rather the result of Weber's despair in the face of that conflict. By realizing this and the absurd consequences of Weber's thesis, we free ourselves completely from the distinction between facts and values and can once again take moral and political questions seriously. Since Weber never proved that the political part of the theological-political problem is insoluble, there is reason to hope that a solution to that part of the problem will allow us to see more clearly the strictly theological problem.

WORKS CITED

Works by Leo Strauss

1936. *The political philosophy of Hobbes: Its basis and its genesis.* Translated by Elsa M. Sinclair. 1936; reprint, Chicago: University of Chicago Press, 1952.

1949. *Natural right and history.* Charles R. Walgreen Lectures, delivered at the University of Chicago.

1952. *Persecution and the art of writing.* Glencoe, Ill: Free Press.

1953. *Natural right and history.* Chicago: University of Chicago Press.

1958. *Thoughts on Machiavelli.* Chicago: University of Chicago Press.

1959. *What is political philosophy? and other studies.* Glencoe, Ill.: Free Press.

1961. "Relativism." In *Relativism and the study of man,* edited by Helmut Schoeck and James W. Wiggins, 135–57. Princeton: Van Nostrand.

1963a. *On tyranny.* Glencoe, Ill.: Free Press.

1963b. "Replies to Schaar and Wolin." *American Political Science Review* 57: 152–55.

1964a. *The city and man.* Chicago: Rand McNally.

1964b. "The crisis of our time." In *The predicament of modern politics,* edited by Harold Spaeth, 41–54. Detroit: University of Detroit Press.

1965. *Spinoza's critique of religion.* Translated by E. M. Sinclair. New York: Schocken.

1968. *Liberalism ancient and modern.* New York: Basic.

1983. *Studies in Platonic Political Philosophy.* Chicago: University of Chicago Press.

1988. "Correspondence of Karl Loewith and Leo Strauss." Translated by George Elliot Tucker. *Independent Journal of Philosophy/Unabhaengige Zeitschrift für Philosophie* 5–6: 177–92.

1989a. *An introduction to political philosophy: Ten essays by Leo Strauss.* Selected and introduced by Hilail Gildin. Detroit: Wayne State University Press.

1989b. *The rebirth of classical political rationalism: An introduction to the thought of Leo Strauss.* Selected and introduced by Thomas L. Pangle. Chicago: University of Chicago Press.

1991. "The Strauss-Kojève correspondence." In *On tyranny*, edited by Victor Gourevitch and Michael S. Roth, 217–314. New York: Free Press.

1993. "The Strauss-Voegelin correspondence." In *Faith and political philosophy*, translated and edited by Peter Emberley and Barry Cooper, 3–106. University Park: Pennsylvania State University Press.

1995a. "Existentialism." *Interpretation* 22: 303–20.

1995b. *Philosophy and law: Contributions to the understanding of Maimonides and his predecessors.* Translated by Eve Adler. Albany: State University of New York Press.

1995c. "The problem of Socrates." *Interpretation* 22: 321–38.

1996. *Gesammelte Schriften.* Stuttgart: Verlag J. B. Melzer.

1997. *Jewish philosophy and the crisis of modernity: Essays and lectures in modern Jewish thought.* Selected and introduced by Kenneth Hart Green. Albany: State University of New York Press.

1999. "German nihilism." *Interpretation* 26: 353–78.

Works by Other Authors

Almond, Gabriel A. 1966. "Political theory and political science."*American Political Science Review* 40: 868–79.

———. 1977. "Clouds, clocks, and the study of politics." *World Politics* 29: 489–522.

———. 1990. *A discipline divided: Schools and sects in political science.* Newbury Park, Calif.: Sage.

Almond, Gabriel A., and Sidney Verba. 1963. *The civic culture: Political attitudes and democracy in five nations.* Princeton: Princeton University Press.

Ambler, Wayne. 1985. "Aristotle on acquisition." *Canadian Journal of Political Science* 17: 487–502.

Aquinas, Thomas. 1945. *Basic writings of Saint Thomas Aquinas.* Edited by Anton C. Pegis. New York: Random House.

Aristotle. 1941. *The basic works of Aristotle.* Edited by Richard McKeon. New York: Random House.

Backus, John. 1969. *The acoustical foundations of music.* New York: Norton.

Banfield, Edward C. 1991. "Leo Strauss: 1899–1973." In *Remembering the University of Chicago: Teachers, scientists, and scholars*, edited by Edward Shils. Chicago: University of Chicago Press.

Barrett, William. 1958. *Irrational man: A study in existential philosophy.* Garden City, N.Y.: Doubleday.

Bay, Christian. 1967. "Politics and pseudopolitics: A critical evaluation of some behavioral literature." In *Apolitical politics: A critique of behavioralism*, edited by Charles McCoy and John Playford, 12–37. New York: Thomas Y. Crowell.

Baynes, Kenneth, James Bohman, and Thomas McCarthy. 1987. "General introduction." In *After philosophy: End or transformation?* edited by Kenneth Baynes, James Bohman, and Thomas McCarthy, 1–18. Cambridge: MIT Press.

Becker, Carl. 1948. *The Declaration of Independence: A study in the history of political ideas*. New York: Knopf.

Bendix, Reinhard, and Guenther Roth. 1971. *Scholarship and partisanship: Essays on Max Weber*. Berkeley: University of California Press.

Bentley, Arthur F. 1967. *The process of government*. 1908; reprint, Cambridge: Harvard University Press.

Berelson, Bernard R., Paul F. Lazarsfeld, and William N. McPhee. 1954. *Voting: A study of opinion formation in a presidential campaign*. Chicago: University of Chicago Press.

Berns, Walter. 1961. "The behavioral sciences and the study of political things: The case of Christian Bay's *The Structure of Freedom*." *American Political Science Review* 55: 550–59.

———. 1985. *The First Amendment and the future of American democracy*. Washington, D.C.: Regnery Gateway.

Bloom, Allan. 1977. "Political science and the undergraduate." In *Teaching political science: The professor and the polity*, edited by Vernon Van Dyke, 111–27. Atlantic Highlands, N.J.: Humanities.

———. 1990. *Giants and dwarfs*. New York: Simon and Schuster.

Bolotin, David. 1998. *An approach to Aristotle's* Physics. Albany: SUNY Press.

Bruell, Christopher. 1995. "On reading Plato today." In *Political philosophy and the human soul*, edited by Michael Palmer and Thomas L. Pangle. Lanham, Md.: Rowman and Littlefield.

Bruun, H. H. 1972. *Science, values and politics in Max Weber's methodology*. Copenhagen: Munksgaard.

Burton, David Henry. 1992. *Political ideas of Justice Holmes*. Rutherford, N.J.: Fairleigh Dickinson University Press.

Burtt, E. A. 1999. *The metaphysical foundations of modern physical science*. 1924; reprint, New York: Humanities.

Catlin, G. E. G. 1964. *The science and method of politics*. 1927; reprint, Hamden, Conn.: Archon.

Ceaser, James W. 1990. *Liberal democracy and political science*. Baltimore: Johns Hopkins University Press.

Chomsky, Noam. 1967. *American power and the new mandarins*. New York: Pantheon.

Churchill, Winston. 1942. *Great contemporaries*. London: Macmillan.

Cobban, Alfred. 1953. "The decline of political theory." *Political Science Quarterly* 68: 321–37.

Comte, Auguste. 1974. *The positive philosophy.* Translated by Harriet Martineau. New York: AMS, 1974.

Cook, Thomas I. 1955. "The prospect of political science." *Journal of Politics* 17: 265–75.

Corwin, Edward S. 1929. "The democratic dogma and the future of political science." *American Political Science Review* 23: 569–92.

Crick, Bernard. 1959. *The American science of politics: Its origins and conditions.* Berkeley: University of California Press.

Cropsey, Joseph. 1999. "Leo Strauss at the University of Chicago." In *Leo Strauss, the Straussians, and the American regime,* edited by Kenneth L. Deutsch and John A. Murley, 39–40. Lanham, Md.: Rowman and Littlefield.

Dahl, Robert A. 1958–59. "Political theory: Truth and consequences." *World Politics* 11: 89–102.

———. 1961. "The behavioral approach in political science: Epitaph for a monument to a successful protest." *American Political Science Review* 55: 763–72.

Dannhauser, Werner. 1973–74. "Leo Strauss: Becoming naïve again." *American Spectator* 44: 636–42.

Derrida, Jacques. 1990. "Force of law: The 'mystical' foundation of authority," translated by Mary Quaintance. *Cardozo Law Review* 11: 920–1038.

Descartes, René. 1988. *Selected philosophical writings.* Translated by John Cottingham, Robert Stoothoff, and Dugald Murdoch. Cambridge: Cambridge University Press.

Downs, Anthony. 1957. *An economic theory of democracy.* New York: Harper and Row.

Durkheim, Emile. 1950. *The rules of sociological method.* Translated by Sarah A. Solovay and John H. Mueller and edited by George E. G. Catlin. 1938; reprint, Glencoe, Ill.: Free Press.

Easton, David. 1953. *The political system: An inquiry into the state of political science.* New York:Knopf.

———. 1969. "The new revolution in political science." *American Political Science Review* 63: 1051–61.

Eulau, Heinz. 1963. *The behavioral persuasion in politics.* New York: Random House.

Geertz, Clifford. 1989. "Anti-anti-relativism." In *Relativism: Interpretation and confrontation,* edited by Michael Krausz, 12–34. Notre Dame, Ind.: University of Notre Dame Press.

Green, Donald P., and Ian Shapiro. 1994. *Pathologies of rational choice theory: A critique of applications in political science.* New Haven: Yale University Press.

Gunnell, John G. 1993. *The descent of political theory: The genealogy of an American vocation.* Chicago: University of Chicago Press.

Hallowell, John H. 1942. "The decline of liberalism." *Ethics* 52: 323–49.

Hand, Learned. 1952. "Democracy: Its presumptions and its realities." In *The spirit of liberty: Papers and addresses of Learned Hand,* edited by Irving Dilliard, 90–102. New York: Knopf.

Havard, William C. 1984. *The recovery of political theory: Limits and possibilities.* Baton Rouge: Louisiana State University Press.

Heidegger, Martin. 1968. *What is called thinking?* Translated by Fred D. Wieck and J. Glenn Gray. New York: Harper and Row.

———. 1977. *Basic writings.* Edited by David Farrell Krell. New York: Harper and Row.

Herring, E. Pendleton. 1940. *The politics of democracy: American parties in action.* New York: Norton.

Holmes, Oliver W. 1952. *Collected legal papers.* New York: Peter Smith.

Horowitz, Robert. 1962. "Scientific propaganda: Harold D. Lasswell." In *Essays on the scientific study of politics,* edited by Herbert J. Storing. New York: Holt, Rinehart.

Husserl, Edmund. 1970. *The crisis of European sciences and transcendental phenomenology.* Translated by David Carr. Evanston: Northwestern University Press.

Kant, Immanuel. 1949. *The philosophy of Kant.* Edited by Carl J. Friedrich. New York: Random House.

Kelsen, Hans. 1948. "Absolutism and relativism in philosophy and politics." *American Political Science Review* 42: 906–14.

Kuhn, Thomas S. 1970. *The structure of scientific revolutions.* Chicago: University of Chicago Press.

Lasswell, Harold D. 1927. *Propaganda technique in the world war.* New York: Peter Smith.

———. 1942. "The developing science of democracy." In *The future of government in the United States,* ed. Leonard D. White, 25–48. Chicago: University of Chicago Press.

———. 1951. *The political writings of Harold D. Lasswell.* Glencoe, Ill.: Free Press.

———. 1956. "The political science of science: An inquiry into the possible reconciliation of mastery and freedom." *American Political Science Review* 50: 961–79.

———. 1963. *The future of political science.* New York: Prentice-Hall, Atherton Press.

———. 1971. *A pre-view of policy sciences.* New York: American Elsevier.

Lasswell, Harold D., and Abraham Kaplan. 1950. *Power and society: A framework for political inquiry.* New Haven: Yale University Press.

Lincoln, Abraham, and Stephen Douglas. 1965. *The Lincoln-Douglas debates of 1858.* Edited by Robert W. Johannsen. New York: Oxford University Press.

Lindblom, Charles E. 1982. "Another state of mind." *American Political Science Review* 76: 9–21.

Lipset, Seymour M. 1963. *Political man: The social basis of politics.* 1960; reprint, New York: Doubleday, Anchor Books.

Lowi, Theodore J. 1972. "The politics of higher education: Political science as a case study." In *The post-behavioral era: Perspectives on political science,* edited by George J. Graham Jr. and George W. Carey, 11–36. New York: David McKay.

Lukács, Georg. 1981. *The destruction of reason.* Translated by Peter Palmer. Atlantic Highlands, N.J.: Humanities.

MacIntyre, Alasdair. 1987. "The relationship of philosophy and history: Postscript to the second edition of *After Virtue.*" In *After philosophy: End or transformation?* edited by Kenneth Baynes, James Bohman, and Thomas McCarthy, Cambridge: MIT Press.

Maimonides. 1963. *The guide of the perplexed.* Translated by Shlomo Pines. Chicago: University of Chicago Press.

Merriam, Charles E. 1921. "The present state of the study of politics." *American Political Science Review* 15: 173–85.

———. 1925. *New aspects of politics.* Chicago: University of Chicago Press.

———. 1950. *Political power.* Glencoe, Ill.: Free Press.

———. 1968. *A history of American political theories.* 1903; reprint, New York: Russell and Russell.

Michels, Robert. 1966. *Political parties: A sociological study of the oligarchical tendencies of modern democracy.* Translated by Eden and Cedar Paul. 1962; reprint, New York: Free Press.

Miller, Eugene F. 1972. "Positivism, historicism, and political inquiry." *American Political Science Review* 66: 796–817.

Munro, William B. 1928. "Physics and politics—an old analogy revised." *American Political Science Review* 22: 1–11.

Nietzsche, Friedrich. 1954. *Thus spoke Zarathustra.* Translated by Walter Kaufman. New York: Viking.

———. 1967a. *Beyond good and evil: Prelude to a philosophy of the future.* Translated by Walter Kaufman. New York: Vintage.

———. 1967b. *The will to power.* Translated by Walter Kaufman. New York: Vintage.

———. 1974. *The gay science.* Translated by Walter Kaufman. New York: Vintage.

———. 1982. *Daybreak: Thoughts on the prejudices of morality.* Translated by R. J. Hollingdale. Cambridge: Cambridge University Press.

Olson, Mancur, Jr. 1971. *The logic of collective action.* Cambridge: Harvard University Press.

Paine, Thomas. 1969. *Rights of man.* Harmondsworth: Pelican Classics.

Pangle, Thomas. 1988. *The spirit of modern republicanism: The moral vision of the American founders and the philosophy of Locke.* Chicago: University of Chicago Press.

Pye, Lucien. 1990. "Political science and the crisis of authoritarianism." *American Political Science Review* 84: 3–19.

Rawls, John. 1985. "Justice as fairness: Political not metaphysical." *Philosophy and Public Affairs* 14: 223–51.

Ricci, David M. 1984. *The tragedy of political science: Politics, scholarship, and democracy.* New Haven: Yale University Press.

Rogowski, Ronald. 1978. "Rationalist theories of politics: A midterm report." *World Politics* 30: 296–323.

Rorty, Richard. 1991. *Objectivity, relativism, and truth.* Cambridge: Cambridge University Press.

Ross, Dorothy. 1991. *The origins of American social science.* Cambridge: Cambridge University Press.

Schaar, John H., and Sheldon S. Wolin. 1963. "Essays on the scientific study of politics: A critique." *American Political Science Review* 57: 125–50.

Simon, Herbert A. 1945. *Administrative behavior.* New York: Free Press.

Somit, Albert, and Joseph Tanenhaus. 1967. *The development of political science: From Burgess to behavioralism.* Boston: Allyn and Bacon.

Soroush, Abdolkarim. 2000. *Reason, freedom, and democracy in Islam.* Oxford: Oxford University Press.

Spinoza, Benedict de. 1951. *A theological-political treatise* and *A political treatise.* Translated by R. H. M. Elwes. New York: Dover.

Storing, Herbert. J. 1962. "The science of administration: Herbert A. Simon." In *Essays on the Scientific Study of Politics,* edited by Herbert J. Storing, 63–150. New York: Holt, Rinehart.

———. 1963. "Replies to Schaar and Wolin." *American Political Science Review* 57: 151–52.

Tocqueville, Alexis de. 2000. *Democracy in America.* Translated by Harvey C. Mansfield and Delba Winthrop. Chicago: University of Chicago Press.

Troeltsch, Ernst. 1934. "The ideas of natural law and humanity in world politics." In *Natural law and the theory of society,* by Otto Gierke, translated by Ernst Barker, 201–222. Cambridge: Cambridge University Press.

Vieta, François. 1968. "Introduction to the analytical art." In *Greek mathematical thought and the origin of algebra,* translated by Jacob Klein, 315–53. New York: Dover.

Voegelin, Eric. 1952. *The new science of politics*. Chicago: University of Chicago Press.

Wallas, Graham. 1921. *Human nature in politics*, 3d ed. New York: Knopf.

Weber, Max. 1920. *Gesammelte Aufsaetze zur Religionssoziologie*. Tübingen: Mohr.

———— 1924. *Gesammelte Aufsaetze zur Soziologie und Sozialpolitik*. Tübingen: Mohr.

————. 1946. *From Max Weber: Essays in sociology*. Translated and edited by H. Gerth and C. Wright Mills. New York: Oxford University Press.

————. 1949. *Max Weber on the methodology of social sciences*. Translated and edited by Edward Shils and Henry Finch. Glencoe, Ill.: Free Press.

————. 1951a. *The religion of China*. Translated by Hans H. Gerth. New York: Free Press.

————. 1951b. *Gesammelte Aufsaetze zur Wissenschaftslehre*. Tübingen: Mohr.

————. 1956. *Wirtschaft und Gesellschaft*. Tübingen: Mohr.

————. 1958. *The Protestant ethic and the spirit of capitalism*. Translated by Talcott Parsons. New York: Charles Scribner's Sons.

————. 1975. *Roscher and Knies: The logical problems of historical economics*. Translated by Guy Oaks. New York: Free Press.

————. 1994. *Political writings*. Edited by Peter Lassman and Ronald Speirs. Cambridge: Cambridge University Press.

Wolin, Richard. 1995. "Karl Loewith and Martin Heidegger—contexts and controversies: An introduction." In *Martin Heidegger and European nihilism*, edited by Richard Wolin, 1–25. New York: Columbia University Press.

Wolin, Sheldon. 1969. "Political theory as a vocation." *American Political Science Review* 63: 1062–82.

Wright, Quincy. 1950. "Political science and world stabilization." *American Political Science Review* 44: 1–13.

INDEX

Adams, John, 41
Almond, Gabriel A., 3, 18, 19, 23, 24
Ambler, Wayne, 157n
Aquinas, Thomas, 34, 60
Arendt, Hannah, 16
Aristotle, 23n, 60, 68, 125, 148–68, 169–70, 173, 174, 178, 180, 182, 185, 194

Babeuf, 120
Bacon, Francis, 88, 110
Baemler, Alfred, 43
Banfield, Edward C., 45–46
Barrett, William, 3
Bay, Christian, 35
Baynes, Kenneth, 30
Beard, Charles, 1
Becker, Carl, 42
Bekesy, Georg von, 6
Benda, Julian 106
Bentley, Arthur F., 11n, 13, 20, 141, 171, 174, 191
Berelson, Bernard R., 18, 19, 20n, 27
Berlin, Isaiah, 31, 57
Bloom, Allan, 30
Bolotin, David, 60n
Bryce, James, 18n
Burke, Edmund, 187
Burtt, E. A., 155n

Calvin, 107–9, 112–13
Catlin, G. E. G., 12, 15, 16, 27

Chomsky, Noam, 36
Churchill, Winston, 11
Cobban, Alfred, 28
Comte, Auguste, 9–10, 11
Cook, Thomas I., 12n
Corwin, Edward S., 12, 13, 15
Crick, Bernard, 142
Cropsey, Joseph, 142

Dahl, Robert A., 23, 149n, 179
Dannhauser, Werner, 208
Derrida, Jacques, 29, 32
Descartes, René, 34, 159n
Dewey, John, 15, 57
Douglas, Stephen , 13n
Downs, Anthony, 25
Durkheim, Emile, 11n

Easton, David, 17, 18, 19, 21–23, 24, 26, 28, 37, 142
Einstein, Albert, 23n, 124n
Eulau, Heinz, 17, 156, 160, 166, 174, 176

Foucault, Michel, 29
Freud, Sigmund, 197, 198
Friedrich, Carl J., 16

Gadamer, H.–G., 29
Goethe, J. W. von, 58n
Green, Donald P., 25

Gunnell, John G., 16, 42
Gurian, Waldemar, 16

Habermas, Juergen, 29, 207
Hallowell, John H., 16, 29
Hand, Learned, 12
Havard, William, C., 142
Hegel, G. W. F., 15, 32, 43, 49, 58–59, 67, 69, 180
Heidegger, Martin 3, 30, 33, 35, 41, 43, 53, 54–57, 58, 65, 104–5, 137
Herring, E. Pendleton, 19
Hitler, Adolf, 1, 16, 41, 77, 187–88
Hobbes, Thomas, 49, 58–59, 72, 110, 159n, 168, 195, 200, 201, 207
Holmes, Oliver W., 38–39
Hooker, Richard, 28
Horowitz, Robert, 142, 146, 201
Husserl, Edmund, 30, 34, 137

Infeld, Leopold, 124n

Jefferson, Thomas, 40
Juenger, Ernst, 43

Kant, Immanuel, 31, 35, 49, 58, 77, 78, 109, 180
Kaplan, Abraham, 18n
Kelsen, Hans, 16, 39–40, 42
Kierkegaard, Søren, 58n.
Kojève, Alexandre, 2, 58, 143n
Kuhn, Thomas, 22–23

Lasswell, Harold D., 6, 13, 14, 17, 18n, 20, 142, 145, 146, 165n, 172, 173, 174, 191, 201
Lincoln, Abraham, 13n
Lindblom, Charles E., 18, 166
Lipset, Seymour M., 20
Locke, John, 49
Loewith, Karl, 58n
Lowi, Theodore J., 36
Lukács, Georg, 56, 58
Lyotard, Jean-François, 29

Machiavelli, Niccolò, 33, 46, 110, 144, 170, 195
MacIntyre, Alasdair, 29

Maimonides, 125, 157n
Marx, Karl, 32, 58n, 197, 198
Merriam, Charles E., 11, 15, 16, 41, 171–72, 174, 188n
Michels, Robert, 14
Mill, John Stuart, 57
Miller, Eugene F., 21
Morgenthau, Hans, 16
Montesquieu, 170
Munro, William B., 14, 16

Nero, 144
Neumann, Franz, 16
Neumann, Sigmund, 16
Newton, Isaac, 23n
Nietzsche, Friedrich, vii, 3, 4, 7, 10, 14, 15, 21, 30, 32, 51, 57, 58n, 72, 91, 94, 95, 97n, 163–64, 168, 204–5, 206, 209

Olson, Mancur, Jr., 24–25

Paine, Thomas, 40
Plato, 4, 5, 31, 58, 67, 68, 105–6, 159n, 186n
Putnam, Hilary, 29
Pye, Lucien, 24, 26

Rawls, John, 30–31, 207
Ricci, David M., 18n
Rogowski, Ronald, 47
Rorty, Richard, 29, 30
Roscher, Wilhelm, 68, 71n
Roth, Guenther, 77n
Rousseau, Jean-Jacques, 49

Schaar, John H., 141, 142, 178
Schmitt, Carl, 43, 52, 115n
Schmoller, Gustav, 120
Shapiro, Ian, 25
Simon, Herbert A., 142, 163, 191, 192, 201
Socrates, 33, 66, 67, 68, 76, 77, 135
Somit, Albert, 16
Soroush, Abdolkarim, 102–3
Spengler, Oswald, 30, 43, 53
Spinoza, Benedict de, 32, 40
Stalin, 1, 179

Storing, Herbert J., 141, 142, 148, 201

Tanenhaus, Joseph, 16
Taylor, Charles, 29
Thucydides, 106, 195
Tocqueville, Alexis de, 18n, 57, 139, 209
Troeltsch, Ernst, 40
Truman, David, 18

van den Bruck, Moeller, 43
Verba, Sidney, 18, 19
Vieta, François, 33

Voegelin, Eric, 16, 28, 29

Wallas, Graham, 12, 13
Washington, George, 119
Weber, Max, 5, 10–11, 15, 16, 30, 50,
    65–137, 141, 183, 193, 197–98,
    203, 210
Wolin, Sheldon, 21, 33, 141, 142, 178
Wright, Quincy, 43, 178–79

Xenophon, 2, 170